William Watts Ball (1868–1952) was a newspaperman, social critic, and a political force. In the course of his long life he was editor of the four most influential newspapers in South Carolina. Politics was his obsession, editorials his métier. His career touched on many important events and influenced some of them. And as he approached legendary stature, he mingled with a remarkable assortment of prominent personalities: Ben Tillman, Cole Blease, Bernard Baruch, "Cotton Ed" Smith, Franklin D. Roosevelt, Wendell Willkie, James F. Byrnes, and Strom Thurmond.

Reliably controversial, Ball was praised by some as a steadfast defender of all that was fine in Jeffersonianism and the Old South; to others he seemed an old-fashioned and tedious curmudgeon. But to all he was a symbol, and his importance lay in his persistence as a symbolic figure.

Ball was perhaps the last public spokesman of a diminishing breed in the South and the nation—the rigid traditionalist. Rugged individualism, held as a dogmatic principle, was his stock in trade. As he pursued his relentless course, he came to epitomize the sort of aristocratic conservatism so often associated with John Randolph of Roanoke.

When Ball fell to self-reflection, he often described himself simply as an upcountryman. "Upcountry" has enjoyed a special meaning in the South. Although the upcountry may be equated with the Piedmont, Ball himself regarded all but the five coastal counties as comprising the South Carolina upcountry. No matter, "upcountry" is more a state of mind than a geographic location, and an upcountryman is one who holds high (or pretends to) a long-

DAMNED UPCOUNTRYMAN

Duke Historical Publications

DAMNED UPCOUNTRYMAN:
WILLIAM WATTS BALL

*A Study in American conserv-
atism by* John D. Stark

Durham, N. C.
DUKE UNIVERSITY PRESS
1968

Printed in the U. S. A.
by Kingsport Press, Inc.

PREFACE

I HAVE WRITTEN a biography of William Watts Ball in order to describe the life and thought of a man who was an important Southern editor and out-spoken critic of democracy. He was, besides, something of a symbolic figure, representative of a point of view rapidly fading in American life. Conse-quently I have commented also upon the dilemma of the traditional conserva-tive in the modern political and social environment. To date, Ball has received scant appraisal. In 1954 some of his essays were published in a volume en-titled *The Editor and the Republic*, edited by Anthony Harrigan, who worked with Ball on the Charleston *News and Courier*. The biographical introduction by the editor is brief and uncritical.

The principal source of my information has been the Ball papers, obtained by Duke University soon after Ball's death in 1952. The collection contains more than twenty-six thousand items of correspondence and a fifteen-volume diary. Other research done in smaller personal collections provided slight additional material.

I should like to express my appreciation to Professor Robert H. Woody, of Duke University, who suggested that I undertake this study and who has since given me many helpful suggestions; and to Professor Robert C. John-son, my colleague at Temple University, who read my manuscript and gave advice. I owe special thanks to Dr. Mattie Russell, archivist of the Manu-script Division of Duke University Library, who gave me her full co-opera-tion; Miss Virginia Rugheimer and her staff at the Charleston Library Society were equally generous. I am grateful also to Temple University for making available some of the time and money necessary to the completion of this study.

I am especially indebted to members of the family of W. W. Ball. They have shown their interest and willingness to lend assistance on many different occasions. Most particularly, however, I should like to thank Eleanor Ball Hewitt-Myring for giving me permission to quote from her father's diary; and Margaret Ball Hickey, who helped arrange interviews for me in Charleston.

J. D. S.

CONTENTS

DAMNED UPCOUNTRYMAN

CHAPTER ONE

UPCOUNTRYMAN: MAN AND SYMBOL

In the summer of 1964 a movement which had gathered force for a decade at last came to fruition amidst a clamor for revenge. The nomination of Barry Goldwater as Republican candidate for the presidency of the United States was proof of the resurgence of American conservatism and must, therefore, be regarded as a significant political development. The conservative spirit, or at least those aspects which were vocal and politically ambitious, had been muted during all those years when the nation was obsessed with the problems of depression, war, and postwar adjustment. The conservative voice rose chiefly from brooding Republican conventioneers who time and again saw their cohorts nominate presidential candidates from the left wing of the party and from defiant Southern Democratic politicians caught in the frustrations of minority politics. But the comparative calm of the fifties offered a gestation period for a renewal of conservative strength; prodded by their distaste for the liberal veneer of Eisenhower Republicanism, party conservatives began to organize. Goldwater's nomination represented the peak of their efforts.

As the political activity of the conservatives accelerated, scholars displayed renewed interest in the entire issue of conservatism and its role in the national life. Clinton Rossiter, who has specialized in the study of American political institutions, reminded us that American and European conservatism were different; the native variety had been marked by the effects of democracy and industrialism; hence it emerged more optimistic, more materialistic, more individualistic than its European counterpart. Rossiter described once again the conservative's ideal government of limited objectives, one which defends against attack, provides a symbol of unity and patriotic fervor, establishes and administers an equitable system of justice, protects against violence, secures the rights of property, adjusts conflicts between groups, promotes public and private morality in league with church and family, removes obstacles in the path of man's individual development, and acts as an humanitarian agency in cases of clear necessity.

Statements of basic conservative principles emerged from a flurry of redefinition. None were identical but all had some common elements. Rossiter and Russell Kirk, often described as the philosopher of "contemporary conservatism," both emphasized the importance of religious belief in conservative philosophy. They described the conservative as one who believed in the imperfectibility of man, yet accepted his equality only in the moral sense; therefore, the conservative placed his faith in a society which recognized social classes and submitted to the orders of a serving aristocracy.

Peter Viereck, like Rossiter, found that conservatives combined respect for history and historical continuity with the realization that not all the past was worth keeping. Viereck, one of the most prolific conservative thinkers, also cited the conservative penchant for fruitful nostalgia for the permanent beneath the flux, but unlike the others he emphasized the humanism rather than the divine interest inherent in the conservative attitude. Finally, preservation through reform was found by all critics to be a canon of true conservatism, with Kirk insisting that all change was not reform and denying that economic leveling represented economic progress.[1]

Definition of conservatism led inevitably to a discussion of its varieties and their exponents. Robert A. Taft seemed the model of the conservative; liberals like Walter Lippmann, Earl Warren, and Clifford Case appeared less genuine. Richard Hofstadter called the styles of Joe McCarthy and John Birch paranoic;[2] with few exceptions, other delineators of conservatism also branded them as aberrations, as nationalist demagogy seeking respectability in the guise of conservatism. Likewise, the philosophy of William Buckley and *The National Review* was generally rejected, with Viereck seeing Buckley's "New Conservatism" becoming a facade for attempted thought control tyranny in America[3] and discounting its philosophy because it is irrelevant to real needs, rootless in its nostalgia for roots, a conservatism of yearning based upon roots never present or no longer existent.[4]

Regarded also as pseudo-conservative was that minority variously

1. Russell Kirk, *The Conservative Mind* (Gateway Edition; Chicago, 1960), *passim;* Clinton Rossiter, *Conservatism in America* (New York, 1955), *passim;* Peter Viereck, *Conservatism Revisited* (Collier Books Edition; New York, 1962), *passim.*

2. Richard Hofstadter, *The Paranoid Style in American Politics and Other Essays* (New York, 1965), pp. 3–141, *passim.*

3. Viereck, *Conservatism Revisited*, p. 18.

4. *Ibid.*, p. 124.

described as traditionalist, reactionary, sentimental—the romantic conservatives. Their stronghold was the defeated South and their doctrine aristocratic agrarianism. In 1955 Rossiter found it virtually impossible to find an articulate spokesman for this tiny company who "indulged with emotion in the ritualistic remembrance of things past."[5] And yet only three years before such a man had died in Charleston, the legendary seat of elitism. William Watts Ball was a newspaperman, social critic, political force. In the course of his long life he was editor of the four most influential newspapers in South Carolina. Politics was his obsession, editorials his metier. His career touched on many important events and influenced some of them. And as he approached legendary stature, he mingled with a remarkable assortment of prominent personalities. Reliably controversial, he was praised by some as a steadfast defender of all that was fine in Jeffersonianism and the Old South; to others he seemed an old-fashioned and tedious curmudgeon. But to all he was a symbol, and his importance lay in his persistence as a symbolic figure.

Ball was perhaps the last public spokesman of a diminishing breed in the South and in the nation—the rigid traditionalist. Rugged individualism, held as a dogmatic principle, was his stock in trade. As he pursued his relentless course, he came to epitomize the sort of aristocratic conservatism so often associated with John Randolph of Roanoke. A stubborn defender of tradition in the Old South, Randolph is remembered for his proclamation "I love liberty. . . . I hate equality." In the New South, Billy Ball frequently boasted that he was always a Democrat but never a democrat.

When Ball fell to self-reflection, he often described himself simply as an upcountryman. "Upcountry" has enjoyed a special meaning in the South. Although the upcountry may be equated with the Piedmont, Ball himself regarded all but the five coastal counties as comprising the South Carolina upcountry. No matter, "upcountry" is more a state of mind than a geographic location and an upcountryman is one who holds high (or pretends to) a long-established set of attitudes. Ball viewed the upcountryman as one who was thrifty, stubborn, stiff-necked, forebearing, long suffering. He concluded:

There are gentleman and scholars, there are elders and deacons, there have been crooks and skinflints, roughnecks and drunkards, cardplayers, and dancers, repentant sinners and brethren strong in

5. Rossiter, *Conservatism in America*, p. 177.

prayer among these Upcountrymen. Day was when they could all ride. They have been good soldiers and some of them heroes; others, loafers. They have had wit and they have been dumb. They have made fools of themselves at the heels of the sorriest quack and braggart politicians and howled down men who had been their true guides. Occasionally they have split one another's throats for good cause or no cause and they have toted pistols most insanely. They have had distilleries, barrooms and dispensaries when the law allowed, they have sung hymns and caught step with canting charlatans to the polls, and bootleggers have been seen among them. If they have never followed after strange gods they have followed sometimes after strange evangelists. They have never taken a beating lying down, and they get up most unexpectedly. Some of them are the laziest folk on earth, and it may be dangerous to disturb them. There is good blood in the worst of them, and bad blood that it were better not to stir. They have been known to mix ignorance with righteousness with a resulting intoxication more dangerous than any liquors. They have left undone the things that they ought to have done, and they owe money in consequence. Gentlemen among them have been common, and the common of them have sometimes been the better gentlemen. They are strong and not altogether lovely. Damn them, they are my people. I am one of them, thank God.[6]

Another newspaperman, however, provided the classic hymn to the upcountry and its people. Ben Robertson[7] in his memoir *Red Hills and Cotton* recalled:

We are a strange people, complicated and simple and proud and religious and family-loving, a divorceless, Bible-reading murdersome lot of folks, all of us rich in ancestry and steeped in traditions and emotionally quick on the trigger. . . . We are Puritan Americans as well as Southern, and we are of a paradox—we are believers in an economy of small units, but we are slain by the edge of swords; there is also a quality within our character that makes us dissatisfied until we have bought all the land that joins our land.

6. William Watts Ball, *The State That Forgot* (Indianapolis, 1932), pp. 93–94.
7. Robertson, also a South Carolinian, was killed in the crash of the "Yankee Clipper" at Lisbon during World War II while on his way to head the London bureau of the New York *Herald-Tribune*.

We cannot resist buying land. . . . [We are] a talking people.
. . . [We are] forthright, outspoken, plain, believe in self-reliance,
self-improvement, progress as the theory of history, loyalty, total
abstinence, total immersion, in faithfulness, righteousness, justice,
honoring our parents, living without disgrace, we've set for our-
selves one of the strictest, sternest codes in existence but our
country is Southern, and frequently we fail. . . . It is not defeat
we fear, it is the loss of our intimate honor.[8]

There is no perfect prototype, and Ball's upcountry ways were colored by his Episcopalianism and by the habits of Charleston, the upcountryman's equation for the evils of Egypt. The paradox that is the
South is sufficiently inclusive to cover his seemingly contradictory claim
to being both a "most Charlestonian person" and a "damned upcountryman." For Ball was indeed the fabled upcountryman of an earlier era
who would not make his adjustment to modern America. He who will
not adjust must strive to endure and perhaps, now and then, challenge.
In countless ways the life of William Watts Ball was representative of
that bitter struggle. It began in the upcountry.

8. Ben Robertson, *Red Hills and Cotton* (Columbia, S. C., 1960), pp. 7–10
(reprint).

CHAPTER TWO

THE EDUCATION OF A CONSERVATIVE

LAURENS is a town in the Carolina upcountry where modest hills relieve the flatness of the farmland. The surrounding district in northwestern South Carolina was settled before the Revolution by Scotch-Irish pioneers. The county still exhibits a striking Anglo-Saxon homogeneity; most people are "kin." The Saluda and Enoree rivers, heavy with the red clay from their banks, flow slowly through a worn countryside. Small plantings of corn and cotton are interrupted by unimpressive woods. Roads, paved and dusty, lead to market in the county seat, the traditional center of Southern life.

Except that the visitor today cannot see the red brick hotel from the courthouse steps, Laurens might be the typical Southern Piedmont town. It has chain shops, feed and seed stores, important cotton mills, and a steady Baptist influence. The town can also boast of the site of the tailor shop of that errant apprentice Andrew Johnson. The busy little library takes special pride in its collection of state and county historical materials. Commanding the center square, victorious over "progressive" citizens who would have removed it in the interests of modernization and traffic efficiency, is the handsome courthouse of Laurens County. Built in 1838 of gray stone, the greek Revival structure has two four-column Corinthian porticos and, in the center of the roof, a low elliptical dome.[1] For generations, countrymen and villagers on court and election days have mingled and talked in the nearby streets.

A century ago in Laurens in a log cabin not far from the same courthouse, Beaufort Watts Ball practiced law. "Colonel" Ball's career had been romantic even by Southern standards. Born in 1830 in Laurens District, where his father worked a farm with three or four families of Negroes, Beaufort Ball came to the village after his graduation from the South Carolina College in 1851. At Carolina he "danced and frolicked and drank his share."[2] In his senior year he had been elected president of the Clariosophic Literary Society and had led the debate before the student body advocating the formation of a Southern Rights

1. The Laurens County courthouse was enlarged and remodeled in 1911.
2. Ball, *The State That Forgot*, p. 189.

Association. When he came to Laurens in the fifties it was to read law in the office of Charles P. Sullivan. Ball stood tall and slim, his yellow hair hanging to his shoulders, and in warm weather he wore white linen clothing, a white shirt with "Byronic" collar unbuttoned at the top, and a black silk shoestring tie about his neck.[3] During his first years in Laurens, he boarded in town but was a frequent visitor at the plantation of his mother's cousin, William Dendy Watts. The Watts plantation, about two miles from the courthouse, was a substantial operation employing about seventy-five slaves.[4] By the time Ball left Laurens to go to war in 1861, his young second cousin, Eliza Watts, then just thirteen, had decided that the dashing young lawyer would someday become her husband.[5]

Ball entered the fighting as a private in Company B of the infantry of the Hampton Legion, of which his friend Martin W. Gary was captain. He was a private at First Manassas. In 1862 the infantry of the Legion was expanded to a regiment, Gary was made a colonel, and Ball was appointed a private adjutant. In 1864 Gary became a brigadier; the private became adjutant to the brigade with the rank of captain and was so serving when he marched with the last troops that left Richmond for Appomattox. Although Beaufort Ball had a generous taste of action— three horses were killed under him—"he was a philosopher and had a good time."[6] Confederate officers often had sweethearts in Richmond society.

> The Adjutant's sweetheart was not of the first social circle, but she was a widow and rich, her house was comfortable, her servants plentiful, her cook excellent, her cellar bountifully stocked, and she was fond of the Adjutant. She gave him parties, he gave parties in her house, he took the goods the gods provided while lovely Thais sat beside him.[7]

But when the war was over and Beaufort Ball returned to Laurens, Eliza Watts was waiting.

Miss Watts herself, however, placed several obstacles before the marriage ceremony. She first sought to tame the streak of wildness that persisted in her husband-to-be. As a youth Ball had experimented briefly

3. *Ibid.*, p. 185.
4. William Watts Ball, Diary (16 vols.), Duke University Library, II, 132.
5. Beaufort Copeland, niece of W. W. Ball, in interview with author, June 5, 1957.
6. Ball, *The State That Forgot*, p. 195.   7. *Ibid.*

with opium eating but when he began to feel a craving, he gave it up forever. In his twenties and thirties he sometimes drank "not wisely but too well" for a day or a week.[8] Eliza Watts stipulated that before the betrothal could become official, her cousin should lead a sober life for one year, and after their marriage, drink only when she handed him the glass. Ball complied, and although Eliza was no prude, her husband had his liquor at home or in her presence.[9] Eliza Watts insisted also that when she married she must have a house of her own.[10] Though he had no money, Ball bought for his bride "Double Chimneys," a long house one block from Laurens courthouse. In November, 1867, Beaufort Ball, thirty-seven, and Eliza Watts, not yet twenty, were married. For a while they lived in "Double Chimneys" while Ball practiced law, wrote editorials for the county paper, and accumulated property. He helped his mother-in-law run the Watts plantation,[11] where he raised "the best watermelons and cantelopes and strawberries."[12] When it came time for Eliza to deliver her first child she returned to the big house set in an oak grove about fifty years from the Spartanburg Road. There, in the frame dwelling at the end of a front walk rimmed with boxwood hedges and crepe myrtles, her son was born on December 9, 1868. He was named William Watts Ball.[13]

South Carolina, at the time of young Ball's birth, was a land of turbulence and strain. Reconstruction was in progress and federal troops were in the state. Carpetbaggers, scalawags, and Negroes controlled the government, while the excluded white minority yearned, and then plotted, for the return of "home rule."[14] One October morning in 1870, a white man and a state constable quarreled; another fired a shot. The crowd in the courthouse heard the shooting; everyone, including the defendants on trail, rushed out to participate, leaving the judge to preside over an empty courtroom.[15] The pervading tension had been broken and the famous Laurens Riot ensued. Armed Negroes, who comprised the local militia, set out to burn the town. White townsmen

8. *Ibid.*, p. 190.
9. Beaufort Copeland, in interview with author, June 5, 1957.
10. *Ibid.*
11. William Dendy Watts died in 1861, a few months after returning from the South Carolina secession convention.
12. Ball, *The State That Forgot*, p. 197.   13. *Ibid.*, p. 13.
14. See Francis B. Simkins and Robert H. Woody, *South Carolina during Reconstruction* (Chapel Hill, N. C., 1932).
15. Rosser H. Taylor and Raven I. McDavid, eds., *Memoirs of Richard Cannon Watts* (Columbia, S. C., 1938), p. 23.

answered their cries of "Matches are cheap" by striking back and quelling the riot. William Ball was two years old, and although he remembered nothing of the disturbance, he knew all about it:

> Certainly seven, possibly eleven men were killed the day and the night, for there was great riding. By five o'clock of the afternoon five hundred men had gathered in the village and all the hours of the night the Rebel yell reverberated down the roads worn deep in the red clay hills across the creeks to Laurens, and my mother said that it seemed that the world was filled with riding men. There were about nineteen hundred white men in the county, but the number in the village was guessed as high as twenty-five hundred, for they came from Union, Spartanburg, Newberry, Abbeville, Greenville.[16]

In Spartanburg and Union the Ku Klux Klan had been organized, and although W. W. Ball stated later that there was no club in Laurens, his kinsman Richard Cannon Watts insisted there was indeed a Klan there and that Beaufort Ball was its leader.[17] If there was a formal Klan in Laurens it was not active; violence of this sort did not recur in the town during the remaining six years of Republican hegemony. During this time Billy Ball grew into boyhood.

As a boy, young Ball lived in "Double Chimneys," next door to the law office, and also on his grandmother's nearby plantation, where the pleasures of a Southern rural life were available to him. Although he liked horses, he was afraid of cows and dogs; a dog bit him when he was six. Until he was nearly grown, he refused cold ham at supper because it gave him bad dreams, vague and gloomy, in which dogs persistently appeared.[18] But when he was very little he rode on the pommel of the "Colonel's" saddle and together they fished for catfish and perch.[19] For his fifth birthday he received from his father a flat English saddle brought from Charleston.[20] When Billy was big he rode both horses and

16. Ball, *The State That Forgot*, p. 153.

17. Taylor and McDavid, *Watts Memoirs*, p. 24. Other commentators disagree also. Edwin P. McCravy in his *Memories* (Greenville, S. C., 1941) states that the Klan at Laurens performed much good and needed service in the intimidation of Negroes. But another says, "There never has been a Ku-Klux organization in the county of Laurens, either before, during or since the riot of 1870." See John A. Leland, *A Voice from South Carolina* (Charleston, S. C., 1879), p. 56. The contradiction probably results from the observer's use of different standards to determine the existence of a "klan."

18. Ball, Diary, XII, 108, April 26, 1944.

19. *Ibid.*, X, 169, April 10, 1937.   20. *Ibid.*, II, 196, Dec. 7, 1916.

mules; he went squirrel and rabbit hunting at fourteen, fox hunting at seventeen. Still, he was not an athlete; neither was he at heart a "country boy." Occasionally for the fun of it he would go into the fields, his bag tied to his waist, to pick cotton. He was paid fifty cents for every hundred pounds picked just as the Negroes were. Once, in competition with a cousin, he picked one hundred and nineteen pounds, but it tired him. Once or twice Ball plowed a furrow, but he never really learned to plow. He was no farmer; he had little interest in such activities.[21]

Ball admitted to being a "good little boy"[22]—conscientious, sensitive, timid. He seldom had fights with other boys. Although he had sweethearts when he was nine, between the ages of ten and seventeen he had almost nothing to do with girls. His bashfulness, however, did not prevent his attending dancing school when a teacher came to Laurens. But Ball was, from a very early age, "a reading boy,"[23] and it was from books that he got his greatest satisfaction. From the time he was five his father read aloud to him from Robert Burns and from Southern poets too. As the boy grew older Beaufort Ball urged him to read good books, particularly the English classics. Billy read *The Swiss Family Robinson* so many times that his mother stopped him. He then found *David Copperfield* and *Robinson Crusoe*, and by the time he was nine, he knew something of Tennyson and Shakespeare. At the same time he did not neglect the literature of his area. One of his favorite books was *Georgia Scenes*, A. B. Longstreet's tales of the frontier of the Old Southwest.[24]

Just before he started attending school, the boy's routine was interrupted by an event which was to delight and impress him—a visit to Charleston. To any boy the first trip is exciting; to a quiet boy like Billy Ball, it was filled with wonder. Already his upcountry imagination had been stirred by the articles which had come in Christmas boxes from the seaport "metropolis": oranges, Albert biscuits, French sugarplums, coconuts, firecrackers, and red bananas.[25]

In December, 1874, when he was six, young Ball accompanied his parents on the nearly two-hundred-mile journey to the coast. Starting by buggy, they crossed the abandoned track of the Laurens and Newberry Railroad, which had not operated for the past five or six years, and proceeded to the home of a relative, just west of Clinton, where they spent the night. The next morning the Ball party arrived in Newberry

21. *Ibid.*, XII, 105–106, April 26, 1941.
22. *Ibid.*, XII, 96, April 26, 1941.   23. *Ibid.*, X, 170, April 10, 1937.
24. *Ibid.*   25. *Ibid.*, XII, 91, April 26, 1941.

just before noon and waited there until two o'clock for the Charleston train. In the waiting room there, young Billy, who usually wore a hat, saw a black velvet cap on another boy and he coveted it. Once inside the coach, the boy marveled at its sumptuousness, the paintings on the arched roof, the paneled decoration of the sides, and the plush-covered seats. The Balls rode all night in the coach (there were no berths available) and the next morning they were in Charleston.[26]

The station, decked with hotel posters, provided an arena for shouting cab drivers who almost fought as they bid for debarking travelers. The Balls' lodgings were in the Waverly, an unpretentious hotel about two blocks south of the bend in King Street. Billy never had seen his family's money spent so freely. He noted with admiration the hotel and particularly its food, for ocean fish and oysters were novelties to an upcountry boy. Around the city he went: to the Battery to see the Ashley and Cooper rivers meet and together pass around Fort Sumter, where not fifteen years before the ominous bombardment had begun; back up the peninsula on horse cars to Magnolia Cemetery; and back to East Bay Street to watch cotton ships load. Young Ball saw a mule power the rope and pulleys which hoisted the bales high in the air and onto the ship. Every few minutes the mule trotted one hundred feet or more, and a bale rose high along a rope. To Billy it was a "wonderful spectacle." But when he left Charleston it had to vie with other excitements in his young memory: the view of sea and harbor, the fire alarm that frightened him at night, the incredibility of his first book store.[27]

The emphasis placed on literacy in his home meant that when young Ball started to school he had already been introduced to the basic skills needed by an upcountry boy. He knew his *A B C*'s and a few simple words. He could recite from the Bible and sing hymns which he had learned from his mother or in the Presbyterian Sunday School. Before he was seven, Ball was sent to Mrs. Anna Leland Kennedy's school about a mile and three-quarters from "Double Chimneys," and there he received, along with eight other youngsters, his first schoolroom instruction. He proved to be a star speller, but although he could easily memorize multiplication tables, he was no problem solver.[28]

While Ball was a pupil at Miss Annie's school he moved with his family from "Double Chimneys" into the magnificent John D. Williams house on a hill less than a mile from the courthouse square. Early in

26. *Ibid.*, VII, 28–32, Sept. 27, 1925.   27. *Ibid.*
28. *Ibid.*, XII, 99, April 26, 1941.

1875 Beaufort Ball purchased the one-hundred-and-twenty-two-acre estate with seventy-five hundred dollars in borrowed money. The mansion
was begun by slave artisans in 1859 and completed two years later. The
twelve-room main house, with its large halls and broad piazzas, was
built of plastered-over brick and set in a forest of oak and hickory
interspersed with dogwood. Rising out of the center of the cross formed
by the intersecting rooms was a low rectangular tower, ideal for use as a
look-out post. Eliza Ball suspected that the "Colonel" had bought the
Williams property not for her but as a meeting place for local Democrats in the coming campaign.[29]

The election of 1876 is perhaps the most celebrated in South Carolina
history. After eleven years of Reconstruction, federal troops were still
garrisoned there, although they had been removed from most other
Southern states.[30] The frustrated Democrats were more determined than
at any time since 1865 to end Republican control and restore native
white rule, but with a Negro voting majority of twenty thousand in the
state, Democratic leaders divided over strategy. One faction, the Fusion-
ists, believed success could come only from co-operation with sympathetic Republican governor Daniel H. Chamberlain. The Straightouts,
on the other hand, stood for a direct independent fight for all officers
from top to bottom. In the August convention the Straightouts won a
narrow victory and the venerated Confederate soldier Wade Hampton
was nominated for governor. Having decided on an independent contest,
the Democrats had still to decide whether they were fighting for a return
of good government which would include participation by the Negro, as
Wade Hampton and the official platform stressed; or whether as M. W.
Gary, the influential Straightout leader insisted, the issue was race
against race. The campaigns of both parties and the events which
followed proved that the question of which race would rule the other was
undeniably dominant.

The Democratic State Committee, anticipating the vital 1876 election, had already begun strengthening local organizations, and Beaufort
Ball was appointed to reorganize Laurens. It had always been the
"Colonel's" habit to bring home his country friends and clients to spend
the night. But in the spring of 1876 it seemed to his young son that the
County Democratic Chairman began to receive more callers. The visitors were influential men in their neighborhoods and were almost exclu-

29. Beaufort Copeland, in interview with author, June 5, 1957.
30. Federal troops remained in Florida, Louisiana, and South Carolina.

sively middle-aged Confederate veterans; they talked politics constantly.[31] From the time of the August convention, hard riding began in Laurens and almost every man was armed, for the aim of the Straightouts was to intimidate the Negro in order to keep him from the polls in November. Red flannel was the badge of the riding Democrat, and every two or three days a squadron of red-shirted men came into Laurens village. Every man and youth seemed to be on horseback. A Red Shirt Club from Cross Hill Township was named for Beaufort Ball, and many of its members, some prominent and some poor, were related to him by blood or marriage.[32]

Nearly every night the big Ball home was crowded with visitors from all over the county. At any hour, squadrons of these men might ride to the house, stable their horses and mules, eat and spend the night. Young William Ball was just eight years old, but he later recalled:

> One night exactly twenty-three, most of them young men, were in the house, and exactly three of them had not had too much whiskey. The Democrats had demanded a "division of time" with the Radical speakers that day and the Red Shirts had been hurriedly summoned. Those boys had no suitcases or nightshirts, and they should not have brought whiskey with them. One of them had to be lifted to his room from the supper table. After supper they went downtown and came back about eleven to dance and sing till two. Only the dependably sober men, none of the youngsters, had access to the Colonel's demijohn, our household did not approve of this drinking, but was not nearly so much shocked as would be expected of it nowadays—in fact my mother was up at six-thirty next morning thinking more about the need of those boys for black coffee hot and strong at breakfast than of the whiskey they drank the night before.[33]

When the Radicals held meetings, shouting Red Shirts sometimes galloped in, rearing their horses within ten feet of the speakers. An open clash with the "Rads" might come at any time, as it had already in other parts of the state. The women of the county lived with fear; news of bloodshed would have startled but not astonished them.[34]

Excitement grew in Laurens as the day of the Hampton meeting

31. W. W. Ball, *A Boy's Recollections of the Red Shirt Campaign of 1876 in South Carolina* (Columbia, S. C., 1911), p. 7.
32. *Ibid.*, p. 8.   33. Ball, *The State That Forgot*, pp. 156–157.
34. *Ibid.*

approached. By this time Billy Ball owned a red shirt, made for him by
his grandmother, and he was very proud even though the shirt was of
calico instead of the regulation flannel. One fall day at sundown, four
hundred Laurens Red Shirts rode out to meet the Democratic candidate
for governor and escort him into town. Hampton's party had made so
many stops along the road, however, that it was ten o'clock before they
arrived and most of the townspeople did not see them until morning.
The spectacle of that day became one of W. W. Ball's brightest
memories:

> The October sun rose next morning on such a day as the village of
> Laurens had never seen before and would not see again. Long
> before daylight every road leading to the town was crowded with
> buggies, wagons, men on horseback. All the vehicles, some of them
> almost falling apart, every horse and mule in the county, and
> hundreds in the adjoining counties, must have been called into
> service. Everybody was shouting, laughing, cheering. I was in the
> carriage with the women of my family; to my sorrow I was not
> allowed to ride in the procession; they thought I was too young.
> . . . About ten o'clock the procession formed in the Public Square
> and the five radiating streets. I had not dreamed that there were so
> many men in the world or half so many horses and mules. Com-
> pany after company, some of them stretching hundreds of yards,
> about twenty of them, swept across the Square, and the yelling and
> cheering never stopped, it only rose and fell in waves of sound. The
> red shirts were not all alike, for many of them were elaborately
> trimmed with blue and yellow. Here and there was a marshal with
> plumed hat and clanking sword. . . . The Greenville band with
> another perhaps which could play more than a single tune were in
> the procession and martial music was abundant, though the sound
> of it died in the music of the cheers. . . . In most of the companies
> were a few red-shirted Negro Democrats—the campaign managers
> were solicitous about them and gave them front seats at the
> stand.[35]

"Colonel" Ball as county chairman, sat on the speakers' platform,
and to Billy's astonishment and delight, his father allowed him to sit
there too. The boy listened to the speakers: he observed how Wade
Hampton spoke to the Negroes in the front seats in a way that was both

35. *Ibid.*, pp. 160–161.

persuasive and conversational; and he was a little disappointed that the General's manner was so easy and calm.[36] Ball himself described why he left the platform and how he failed his own special assignment that day:

> Disaster befell me. I got the stomachache and had to be taken to my mother in the carriage. Now General Hampton when he began to speak asked me to take care of his hat. It was a sacred trust, and I watched the hat, on the table, till I got sick. Some stranger took the General's hat, leaving one three sizes too small for him, and as he had a large head he could not find a hat in a Laurens store that fitted. I was well again in an hour, but the affair of the hat was long on my conscience, or stomach.[37]

As November grew nearer the riding increased and the Rebel yell echoed throughout the country. In two townships of Laurens County people resorted to violence; a few Negroes were killed. But for these exceptions there was no blood let in Laurens; the White Democrats instead "bulldozed, frightened, and bribed the darkies."[38] Eliza Ball offered half a dozen Negro laborers five dollars apiece in gold if, on election day, they would report at her house at seven o'clock and remain there without doing any work until the polls closed that evening. Only one accepted her offer, and he demanded (and received) besides his gold piece, all the sweet potato custard he could eat.[39] On the evening before the election, hundreds of Negroes camped in the courthouse ready to cast their ballot early the next day. But in the morning the Red Shirts made the square their circus track as they whooped and shouted, firing pistol shots into the air and throwing rocks at the courthouse walls. Most of the Negroes became so frightened that they fled and did not return to vote.[40] The Federal garrison stayed in its camp all day; no soldiers came to the square.

Accounts differ as to the prevalence of fraud that day in Laurens,[41] but one thing was certain. The Democrats carried Laurens County by a majority of more than eleven hundred votes. The Republican state board of canvassers later refused certificates of election to the members of the

---

36. *Ibid.*   37. *Ibid.*, pp. 161–162.
38. Taylor and McDavid, *Watts Memoirs*, p. 45.
39. Ball, *A Boy's Recollections*, p. 16.
40. Taylor and McDavid, *Watts Memoirs*, p. 45.
41. Ball, *A Boy's Recollections*, p. 22: election frauds infrequent; Taylor and McDavid, *Watts Memoirs*, p. 45: the Democrats seized the polls on election day (considerable dishonesty implied).

House elected from Laurens and Edgefield counties and rival Houses convened in Columbia, one with a Democratic speaker, the other under Republican control. It was not until April, 1877, after President Hayes's removal of federal troops from South Carolina, that the White Democrats recaptured control of the state government. But the victory had been celebrated months before in Laurens. For two or three days after the election, reports of the results conflicted. When at last it seemed that the Democrats had won, the town exploded in wild rejoicing. That evening a delegation of exuberant townspeople came to serenade Beaufort Ball. The band played and the "Colonel" spoke from the front steps while the household buzzed inside. When Ball had finished speaking, having been warned by his son not to stop too soon, the doors of the big house were thrown open and the crowd invited in for cake and nog hastily prepared from nearly seven dozen eggs.[42]

When the day of the Red Shirts had passed Billy Ball was eight years old and attending the Male Academy in Laurens, where he played all the games but excelled in none. At nine he studied Latin and at eleven he began Greek. After a year as a special student in the Laurensville Female Academy, Ball entered Adger College in the village of Walhalla at the extreme northwestern tip of the state. The preparatory school's five-man faculty included specialists in Greek, Latin, mathematics, the physical sciences, and moral philosophy.[43] Young Ball lived at the home of the headmaster, and it was there that he began his career as a journalist.

Ball and the other boarding students published for a time a weekly sheet which they called "Angellos." The paper, handwritten and offered for five cents a copy, reported locals, personals, riddles, jokes. It announced the topics for the school debates: "Resolved—that the abolition party of the north was more to be blamed for the late war than the secession party of the South."[44] W. W. Ball was listed as manager of the editorial and local department. In "Angellos" appeared his earliest attempt at criticism (sour feet in church) and his first editorial, "Indulgences of Students." As a class, wrote editor Ball, students were more susceptible to temptation than any other group. All time should be devoted to study except the modicum necessary for healthful exercise

42. Ball, *The State That Forgot*, p. 168.
43. Ball, Diary, VII, 363, June 11, 1930.
44. "Angellos," Vol. 1, Feb. 16, 1883, Papers of William Watts Ball, Duke University Library. Note that while "South" is capitalized, "north" is not.

and literary pursuits. Particularly damaging to the student was time lost in calling on the ladies. Courting, Ball maintained, "fills the mind of the student with anxiety, consumes large portions of his time without improving his mind, destroys his appetite which causes dyspepsia, sometimes breaks his heart and causes him to commit suicide."[45]

After a year at Adger, Ball entered South Carolina College. He was not yet fifteen, and for a time his interest in amateur journalism persisted. In the summer after his first year at Carolina, the firm of Ball and Ball compiled a household organ they called "The Domestic Regulator." This paper was written every few days and submitted to the neighborhood public for twenty-five cents a month. Advertising could be had for seventy-five cents per square. Eliza Ball at first consented to be her son's co-editor but resigned after the first issue; her partner had published a plea for the neighbors to supplement his dinner menu, which was composed of nothing but bacon and cabbage.[46] The editor's young sister Sara—seven, and a suffragette—was the paper's fashion editor although she apparently did not contribute copy. This was Billy Ball's paper and he read it aloud to his family hoping to amuse them by making fun at their expense. His Aunt Sue Simpson's collection of curios and shells he termed the "Simpsonian Institution."[47] But there was the serious side, too; the proprietor referred to himself throughout as a "fighting editor." In politics "The Domestic Regulator" was conservative Democrat, and, like any respectable newspaper, commented on the important matters of the day. On one such issue, the selection of a new president for his college, Billy sought an interview from his father. Beaufort Ball was pessimistic about the future of Carolina. The people of the state, he said, were nothing but shopkeepers—had no large views, didn't think it their interest to have a college, would rather see ten cents come in for a box of matches.[48] The Younger Ball, nevertheless, returned to his college in September, and when he did, "The Domestic Regulator" expired. The last issue extant was dated September 11, 1884.

Ball's years at South Carolina College were critical ones for the old school. First opened in 1805, it had become a Negro college during the Reconstruction Era, and finally closed, a victim of racial problems and political squabbling. It reopened in Columbia in 1880 as an agricultural

45. *Ibid.*
46. "The Domestic Regulator," Vol. 1, no. 1, Aug. 30, 1884, Ball Papers.
47. Ball, Diary, VII, 362, June 11, 1930.
48. "The Domestic Regulator," Vol. 1, no. 3, Sept. 6, 1884, Ball Papers.

and mechanical school supported by federal grants and in 1882 a school of liberal arts was added by the state. Before the re-created college graduated its first class it was attacked by Ben Tillman, just beginning the political career that was to take him to the governorship, the United States Senate, and the dictatorship of South Carolina. Tillman charged that the agricultural college had been overpowered by the college of liberal arts, and that a new independent college must be established for the education of farmers' sons. The present college, he scoffed, was an institution for the sons of lawyers and the well-to-do.[49] Ball, reflecting later on these exaggerated charges, admitted to being one of the richest of the two hundred students at the South Carolina College. His father was able to give him three hundred and fifty dollars a year, four hundred when he was a senior. With two hundred and fifty dollars a year, a man could pay board nine months and look well dressed if he were careful.[50] Young Ball, with his grander allowance, could dance at least one night a week and wear a fraternity pin.[51] He joined the Phi Delta Theta fraternity; there and elsewhere at Carolina he made half a dozen good friends he was to keep throughout his adult life. The Reverend J. W. Alexander, Professor of Moral Philosophy, instilled in Ball the determination to maintain his intellectual integrity. But R. Means Davis, Professor of History and Politics, of all Ball's instructors, made the deepest impression on him. The textbook for Davis's course was John Stuart Mill's *Principles of Political Economy.* Mill's theories, Ball acknowledged, "got into his system."[52] In his last year Ball was elected president of the Clariosophic Literary Society, an honor which pleased him chiefly because his father had held the same office about thirty-six years before.[53]

By this time Billy Ball had formed his prejudices and found his causes. How like his father's they were, for the young man was an unblushing idolator. He once wrote: "All men have their faults, they say. He had his share I suppose. I knew them not."[54] Young Ball had grown up in his father's friendship, shared his thoughts, and drawn from him

49. Ball, *The State That Forgot,* p. 212.
50. W. W. Ball to Helen C. Bennett, Jan. 22, 1929, Ball Papers.
51. Ball, *The State That Forgot,* p. 212.
52. W. W. Ball, *The Editor and the Republic,* ed. Anthony Harrigan (Chapel Hill, N. C., 1954), p. x. Ball seems to have been most influenced by Mill's claim that modern democracies tended to crush individual development and tyrannize minorities, and by his suggestion that the problems of Ireland might be solved by the establishment there of peasant-proprietorships.
53. Ball, Diary, II, 167, Nov. 2, 1916.
54. Ball, *The State That Forgot,* p. 201.

what he knew of things and men and books. The "Colonel's" friends and acquaintances were judges, lawyers, ministers, and Confederate officers, members of the ruling class of the ante-bellum South. They visited Beaufort Ball, and his son grew up listening to their talk. From them he acquired his distrust of the political democracy which he could see expanding about him. Postwar constitutional developments in the state had expanded the suffrage to include large portions of the "great unwashed," and now as Ball prepared his commencement speech, the "wool hat" farmers had indeed embarked on the jihad which, a few years hence, was to turn the "aristocrats" from Columbia. During these same years Ball was settling into the cult of aristocracy. He had accepted the opinions of the "Bourbon Democrats"; he cherished their philosophies; and forever he stood by them, rejecting nothing.[55]

But Beaufort Ball imparted to his son more than a vague indoctrination in the Bourbon traditions; he gave him his heroes. The "Colonel" knew his Jefferson, his Calhoun, and his Dr. Thomas Cooper, and their doctrines were his political opinions.[56] From Jefferson, Billy adopted a deep respect for "small" government and a distaste for a national life centered about large urban industrial centers. He was proud that his birth outside the village of Laurens entitled him to call himself a "countryman." From his reading of Calhoun he became convinced of a need for safeguarding the political rights of a minority, removed though it might be from popular currents. Dr. Cooper helped acquaint him with the vulgarities of popular government. From all three men, and from countless other sources too, he absorbed enough of the wine of states rights—that perennial Southern potion—to exhilarate him for the rest of his life.

The first public announcement of Ball's serious young conservatism came in his graduation speech delivered at the South Carolina College on June 22, 1887. Written as an editorial, it was a defense of primogeniture reflecting in part an Anglophilia not uncommon among educated South Carolinians. What do Englishmen do with bequests they get

55. *Ibid.*, p. 14.
56. *Ibid.*, p. 200. Dr. Thomas Cooper was English by birth and Oxford educated. Although he was a liberal in England, he became disgusted with practical democracy in America and supported aristocratic control of government here. In 1820 he was made Professor of Chemistry at South Carolina College and soon afterward was elected president of the college. During these years he also taught political economy and was recognized as a prominent academic spokesman for states rights. He was an early advocate of secession. See Dumas Malone, *The Public Life of Thomas Cooper* (New Haven, Conn., 1926).

because they were first born? Some of them, Ball suggested, used them in a way which was beyond the conception of American railroad, cattle, and cotton kings, because those Englishmen alone "recognized in wealth a power to kindle their own talents into lights for their inferiors."[57] In England, Ball continued, genius traveled by the side of wealth, each descending from father to son; critics of primogeniture might point to examples of self-made men but they could not show a finished one. Experience had shown that every nation has a wealthy class, it had demonstrated that the fixed class is the superior; it followed then that primogeniture would benefit a new country:

> The American Eagle should learn that the plumage of youth is neither fitting in quality or quantity to his present dignity and future majesty. There are feathers in the mother bird's wing which might add strength and luster to his own opinions. Perhaps to advocate primogeniture would be considered treason in America; perhaps in another century it will sink to a political foundation stone by force of sheer inertia.[58]

With that oration William Watts Ball, a reactionary at nineteen, departed South Carolina College, a member of the "brilliant"[59] class of 1887. During the autumn months he taught school at Johnston in Edgefield County. Johnston was a country village of six hundred residents who were nearly all Methodists or Baptists and very pious. He was once cautioned by the principal not to mention attending a dance in Columbia because public reaction would destroy his usefulness.[60] Ball hated teaching in Johnston, and, when his father became ill early in 1888 he returned to Laurens. That spring he substituted in Laurens schools and in the fall he began a one year's teaching chore in Columbia, at the same time taking postgraduate courses at South Carolina College. With the end of school in the spring, Ball again came home, and having by now decided that although teaching might be "good training" it

---

57. W. W. Ball, "Primogeniture," Ball Papers.   58. *Ibid.*

59. Daniel W. Hollis, *University of South Carolina* (2 vols.; Columbia, S. C., 1951, 1956), II, 264. The class of 1887 contained several men who, like Ball, were to become influential in South Carolina and beyond, including: Robert Wilson, Dean of the Medical College of South Carolina; Charles H. Barnwell, Professor of English and Dean of the University of Alabama; and David F. Houston, Secretary of Agriculture and Secretary of the Treasury during the administrations of Woodrow Wilson.

60. Ball, Diary, IV, 91–92, July 30, 1918.

would not provide him with a satisfying career, he began to read law in his father's office. The next year he was admitted to the state bar.

The year was 1890—a "watershed" date for the nation but a turning point too for South Carolina. Her political life was forever altered when control of the Democratic party, hence the state itself, passed from the Bourbons to the agrarian reformers. A national farmers' revolt was brewing, directed especially against the railroads. Benjamin Ryan Tillman, organizer of the state Farmers Association, had announced in his Shell Manifesto that farmers should not join the Populist movement but should contain their revolt within the Democratic party. Their capture of the nominating convention guaranteed election of their leader as governor. In 1890 Ben Tillman, idol of the wool-hats, ascended to the state house; "democracy" had captured the Democratic party.[61]

At the same moment, while Ball was taking summer law courses at the University of Virginia, events in Laurens County were to have a sharp effect on his future also. The Ball family had always been interested in the press. The "Colonel" had written editorials on a part-time basis for the *Laurensville Herald*; his son's own youthful experiments in reporting and publication were not far behind him. Now the weekly *Laurens Advertiser* was offered for sale. Billy Ball, still in Charlottesville, decided to buy the paper, and with fifteen hundred dollars borrowed at 7 per cent from the National Bank of Laurens, the purchase was made.[62]

Therewith Ball began the career in journalism that was to make him a center of comment and controversy for more than half a century. The simultaneous fall of conservative leadership before rising agrarian discontent proved to be a fateful coincidence. Ball, at the start, stood where he was so often later to be found—*in opposition.*

61. See Francis B. Simkins, *The Tillman Movement in South Carolina* (Durham, N. C., 1926) and *Pitchfork Ben Tillman* (Baton Rouge, La., 1944). Ball often said that Simkins oversimplified by describing Tillmanism as a movement of plain people against the aristocracy. According to Ball, nearly every "aristocratic" family in Laurens was divided. Both his father and mother had cousins who were Tillmanites. See W. W. Ball to David R. Coker, June 7, 1929, Ball Papers.
62. Ball, Diary, VII, 299, Feb. 12, 1930.

CHAPTER THREE

FRUSTRATIONS OF A YOUNG
NEWSPAPERMAN

WHEN BALL returned to Laurens to take over operation of the *Advertiser*, he found the office a shambles. In one corner of the space, which was located on the second floor of a store building, was the editor's private office—a little boarded-off section, six by six, containing an old desk and two or three split-bottom chairs. The bookkeeping system used by the previous owners was, to say the least, primitive. Dates on which subscriptions were paid were kept in type. When a dollar was paid the date was changed. No subscription book was kept and errors were numerous. When a subscriber questioned the record, there was little Ball could do but take his word. The staff of the paper included the printer, who was paid only eight dollars a week, but who drank whiskey in excess and was probably not worth more; a boy of thirteen or fourteen who helped in the office while he learned the printing trade; and a Negro who set type and was the object of spirited community criticism. White men who engaged Negroes for anything but strictly laboring duties caused resentment in Laurens. A complete reorganization of the paper appeared necessary, and Ball began by firing both the Negro and the drunkard and hiring a new printer.[1]

When Ball assumed control of the *Advertiser* he knew nothing of presses or printer's ink. He at first thought he could practice law and run the paper at the same time; if he wrote the editorials, the paper, with a small staff, would "run itself." Consequently, he became his father's law partner in the firm of Ball and Ball. He assisted in the defense of two Negroes accused of homicide and participated in several civil cases, but he did little actual work. Ball soon found he had neither the time nor the inclination for the law and after two or three months he gave up all pretense of practicing. For the next four years he devoted himself principally to developing his investment in the rural press.

Ball's idea was that the county weekly should report the news of its

1. Ball, Diary, VII, 299–302, Feb. 12, 1930.

territory with care and thoroughness, leaving most events of general interest to the daily press, but that its editorial page should speak plainly on any issue the editor deemed provocative.[2] The *Advertiser* carried news of the neighboring towns, for Ball had correspondents in Waterloo, Cross Hill, Ora, and other hamlets, but national news stories were rare in the columns. Because Ball was a young editor of firm opinions on many subjects, the editorial stand of the paper was taken not only on the traditional "page four," but in short quips interspersed between the advertisements for Castoria, syrup of figs, botanic blood balm, and trinkets of the Laurens Jewelry Palace. Ball's editorial verdicts were sometimes long, sometimes short, often expressed in puns; on the free coinage of silver: it will not answer the South's problems which arise from one-crop servitude;[3] on cheap money: dangerous;[4] on hard money: "we are opposed to hard money, that is hard to get";[5] on a divorce: South Carolinians can become divorced across the Savannah River in Georgia, which was "founded as an asylum for unfortunates";[6] on being a Democrat: "a thing of duty and a joy forever."[7]

In the early nineties, however, Ball saw the first of a long series of developments that were to make his loyalty to the Democratic party less a pleasure. As farmers struggled with lower prices and bigger debts, the Bourbons espoused economical government and offered concessions to industrial developers. Mixing polite manners and fond remembrances of the Confederacy, they admonished their critics that white infighting would restore the Negro to political influence; and for a time the Bourbons retained their hold. But then as the Populist movement took form in the nation Tillman and his Alliance men demanded a state government in South Carolina that would take positive steps to aid the farmer, and ultimately they gained control. Although Tillman enjoyed some upper-class support, his victory was essentially a triumph for the underprivileged class.

On the surface the difference between the deposed conservatives and the Tillmanites could hardly have been more striking. Ben Tillman's manners were crude and his methods overbearing, the antithesis of Bourbon reserve. Wielding his figurative pitchfork, he capitalized on racial and class feelings in a fashion too blatant for the Bourbon stom-

2. W. W. Ball to H. H. Woodward, March 30, 1926, Ball Papers.
3. *Laurens Advertiser*, July 4, 1893.
4. *Ibid.*, Oct. 10, 1893.   5. *Ibid.*, July 25, 1891.
6. *Ibid.*, May 12, 1891.   7. *Ibid.*, July 25, 1891.

ach. He turned scores of the old conservatives from office, replacing them with his own men. And so Ball persistently regarded Tillman as if he had turned the state upside down. After all, had he not prevented Wade Hampton's return to the Senate? Hampton—that most exemplary Bourbon who had been one of the richest ante-bellum slaveholders, a Confederate hero, a Redeemer, and one of the few Bourbons who maintained his planting interests in the postwar South! Ball regarded Tillman as a demagogue and the democratic victory as cataclysmic. The difference implied by the capitalization of the letter "d" became a fetish with him: a Democrat he was, a democrat he was not. "Take democracy," he wrote, "just now there is never a fellow with a political fad or phase of foolishness who does not claim some of its leaven."[8]

The farmers' movement acquainted the white masses with political power; and Ben Tillman, though middle class himself, was unquestionably the democratic figurehead. Still, Tillman evoked from Ball and other conservatives a degree of animosity somewhat out of proportion to the governor's actual threat to their ideals. His enacted program included higher corporation taxes, increased appropriations for state medical institutions, and measures encouraging to agricultural and other vocational training at the expense of liberal arts education. He was responsible for a legislative reapportionment which furnished the more populous upland counties with new, if not yet adequate, political strength. Other measures, including a new constitution, further lowered the social and political status of the Negro. But no revolutionary changes in the life of the state accompanied the unfolding of Tillmanism. In fact, the Farmers Alliance, disappointed over the failure of a railroad regulation bill, formally repudiated the governor in 1891, following charges that he had been not only complacent but traitorous as well. The truth was that the gap between reformers and traditionalists was not so wide as both groups insisted. Mutual intolerance brought down both factions, leaving racism without challenge as the predominant philosophy.

Democratic party solidarity was the instrument of racial control, and, to Ball, there was no denying that "white dominancy is the necessity to which all others in Southern politics are secondary and trivial."[9] After the Tillmanites captured control of the gubernatorial nominating convention in 1890, the Conservative Democrats met separately and nominated Colonel A. C. Haskell to oppose Tillman in the general election.[10]

8. *Ibid.*, Aug. 24, 1891. 9. *Ibid.*, Oct. 13, 1891.
10. Haskell's candidacy was endorsed by the Republican executive committee but Tillman won easily: 59,159 votes to 14,828 for Haskell.

Much as Ball deplored the fall of the aristocracy, there is no evidence to indicate that he sanctioned the splinter movement, later charges of his critics notwithstanding. Though he was not able to produce the files of the *Advertiser* and prove his point, Ball insisted he did not either support editorially or vote for Haskell in 1890.[11] In 1893, moreover, Ball called the Haskell movement a blunder and stated explicitly, "The Advertiser was opposed to Judge Haskell in '90."[12] In 1892, nevertheless, he took an active part in the anti-Tillman or conservative campaign in Laurens. The county meeting elected him alternate delegate to the state Democratic convention, where he served as one of its two secretaries[13] and where he again saw Ben Tillman emerge as the party's candidate for governor. Ball despised Tillmanism and the constitution which the democratic revolt was to provide the state in 1895, but to him Democratic solidarity was the insurance for white control in the state. Ball was a Democrat; Tillman was the party's choice; Ball's paper acquiesced.

The responsibilities of editorship also brought Ball for the first time into sharp contact with the ugliest aspects of the South's racial problems. For the second time in Ball's young life the Southern Negro was undergoing a revolution in status. When Reconstruction ended the philosophy of Redemption required that the Negro be stripped of political power. His voting strength was substantially reduced by such devices as gerrymandering and in South Carolina the "eight box law" whereby ballots for each state officer must be placed in appropriately marked boxes which might be rearranged by election officials in order to confuse the Negro and negate his vote. Most Negroes who were not effectively disenfranchised in this way resided in the black belt where their vote was controlled—through threat or promise—by conservative leaders. The combined result was the removal of the Negro from political influence, although its counterpart—social segregation—was not immediately forthcoming.

As Ball reached manhood and began his career as an editor, a movement was underway to complete the political removal of the Negro and to isolate him socially as well, developments which sprang from a configuration of forces. The early impact of industrialization on the

11. Unfortunately, the 1890 files of the *Advertiser* have been lost and absolute corroboration is impossible. Beaufort Copeland, in an interview with the author, June 5, 1957, stated, however, that Ball, her uncle, told her once that he would have voted for Haskell if he had known that Tillman would later prevent conservative Wade Hampton's re-election to the United States Senate.

12. *Laurens Advertiser*, May 30, 1893.

13. Ball, Diary, XI, 175, Aug. 9, 1939.

agrarian South was a key factor. The growth of factories brought more Negroes to the cities. There they posed an economic threat to white workers, who demanded that the Negro's inferiority be established through segregation. In the years surrounding 1890 all Southern states enacted Jim Crow laws providing for racial separation on railway cars. Simultaneously the farmers revolted against Bourbon politicians partly because they seemed to favor industry over agriculture. Since one-party politics was the instrument of racial controls, most South Carolina farmers remained in the Democratic party, as did most Southern ones. But independent parties emerged in some states and in North Carolina a Populist party fused with white Republicans and Negroes for the campaign of 1894. The election of several Negroes to important state offices demonstrated to the entire South the dangers of white political rivalry. Only if disenfranchisement were made complete could white men be sure that they would not again be tempted to enlist Negro support. That realization encouraged other Southern states to follow the lead provided by Mississippi in 1890.

Events in South Carolina were typical of the region. Tillmanites had long resented the manipulation of the Negro vote by conservatives, and the farm leader insisted on the constitutional convention which met in 1895. To insure success Tillman solicited conservative aid; and although reformers outnumbered conservatives almost three to one in the convention, its work was achieved through the co-operation of the rival factions. The Constitution of 1895 incorporated safeguards against Negro suffrage with provisions designed to protect white manhood suffrage. The vote was granted to all men who were able to read or write the Constitution or who paid taxes on property valued at three hundred dollars. White illiterates who could interpret the Constitution when it was read to them were to be registered for life provided they made application by January 1, 1898. Under the impact of these arrangements, the Negro vote fell to two or three thousand by the end of the century.

Moreover, the accomplishment of the Negro's political isolation stimulated demands for his social separation, especially from lower-class whites who looked upon segregation as the badge of their biological superiority. The new constitution itself forbade mixing in schools and intermarriage between white persons and those with one-eighth or more Negro blood. There followed in South Carolina, as in other Southern States, a series of enactments, both constitutional and legislative, which

provided for racial separation in hotels, theaters, restaurants, and virtually all other places of public accommodation. Thus, as Northern interest in the Negro faded and the Supreme Court seemed ready to accept all
local arrangements save those which blatantly violated the Fourteenth
Amendment, the definition of caste was established in the South.

That the democratization of politics robbed the Negro of his democratic rights is one of the most frequently stated ironies of Southern life.
Conservative elements, of course, co-operated in disenfranchisement, in
part because they had hoped it would reduce election fraud and bribery.
But because they enjoyed the comfort of status, they had no psychologi-
cal need for legalized social segregation. Still, they acquiesced in its
establishment, confining their racial criticism to the increasing practice
of lynching. W. W. Ball abhorred lynch justice—but then so did Ben
Tillman except as punishment for the rape of white women. As a
newspaper editor, Ball could not ignore a lynching bee. One spring day
news circulated in Laurens that a Negro youth had attacked the young
daughter of a well-to-do farmer as the girl walked from school. He had
grabbed her arm and snatched the satchel she had been carrying. When
the white girl screamed, the boy fled. He was later arrested by neighbors
of the girl's father, who did not bring him to jail, arranging instead for a
hanging in the public square with the prominent men of the town
participating. Ball, as editor of the *Advertiser* and Laurens correspondent for the Columbia *State*, the *Greenville News*, and the Charleston
News and Courier, believed that he must "cover the story." He set out,
reluctantly, driving his two-wheeled cart; but after he had gone less than
a mile, he changed his mind. A young fellow of nineteen, also going to
the "show," agreed to report to him the details of the lynching. Ball was
able to send out his story and afterward "a thousand times rejoiced"[14]
that second thought had kept him from being an eyewitness. He never
had opportunity to see another, yet he began a lifelong editorial campaign against lynch-mob justice. Even in the South, Ball charged repeatedly, where racial taboos made white girls especially shy to testify about
rape, there was no excuse for murder.[15]

Besides news of politics and local incidents, readers of the country
weekly also expected, and received from the *Advertiser*, scrupulous
coverage of the local social scene. When a wedding account was sent to
the paper, a piece of wedding cake for the editor was often enclosed.[16]

14. *Ibid.*, VII, 355, June 30, 1930.   15. *Ibid.*
16. *Ibid.*, XI, 169, Aug. 6, 1939.

Ball always needed items of personal interest to fill his columns, but he had to learn to use discretion in accepting contributions. One day when the editor was walking in the street, an acquaintance (a Northern woman) suggested that, as a joke, he report in the *Advertiser* the fact that four Laurens men, all widowers over fifty and all Confederate veterans, had spent a week end in Augusta, Georgia. Although instinct warned him against it, Ball printed the seemingly harmless story. The men were offended, or embarrassed; two of them protested, and Ball had learned his first important lesson as a newspaperman. "A joke told in the street at which men laugh is quite different from a joke in cold print."[17]

There was much about Ball's four-year active editorship of the *Advertiser*, however, that was light and pleasant. The young editor was a "society man." He had better clothing than most other men in the village, and by his own reckoning, a better income than the young lawyers and teachers.[18] There were dances and baseball tournaments in Laurens and neighboring towns; special events like the cotillion of the Greenville dancing club and the State Ball in Columbia during fair week;[19] interludes at Glenn Springs, a fashionable spa near Spartanburg and one of the social centers of South Carolina.[20] Ball and his sister entertained at home, too, where the dancing and drinking of the young people precipitated a row in the Presbyterian Church. Eliza Ball responded by leading her family out of the disapproving church and into the tiny Church of the Epihany, and the more liberal shelter of Episcopalianism.[21]

During those four years in Laurens, Ball's social life was diverting and his career as a country editor a modest financial success, but after the first six months he became restless. The *Advertiser* was small, the pace of rural publishing slow, and Ball's own habits lazy.[22] Temporary assignments placed him in more stimulating surroundings. In November, 1892, J. C. Garlington of Spartanburg asked Ball to write editorials for the *Herald* while he took a two-week vacation in New York. Soon after, at the invitation of publisher Ambrose Gonzales, he spent a month in Columbia covering the Senate proceedings for *The State*. That was his first experience in reporting and he found the work difficult and exacting.[23] Gradually his name was becoming known in state newspaper

17. *Ibid.*, XI, 174, Aug. 9, 1939.   18. *Ibid.*, VII, 302, Feb. 12, 1930.
19. *Ibid.*, XI, 174, Aug. 9, 1939.
20. Sara Ball Copeland, in interview with author, June 5, 1957.
21. Beaufort Copeland, in interview with author, June 5, 1957.
22. Ball, Diary, XI, 174, Aug. 9, 1939.   23. *Ibid.*

circles. He hoped for a position on a daily paper, but vacancies did not occur on the leading dailies. It did not occur to Ball that he might leave South Carolina.[24]

In the summer of 1894 Ball decided to plunge into the daily publication field in the only way that seemed open to him. With his cousin Larry Boyd as partner, he organized a new paper in the capital. Leaving the *Advertiser* in the care of his father and sister, Ball, who had had no previous permanent connections with a daily newspaper, and Boyd, who had been in the railroad business but was now to act as business manager, embarked on the Columbia adventure. Ball had realized thirty-five hundred dollars in profit from the *Advertiser*,[25] and part of this money he contributed to the small fifteen hundred dollar capital investment in the *Journal*. The paper had no plant; it was printed by *The State*.[26]

Within six months after the appearance of the first issue of the new afternoon sheet, its owners had abandoned it. The demise of the *Journal* was not difficult to explain. Ball's paper was not the only new one in the capital; the steadily growing *State* had not yet celebrated its fourth anniversary. Futhermore, South Carolina was undergoing hard times. Cotton sold for seven or eight cents a pound. Many of the established papers were struggling to survive. But the faults were certainly not all circumstantial. Ball admittedly did not understand what a daily newspaper, even a small one, was all about; moreover, he was earning one hundred dollars a month as a correspondent for other papers and, therefore, not completely dependent financially on the success of the *Journal*. His heart was never thoroughly involved in the venture. If the returns were not enough to keep his partner and him comfortable without painful effort, then they would engage in no stubborn sacrifice just to keep the paper running. With bills mounting, in December, 1894, the *Journal* closed down and W. W. Ball's brief career as the owner of a daily newspaper ended with it. Ball remained in Columbia, working as correspondent there for an assortment of papers that included the distant Cincinnati *Enquirer*.[27]

In March, 1895, came the opportunity he had sought before his unfortunately premature experiment in independent publication. Benjamin A. Hagood, Charleston attorney and his friend from South Carolina

24. *Ibid.*   25. *Ibid.*, VII, 302, Feb. 12, 1930.
26. Memorandum, April, n. d., 1895, Ball Papers.
27. Ball, Diary, VII, 302, Feb. 12, 1930.

College days, wrote Ball that the directors of the floundering *Charleston Evening Post* wanted him to come to Charleston. The young paper, waning beside the venerable *News and Courier*, was not earning expenses. Ball, the stockholders hoped, might make the paper pay. They were prepared to raise as much as four hundred dollars immediately to secure the enterprise. Would Ball come to the aid of the *Post* as editor and bring with him Fitz Hugh McMaster, another college friend, to act as business manager? If after a month Ball and McMaster could bring the paper out of the "slough of despond," D. C. Heyward, one of the directors, promised to contribute a thousand dollars himself to help rejuvenate the paper. If he were successful, Ben Hagood reminded Ball, his reputation would be established.[28]

Ball hesitated. He had experienced recent failure. With his limited experience in the daily press, assuming the editorship of a shaky paper might mean failure again. In his consternation he sought advice from the man he had always emulated. Beaufort Ball responded by asking his son, first, whether he had decided to make journalism *the* business of his life. Whatever his career, the elder Ball continued, he should stay in South Carolina, where he enjoyed some regard as a man of sense and intellectual promise. And if he were to remain in the state, was there any better place than Charleston, where life was more cosmopolitan, broader, richer? Charleston was certainly much better than Columbia. Beaufort Ball judged that there was a promising element surrounding the Charleston opportunity but urged his son, if he accepted the responsibility to work exclusively on the paper; to study politics—city, county, state, nation; to read history; to know Calhoun, Jefferson, Hamilton, and the others. If Ball's goal was a permanent place on one of the state newspapers, his father said, he must accept either a subordinate job on a leading paper or a top position on a smaller paper and fight the competition. If it became necessary for Ball, as editor of the *Evening Post*, to antagonize *The News and Courier*, then he would have to do it. Above all, he must have a line of policy. If the paper should not recover, he stressed, Ball would not be identified with its failure. Finally, with confidence and affection, Beaufort Ball directed his son to "consult himself" in making the decision.[29]

Whether encouraged by his father's calm words or affected by the allure of Charleston for a man of the upcountry who cherished tradition

28. B. A. Hagood to W. W. Ball, March 31, 1895, Ball Papers.
29. B. W. Ball to W. W. Ball, March 31, 1895, Ball Papers.

and gentility, Ball dispatched his acceptance to the directors of the *Evening Post*. He demanded a weekly salary of fifteen dollars in cash and ten dollars in stock and emphasized that his willingness depended on the assurance that the owners would stand by the paper long enough to demonstrate fairly whether success was possible. That success, he predicted, would not be likely without the employment of an experienced and capable reporter at fifteen dollars a week and another at seven dollars.[30]

Ball's first concern, however, was the editorial policy of the paper. The editing of the news columns and choice of what should be published, he expected, would be left for him to determine. He emphasized, however, that the directors should find him generally attentive to their expressions and grateful for their advice, especially in municipal politics. Ball suggested that, from a business point of view, an anti-Tillman policy would be best in state affairs—"candid and positive"[31] but not "ill-natured or petulant."[32] The official editorial position of the paper ought to be independent and should avoid permanent factional alignment. Ball admitted frankly that he thought the *Evening Post* had been started on too small a scale, but in pledging his and McMaster's best efforts he expressed his faith that the paper had a "fine chance to survive and become a handsome property."[33]

With Ball's formal letter of acceptance to his new employers, he enclosed a note to his friend Ben Hagood. "If I fail in Charleston," he confided, "I should feel inclined to sneak out of South Carolina."[34] In April, 1895, stifling his uneasiness, Ball left Columbia for Charleston.

When Ball arrived in Charleston in the spring of 1895, he found the old town shabby. Although still one of America's most distinctive cities, Charleston had been robbed of much of her vitality by decades of economic stagnation. In colonial and Revolutionary days, she was the queen of the South; her docks bristled with activity; her shops and theaters served one of America's most cultivated and cosmopolitan societies. But in December, 1860, when the first secession ordinance was passed in St. Andrew's Society Hall, Charleston was already in decline. Growing competition from Savannah and Wilmington, poor rail connec-

30. W. W. Ball to the directors of the *Charleston Evening Post*, April 11, 1895, Ball Papers.
31. W. W. Ball to B. A. Hagood, April 2, 1895, Ball Papers.
32. *Ibid.*
33. W. W. Ball to the directors of the *Charleston Evening Post*, April 1, 1895, Ball Papers.
34. W. W. Ball to B. A. Hagood, April 1, 1895, Ball Papers.

tions with the West, and the shallowness of her ship channel were weakening her position as a leading commercial center. By the end of the century she had lost her importance as a port. But her culture was kept alive by the old families who, more and more, were living side by side in that part of the city that lay south of Broad Street. Many of Charleston's elite were impoverished by the war and their fortunes did not substantially improve in the years that followed. As carriages and coachmen became luxuries, the aristocracy discovered that concentration facilitated visiting. The trek to the southern tip of the peninsula which began as a convenience by the end of the century had become a mania. Broad Street became the social equator. Between Broad and the Battery, in a tiny area of narrow and winding streets, Charleston's first families fashioned the society—proud and exclusive—that has become a legend.

Ball's first impression when he arrived from the upcountry, however, was that he had come to a dead town. There were few signs of business activity in the streets. The Charleston Hotel had been handsomely redecorated but the bar was never crowded. Ball saw only four or five old people "lolling on the divans" in the hotel corridors, which reminded him of a mausoleum. Streetcar lines had come to Columbia a year before, but Charleston still had mule-drawn cars and was to retain them for several years more. Ball did not think the houses of Charleston beautiful; to him the town was "ramshackled" and needed paint more than any he had ever seen. One did hear, though, of the beauty of a few private gardens, particularly of the one surrounding the Witte mansion, which Ball was soon to know intimately.[35]

The city editor of *The News and Courier* directed Ball to Mrs. Coates's boarding house, where he obtained food and lodging for twenty-five dollars a month. On Sunday he had dinner with Ben Hagood, and he had a dozen other friends in Charleston with whom he had gone to South Carolina College. He had heard of the St. Cecilia Society but, though he had been a "society man" upstate, thoughts of dancing clubs were remote from his mind when he arrived in Charleston. He must be successful as the editor of the *Post*. Soon after Ball assumed his new responsibilities, *The News and Courier* announced:

> Our evening contemporary, the Post, has made some important changes in its working force. Mr. W. W. Ball, of Laurens, has been elected managing editor in place of Mr. H. M. Ayer, who

35. Ball's description of Charleston in late March, 1895, Ball Papers.

resigned the position; Mr. Fitz Hugh McMaster, of Columbia, has been elected business manager. . . . Mr. Ball is a son of Colonel B. W. Ball, of Laurens, and has had considerable experience in newspaper work, first as editor and proprietor of the Laurens Advertiser, of which he is still the owner, and then as editor of the Columbia Evening Journal. He is a bright young man of good training and fine promise and will fill his new post with great credit to himself. Mr. McMaster is the son of Mr. George H. McMaster, of Winnsboro, S. C., one of the most prominent men in that part of the state and has been engaged in newspaper work in Columbia. . . . With such a force as this our evening contemporary will doubtless take on a new lease of life and render good service to the community.[36]

When Ball and McMaster came to the *Evening Post*, its existence was indeed precarious. The paper had been initiated during the previous year in a little building on the west side of Meeting Street at a cost of not more than two thousand dollars. By the spring of 1895 its capital had been exhausted. Fitz Hugh McMaster began by substituting white for colored newsboys and improving collections. Ball's experience in judging news values was limited; political editorials were his forte and he hoped to use Charleston's unflagging interest in state and local politics as the lever to pry his paper out of the doldrums. In spite of the editorial emphasis on politics, circulation did not improve and the *Evening Post* continued to lose money. Debts mounted steadily and by the end of the year had reached eleven hundred dollars.[37] A search for new backing had been unsuccessful; Ball demanded a free editorial rein, and some prospective investors were possibly discouraged by his insistence. Fitz Hugh McMaster had resigned after seven weeks; by December Ball was ready to quit. Dread of a second quick failure still tormented him.

The directors received notice from Ball that he must resign and seek a secure position, but they asked him to postpone his departure for a week so that they might find a new editor. Ball stipulated, however, that announcement of his resignation be inserted in the next issue of the paper. In this way what little was left of his reputation might be salvaged. His own distress, however, could be assuaged. He did not want to leave Charleston; he had joined St. Andrew's Society and the

36. *The News and Courier*, April 8, 1895.
37. Ball, Diary, VII, 334–335, May 16, 1930.

Carolina Yacht Club; he had begun to move in Charleston society. The injection of a little money, Ball believed, could save the paper and prevent his own humiliation.[38]

The morning after notice of his resignation appeared, help came from "a tall, dark, bony, black-whiskered angel."[39] A. M. Manigault, whom Ben Hagood had introduced to Ball several months before, called to ask why he was resigning. Manigault confessed that he knew nothing about the newspaper business but believed that there was need in Charleston for a paper with the *Post*'s policies. When Ball set at five thousand dollars the amount necessary to invigorate the paper, Manigault proposed that if Ball and his friends could invest fifteen hundred dollars, he would provide the rest. Ball was overjoyed, for that was just the amount of money that he, Hagood, and a few other friends could raise.[40] In late December, 1895, the *Charleston Evening Post* was reorganized. Fitz McMaster returned as business manager and Thomas R. Waring, who had replaced McMaster, stayed on as assistant editor at ten dollars a week. Ball as editor earned fifteen dollars weekly; there was no ten dollars a week in stock now, but he owned five hundred dollars worth of stock in the new company.[41]

Manigault seldom interfered with the news or editorial policies of the paper. In 1896 he approved Ball's position in the national presidential election. In that year the Democratic party chose William Jennings Bryan as its candidate and adopted a Populist-flavored platform which demanded an income tax amendment and condemned trusts, monopolies, the high protective tariff, and the use of injunctions against labor. But the money question was paramount and it was the Democrats' espousal of the free and unlimited coinage of silver at the ratio of 16 to 1 that fired the campaign. Any threat to the gold standard, any hint of inflation or devaluation, incensed the conservatives as few other attacks upon the establishment could. It was so in 1933, and it was so in Bryan's day. Ball thought that cheap money was dangerous and that the fixing by statute of a ratio between the fluctuating value of two metals was preposterous. The *Evening Post* bolted.

When the gold Democrats met in Indianapolis in September, 1896, and nominated John M. Palmer for President and Simon P. Buckner for Vice-President on a platform supporting the gold standard, Ball was a member of the convention. This rare excursion into practical politics (he

38. *Ibid.*, VII, 336, May 16, 1930.   39. *Ibid.*   40. *Ibid.*
41. *Ibid.*, VII, 337, May 16, 1930.

was always an observer and critic but almost never a direct participant)
was made possible by a thirty-dollar contribution from his Aunt Betty
Watts.[42] When he returned to Charleston, the *Evening Post* began its
editorial support of the rebellious Palmer-Buckner ticket, a press policy
that was a "bold departure"[43] for the time and place. In an election in
which McKinley polled over seven million votes and Bryan almost six
and one-half million, the Palmer-Buckner ticket received only 131,529.
For the first time as an editor Ball revealed what was to become one of
his most remarkable characteristics. It seemed to matter to him not at all
what a political candidate's chances to be elected might be; his editorial
choices were made irrespective of any consideration so limiting.

Ball continued as editor of the *Evening Post* for about two years. In
1896 the paper acquired a linotype machine, and became by Ball's
reckoning, the second paper in South Carolina (*The State* had been the
first) to depart from the old system of setting type by hand.[44] The *Post*
made gradual but steady progress and by 1897 it was "on its feet"; the
interjection of five thousand dollars in new capital little more than a year
before had saved what was ultimately to become a million-dollar business. Ball believed himself obligated to Manigault to remain as editor at
least until the success of the paper seemed definite; indeed, during the
first months after its reorganization he had no desire to leave even
though it was difficult to be a "society man" in Charleston on a salary of
fifteen dollars a week; furthermore, Ball came to Charleston with debts
and accumulated more while he was living there.[45] But what did it
matter—he was twenty-seven, independent, unmarried, had no thoughts
of marrying. All of this changed rapidly, however, in the fall of 1896.
His friend Tom Waring brought him an oral invitation from Miss Fay
Witte, whom Ball had met a few months before, to attend a party at her
father's house. That was on November seventeenth. On Christmas Day
Ball and Fay Witte became engaged.

Charles Otto Witte was a well-to-do German banker and cotton
merchant who in 1874, before the penchant to live south of Broad Street
hit its peak, bought a mansion up on Rutledge Avenue in a part of town
which was soon to be outside the "fashionable" district.[46] The Witte

42. *Ibid.*, IX, 180, May 22, 1934.   43. *Ibid.*, VII, 338, May 16, 1930.
44. *Ibid.*, VII, 339, May 16, 1930.
45. Ball's principal new liabilities were a $400 loan from the Bank of Laurens
(see note in Ball Papers, Nov. 1, 1895) and another loan for $180 from the same
bank (see note in Ball Papers, Dec. 10, 1895).
46. W. W. Ball, Jr., in interview with author, May 11, 1959.

house, built about 1816, was an outstanding example of a suburban Regency villa modified by the heavy molding and decorations of Victorian times.[47] In a town where showplaces were common, its distinctive attraction was the extensive garden with its miniature zoo. In cages or houses lived monkeys, opossums, prairie dogs, pheasants, peacocks, cockatoos, parrots, and love birds. A tame bear strolled the grounds, and alligators lived in the fountain until they grew large enough to endanger the safety of the children.[48] Inside the house, C. O. Witte and his wife reared six children, all daughters—Alice, Fay, Beatrice, Carlotta, Belle, Laura. They have a place in Charleston legend as the "six beautiful Witte girls," but by the admission of one of them, they were not beautiful; attractive, yes, but not beautiful.[49]

Fay, the second daughter, according to one of her sisters, was a "darling always," a girl who had a good time, made friends easily, was graceful and quick-witted.[50] Her special interest was speech and dramatic arts. Once when she appeared on the program of the Congress of Expression in Atlanta, *The News and Courier* reprinted a reference to her which appeared in the *Atlanta Journal*: "Miss Florence Horlbeck and Miss Fay Witte of Charleston, S. C. . . . are both cultured, charming and beautiful girls, who have studied elocution as an art and for the sake of accomplishing themselves. They are neither in any sense professional, and are artists for the sake alone."[51] Miss Witte would have liked very much to abandon her amateur status and seek a stage career, but although she had a strong will which belied her slight body, she could not overcome her father's objections. Witte, while he gave the girls everything they wanted in the material sense,[52] exercised rigid control over their activities, including their choice of husbands.[53] Apparently Billy Ball met the requirements, for his betrothal to Fay Witte was announced not six weeks after their first evening together. But Ball could not marry on a salary of fifteen dollars a week.

During the previous months Ball had resisted overtures to replace

47. Historic Charleston Foundation, *Charleston's Historic Houses* (Charleston, S. C., 1957), p. 38. The Witte house is now the Ashley Hall School for Girls.
48. Laura Witte Waring, *You Asked for It* (Charleston, S. C., 1941), pp. 46–50.
49. The words of Beatrice Witte Ravenel as revealed by her daughter, Beatrice Ravenel, in interview with author, May 11, 1959.
50. Waring, *You Asked for It*, p. 30.
51. *The News and Courier*, Dec. 25, 1895.
52. Waring, *You Asked for It*, p. 46.
53. Beatrice Ravenel in interview with author, May 11, 1959.

the departing A. B. Williams as editor of the *Greenville News*. But on January 1, 1897, J. F. Richardson, manager of the *News* company, wrote to Ball formally asking him to assume direction of the editorial department and offering to arrange matters so that Ball could be associated with him in the management of the paper.[54] Though it meant leaving Charleston, a move to the *Greenville News* was a step up. The *News*, founded in 1874, was the leading daily in the northern third of the state. Ball judged that his period of obligation to the *Post* had ended, and the publishers of the *News* offered him a substantial increase in salary. With twenty-five dollars a week, he could get married.[55] In February, 1897, he left for Greenville to become editor of the *News*. In April, Ball returned briefly to Charleston and there he and Fay Witte were married by an Episcopal rector on the twenty-first of the month.

When Ball, not yet thirty, joined the staff of the *Greenville News* he assumed one of the top editorial posts in the state. But within little more than a year he was to suffer the second humiliation of his journalistic career. In May, 1898, he was discharged and replaced by his predecessor, A. B. Williams, a partner in the paper who returned from New York to resume the editorship of the *News*. The official reason for his removal was that the paper was "losing ground," and this Ball did not deny. He at first thought the action was the result of great pressure on Jeff Richardson, and that no charge of neglect or incompetence on his part was implied. He believed, however, that he had not been given a fair trial.[56] His friend Thomas R. Waring, who had succeeded Ball as editor of the *Charleston Evening Post*, suggested that possibly Williams wanted to return to Greenville and Ball had been ousted to make room for him.[57] His mother was "sure" that Williams had failed in New York and was calling on his partner for money, that Richardson could not stand the strain and so replaced Ball.[58] But ultimately the discarded editor became convinced that Richardson had written Williams that affairs demanded his return, and that after Ball's release, his successor's continued reflection on his work was creating a permanent injustice. Richardson replied to Ball's request for a statement by indicating his disappointment that Ball, though he had been in Greenville three times

54. J. F. Richardson to W. W. Ball, Jan. 1, 1897, Ball Papers.
55. Ball, Diary, VII, 341, May 16, 1930.
56. W. W. Ball to J. F. Richardson, May 30, 1898, Ball Papers.
57. T. R. Waring to W. W. Ball, June 2, 1898, Ball Papers.
58. Eliza W. Ball to W. W. Ball, n. d., Ball Papers.

since he left the paper, had not seen him.[59] Ball's reaction to Richardson's letter of friendship was polite but chilly. He wrote back:

> It is my desire and intention to treat you with the utmost courtesy at all times. I had hoped that I made it clear before leaving Greenville that the once close relations between us were at an end and I regret that you did not so understand. I think that any recurrence to the episode of my connection with the *News* could only be unprofitable for us both.[60]

There could be no doubt; Ball's resentment was deep and bitter. He had built a house in Greenville with the help of money borrowed from his father-in-law.[61] On March 20 his first child, his daughter Katharine, had been born to Fay Ball in Charleston. In these dark days Ball tried to re-establish himself in Charleston. The old city had her first hold on him; he had kept his membership in the Charleston Light Dragoons. But there were no suitable opportunities there or anywhere in South Carolina. He tried unsuccessfully to find a newspaper job in Washington or as a correspondent in the war with Spain.[62] First as a conservative, and now as an editor, Ball learned the feeling of continuing frustration. Finally he decided to go North in search of work. In July, 1898, he wrote to his friend J. C. Hemphill, editor of the Charleston *News and Courier*, applying for a position on "my own state's leading paper" whenever it might become available and "almost without regard to salary."[63] Armed with letters of recommendation to prominent newspapermen and Hemphill's promise that, if he could make room for him, he would be glad to have him on *The News and Courier*, Ball left for Philadelphia and New York.[64]

For a few months Ball worked as a reporter on *The Philadelphia Press*, where he "learned the value of a story."[65] Once he was assigned to interview one of *the* Goulds who, during the course of his honeymoon cruise, had anchored his yacht in the Delaware River. He was never able to see Gould, but he did talk with the skipper and the mate. The only real information they gave him was that the yacht was called the *Niag-*

59. J. F. Richardson to W. W. Ball, July 19, 1898, Ball Papers.
60. W. W. Ball to J. F. Richardson, July 20, 1898, Ball Papers.
61. C. O. Witte to W. W. Ball, Feb. 21, 1898, April 11, 1898, May 19, 1898, July 1, 1898, July 19, 1898, Ball Papers.
62. H. V. Boynton to W. W. Ball, July 21, 1898. Ball Papers.
63. W. W. Ball to J. C. Hemphill, n. d., Ball Papers.
64. J. C. Hemphill to W. W. Ball, July 19, 1898, Ball Papers.
65. W. W. Ball to Col. George N. McCain, April 22, 1933, Ball Papers.

ara and had come to Philadelphia from Mt. Vernon (either New York or Virginia, Ball did not discover which). He returned to the office expecting to be fired, but was told that in this case "no story" was *the* story and directed to write it.

In Philadelphia Ball earned twelve dollars a week and lived at a boarding house on Arch Street. Times were hard for a beginner in the metropolitan field. Ball's spirits were low; he had a wife and baby in South Carolina. By October he had decided to return to the South and wrote Hemphill again asking about a place on *The News and Courier.* When he learned that there was still no opportunity for him in Charleston,[66] he yielded to his father's suggestion that he re-enter his law office and consider an eventual political career. By December, 1898, he was back in Laurens.

Ball stayed in Laurens this time for about two years helping run the *Advertiser* and practicing law as a member of the firm of Ball, Simkins, and Ball. It was another period of frustration for him; he could not make a living. In 1899, with his wife expecting her second child, Ball desperately needed money.[67] His five hundred dollars worth of stock in the *Charleston Evening Post* he sold to Julian Mitchell, Charleston lawyer and banker, for six hundred twenty-five dollars.[68] Still William and Fay Ball were compelled to sign notes for money, and once again Ball decided to look beyond the state for opportunity. In the fall of 1900 he went to Jacksonville, where be became city editor of the *Florida Times-Union.*

The Jacksonville job lasted for a year and a half. During this time he widened his general newspaper experience, especially through his responsibility for providing disaster coverage of the great fire that swept the city in 1901. Ball was "in better spirits" in Florida than his difficulties of recent years had previously allowed,[69] but in February, 1902, he resigned and went again to his home village. He was, in part, answering a summons; Beaufort Ball had fallen seriously ill and his son returned to take care of both his father's and his own business affairs in Laurens. These two men, who were so alike and who, in the elder's words, were

66. J. C. Hemphill to W. W. Ball, Oct. 29, 1898, Ball Papers.
67. The Balls' second child, Charlotte, was born in January, 1900, but lived only until May, 1901.
68. Ball, Diary, VII, 337, May 16, 1930. Although at the time Ball thought he was making a good trade, the twentieth-century growth of the *Post* company proved the purchase to be a bargain for Mitchell.
69. B. W. Ball to W. W. Ball, Dec. 17, 1900, Ball Papers.

both inclined to be critical, spent their last month together. On March 27, 1902, "Colonel" Ball died. The physical ideal was gone; but the veneration of the conservative idea passed from father to son and thereby became entrenched, and in time, expanded.

For the next two years Ball stayed in Laurens, dabbling with the law, working on the *Advertiser*, and taking occasional special news assignments as correspondent in other parts of the state. Those years in South Carolina were in some respects as unsettled as Reconstruction days. The defeat of Bryan in 1896, together with new discoveries of gold and increased agricultural prosperity, had demoralized the national Populist crusade. Simultaneously, the Tillman movement disintegrated in South Carolina. Disappointment with state government under agrarian control had affected the rural masses even before their leader went to the United States Senate and there indulged in frequent oratorical outbursts, earning censure from his colleagues in 1902 after a Washington's Birthday brawl with John McLaurin, the other senator from South Carolina, whom Tillman had accused of consorting with the Republican administration. Tillman did indeed earn a national reputation, but as an exponent of white supremacy. His generally mediocre legislative performance helped substantiate later charges by critics that reform leadership had been more personally ambitious than honestly committed to the cause.

Beset with internal trouble, the agrarian radical movement was perhaps also weakened by the rise of tenancy and sharecropping, or so thought V. O. Key, pioneer in the study of Southern political patterns. In any case, with the rise of industrialization the center of the democratic thrust began to shift from farmer to mill operative. By the turn of the century the Tillman movement was dead. Its principal legacies to the state—constitutional revision and dispensary legislation—were not only measures removed from the problems which spawned the movement but also purveyors of trouble to come. For the state liquor monopoly became almost at once a center of violence and corruption; and the constitution of 1895 by providing the ultimate in white supremacy in time evoked the Negro protest that wracked the state.

Although the day of the farmer passed, "Tillman" Democrats and conservative Democrats continued to battle for power and the spoils of office while significant legislative activity was all but suspended. Crimes of violence were frequent and the courts often erratic in their administration of justice. D. D. Wallace, author of the most comprehensive history of South Carolina, characterized the early years of the twentieth century in that state when he remarked: "I think I am warranted in saying that such conditions were worse than either before or since in the period from 1890 to 1915, when political excitement, whiskey dispensary corruption, factional hatred, and race prejudice were putting an unusual strain upon the morals and sanity of South Carolinians."[70] No event lends more striking proof to these generalizations than the murder of N. G. Gonzales, editor of the Columbia *State*.

The gubernatorial election of 1902, in which Ball's friend D. C. Heyward emerged the victor, evoked extreme personal hatreds. During the campaign Gonzales had branded James H. Tillman, nephew of Ben and a candidate for governor, as a liar, gambler, and drunkard. On January 15, 1903, Jim Tillman, then lieutenant-governor, while walking on the State House grounds in Columbia, met and shot the unarmed editor, apparently by deliberate plan. Though many in South Carolina were shocked by the murder, others considered the editor's attacks justifiable provocation. A change of venue brought the case to Lexington, where the jury, responding to a plea of self-defense and the right of revenge, freed Tillman. Ball covered the trial for the *Advertiser* and as correspondent for several out-of-state papers but never pretended that his reporting was good newspaper work; he was defending and vindicating Gonzales. He regarded Tillman and his protectors as typical of the "sordid and depraved" creatures who vulgarized South Carolina politics after 1900, actors in a "wretched farce-tragedy."[71]

The death of N. G. Gonzales, nevertheless, necessitated a reorganization of the staff of *The State* and indirectly provided Ball with the opportunity to re-enter the service of one of the state's major dailies. In the spring of 1904, Ball was in Columbia as head of the news department of *The State*. He was barely established there, however, when his continuing campaign to get back to Charleston—to go to *The News and Courier*—produced results. In September, 1904, the engaging but erratic Hemphill hired him as assistant editor, and Ball returned to the "holy city."

70. David D. Wallace, *South Carolina, A Short History* (Chapel Hill, N. C., 1951), p. 651.
71. W. W. Ball to Jessica B. Mannon, Feb. 10, 1932, Ball Papers.

CHAPTER FOUR

THE TRAINING OF AN EDITOR

THERE WAS a note of finality in this, Ball's second move to Charleston. The Balls' twin daughters, Margaret and Eleanor, had been born in 1902; William, their only son, arrived in 1905 and Fay in 1909. Though cautioned by Eliza Ball not to be too "uppity,"[1] the family established residence in a fine old house on Meeting Street, on the "right" side of Broad, and entered Charleston society. Ball was admitted to the famous old St. Cecilia Society, one of the most exclusive social organizations in America, and the privilege of attending its balls was extended to him and his family.[2] Though Ball had not previously, according to a friend, been "church broken," he became an active layman of St. Michael's Episcopal parish.[3] About this time he also began taking special interest in the alumni activities of the University of South Carolina (previously known as South Carolina College), and in 1908 he was appointed to serve on the legislative committee of the Alumni Association.

Another activity to which Ball began to pay increasingly greater attention was real estate. When he arrived in Charleston he owned a modest amount of property. Besides his interest in his father's estate which included the big house in Laurens, he owned three small lots in Laurens County representing a total value of about one thousand dollars.[4] In 1909 a redistribution of family property was effected whereby Ball sold his interest in the family home to his sister Sara, who had married, and bought from the estate a farm in Cross Hill Township of Laurens County. Though he exhibited the upcountryman's penchant for extending his land holdings, he remarked characteristically that he had no objection if Sara should later sell the old home out of the family since

1. Eliza W. Ball to W. W. Ball, March 29, 1908, Ball Papers.
2. Gustavus M. Pinckney to W. W. Ball, Dec. 10, 1907, Ball Papers. Membership in the St. Cecilia Society, founded in 1762, passes through the male line only. Ball's father had been one of those South Carolinians not residents of Charleston to belong to the society. Exclusivity was not necessarily expensive in Charleston. W. W. Ball's dues for 1908–1909 were fifteen dollars.
3. Lucian Mimminger to W. W. Ball, April 23, 1907, Ball Papers.
4. W. W. Ball's financial statement, March 16, 1907, Ball Papers.

"in this country, ancestral estates cannot be maintained."[5] In 1907 Fay Ball bought a lot in the resort town of Hendersonville, N. C. The next year her father died, leaving Mrs. Ball and her five sisters trustees of a considerable estate encompassing rural lands and Charleston houses.[6] From that time Ball served as manager of his wife's holdings, seeing to repairs and collecting rents. Together, and separately, they bought and sold real estate in Charleston and elsewhere—endlessly speculating.

Ball's position on *The News and Courier* gave him an address convenient for supervising his wife's property interest in Charleston. He could follow the pleasant routine of coming to his office at ten o'clock and remaining until half past two, going home for three o'clock dinner, and returning to work from four until seven. His salary, thirty-five dollars a week, was by far the largest he had yet earned as a newspaper employee. And though he had only the second spot in the editorial department of *The News and Courier*, his reputation as a political observer was gradually growing. In a time when political factions were categorized as "dispensary" and "anti-dispensary," Hemphill, Ball, and *The News and Courier*, along with *The State*, were active campaigners against the state liquor business.

In the South Carolina hurly-burly, the Dispensary was the chief agent of chaos. Responding to a popular referendum, the General Assembly approved a prohibition law in 1892 and passed it to the Senate. While it was under debate there, the Tillman-sponsored dispensary plan was abruptly substituted and approved by both houses, a tribute to the governor's dictatorial powers. Whether as a rejection of prohibition, or an exercise in individualism, or as an effort to raise public funds, the Dispensary became one of his obsessions. The system was administered by a state board of control and commissioner and by local county boards. The wholesale outlet in Columbia furnished supplies to retail dispensaries in each of the thirty-four county seats where liquor could be bought. (It could not be consumed on the premises.) By law the state stores became the only legal outlet for liquor in the state. Profits of the state dispensary went into the state treasury to be used for the support of education; local profits were distributed equally to municipal and county governments.

From the start the Dispensary fell victim to the bitter partisanship that choked the state. It pleased neither the wets nor the drys, town or

5. W. W. Ball to Sara B. Copeland, Jan. 9, 1909, Ball Papers.
6. W. W. Ball to John S. Bryan, March 18, 1908, Ball Papers.

country, upcountry or low country. Many opposed the experiment simply because it was Tillman's self-proclaimed "baby"; still others, regardless of their attitude toward liquor, supported the plan out of loyalty
to the reform leader. Under the circumstances it never had a chance.
Throughout the Dispensary's stormy history the enabling act was frequently amended and the legality of the monopoly was frequently in
question. In 1894 the State Supreme Court declared the law unconstitutional but reversed itself soon afterward when a Tillmanite acceded to
the bench. Later, the United States Supreme Court reversed a circuit
court ruling which had denied the right of the state to be a merchant in
the liquor business.

Fraud appeared early. Because a majority of freehold voters were
required to approve the establishment of local outlets the dispensary
system faced instant failure if voter support was lacking. Where "antis"
formed the town majority, ingenious methods broke down opposition. In
one town a quarter of an acre in a swamp was conveyed to forty whites
and blacks who were thus freeholders and the required majority was
secured.[7] Graft and corruption were also quick to appear. Distilleries
lobbied in Columbia and offered bribes as rewards for contracts to fill
the palmetto-adorned dispensary bottles. In some cases local offices lost
funds through poor bookkeeping or diverted profits through manipula-
tions. Constables were sometimes induced to ignore violations. Bootlegging flourished and saloons operated defiantly. "Social clubs" were
stocked with liquor imported by members after the courts ruled that
attempts to block that traffic violated the interstate commerce clause of
the federal Constitution.

Worse, the Dispensary was the cause of occasional violent clashes
between enforcing officials and recalcitrant townspeople. Charleston—
independent, wet, conservative—was the most consistent rebel. "Blind
tigers," as the illegal saloons were called, abounded. In 1896 Governor
John Gary Evans invoked the metropolitan police law which allowed
him to appoint police commissioners who in turn supervised officers who
might arrest violators of state law. Despite cries of persecution and
heavy press criticism, the metropolitan police administration remained
in effect until ended by Governor W. H. Ellerbe eighteen months after
its inception.

Although Charleston was the most persistent violator of the law, the

7. Ball, *The State That Forgot*, p. 249.

most celebrated episode occured in Darlington, a courthouse town in the Pee Dee region. Already strong feeling against Tillman and the Dispensary was aggravated by the arrival of seventeen constables intent on uncovering a ring suspected of organized resistance to the law. False rumors circulated that houses were to be entered without warrants in a search for illegal whiskey. When a constable shot and killed a townsman during a scuffle on an afternoon in May, 1894, a riot erupted in which several of both camps were killed and wounded. A mob drove the state policemen from town, destroyed the local dispensary, and threatened to lynch any constable who dared to return. When Tillman called for militia, the first counties summoned refused to submit men and he was forced to rely upon companies of his neighbors from Edgefield. Simultaneously he declared Darlington and Florence counties in a state of insurrection and took over the railroads, the telegraph, and the Columbia police force. But when the troops reached Darlington, the crowd had dispersed despite support from elements of the conservative press which in ordinary times would have abhorred mob violence as inconsistent with the code of the gentleman. With the town quiet after a week of turmoil, the "Darlington War" ended. While the excitement lasted, Ball claimed to have made more money as a newspaperman than during any week before or since: "One night *The New York Tribune* replying to my 'query' ordered all I could send, the sky was the limit." He added, "It was a great week."[8]

By 1904 the ultimate demise of the Dispensary system was apparent. In that year the Brice Act, passed with the aid of growing prohibition sentiment, permitted any county to vote out the dispensary. Ball had been a constant opponent of the liquor monopoly both as a violation of free enterprise and as an exercise in bureaucratic centralization. During the campaign of 1906, he urged Fraser Lyon of Abbeville, a man he "hardly knew,"[9] to abandon his plans to run for the office of attorney general and run for governor instead. It was a time of crisis and Lyon's views on the liquor problem pleased Ball. Though he could not speak for *The News and Courier*, he offered the support of the *Laurens Advertiser*:

If the State dispensary is endorsed this year, it means that the state will be surrendered to grafters, they will be impudently ascendant and South Carolina will get down to the level of Pennsylvania,

8. *Ibid.*, p. 252.
9. W. W. Ball to Fraser Lyon, June 4, 1906, Ball Papers.

Rhode Island, Montana and other states where the corrupt ma-
chines are in open and unblushing possession. . . . I don't care
what your platform may be, provided it includes the abolition of
the state dispensary. With the whiskey ring's selling agency out of
the way, the right kind of readjustment will come in time. I believe
that every county should settle the whiskey question for itself.[10]

Though he did not convince Lyon to declare for the governorship, both
the governor and a majority of the legislature elected that year were
anti-Dispensary. Hence, Ball's real objective was accomplished when the
state Dispensary system was abolished in 1907. A temporary solution to
the liquor question was reached through the installation of an option
plan whereby each county might set up its own dispensary or adopt
prohibition.

As Ball offered political advice, so prospective candidates began to
seek his opinion. In the state campaign of 1908 Ball discouraged one
such office seeker from running against incumbent Governor Martin F.
Ansel, not because he preferred Ansel, but because he judged accurately
the Governor's strength.[11] It was perhaps the politician's awareness of a
new voice in the state that prompted Governor Ansel to offer Ball an
honorary position on his personal staff. When Ball declined, explaining
that an editorial writer must maintain complete detachment, he surrendered his opportunity to join scores of South Carolinians who had never
seen a regiment but who might properly be addressed as "Colonel."[12]

Workers for William Howard Taft in the 1908 election asked Ball
for his estimate of the Republicans' chances in South Carolina. Ball
reported that he knew no one who would vote for Taft and that any such
person would be without influence in the state considering the present
condition of politics there. Though he admitted that the establishment of
a healthy local Republican organization respecting existing racial accommodations would benefit the state, and though he confessed high regard
for the conservative national Republican platform and leadership, Ball
explained that he could engage in no activity which might aid the
present state party. The current Republican party of South Carolina he
condemned as opportunistic and racebaiting and a "fatal obstacle" to
the creation of a two-party system.[13]

10. *Ibid.*
11. W. W. Ball to C. C. Featherstone, Jan. 2, 1908; C. C. Featherstone to W.
W. Ball, Feb. 6, 1908; W. W. Ball to C. C. Featherstone, Feb. 11, 1908; W. W.
Ball to C. C. Featherstone, April 12, 1908; Ball Papers.
12. M. F. Ansel to W. W. Ball, Feb. 23, 1907, Ball Papers.
13. W. W. Ball to John G. Capers, Oct. 16, 1908, Ball Papers.

As assistant editor of *The News and Courier*, Ball gained valuable experience assaying the state's political condition and enjoyed increasing repute as a commentator thereon. Considering his haste to return to Charleston and the total advantages of remaining there, it was somewhat surprising that discontent set in so soon after his arrival.[14] Although he was tied to South Carolina in a dozen ways, Ball inquired about opportunities in Virginia, he and Mrs. Ball having decided that living in Richmond was a reasonable substitute for living in Charleston. His overtures to John Stewart Bryan of the Richmond *Times-Dispatch* emphasized that he could not give up his present position without a substantial increase in salary.[15] For his part, Bryan admitted satisfaction with Ball's editorials and interest in obtaining his services, but he ignored Ball's offer to visit the *Times-Dispatch* office. The present situation in his editorial department, the Richmond newspaperman claimed, precluded his making Ball a definite offer.[16]

Meanwhile Ball considered buying a paper of his own. He wrote to Fitz Hugh McMaster, who had helped him revive the *Charleston Evening Post* and who was now State Insurance Commissioner, suggesting that together they buy the Spartanburg *Herald*. Fitz would be manager and Ball editor; they would draw equal salaries. At present, Ball pointed out, the *Herald* was lifeless and "the time has come when I must own a paper and build up a property—or abandon that notion forever."[17] Whether or not McMaster joined him, Ball intended to open negotiations through Spartanburg attorneys. The *Herald* was owned by A. E. Gonzales, publisher of the Columbia *State*. Gonzales had bought the paper believing that one day soon a good morning paper in the growing Piedmont city would be valuable property. He had no inclination at that time to surrender his investment.[18] Having been blocked in an attempt to interest Gonzales, Ball instructed his attorney to negotiate for the purchase of the *Journal*, the afternoon Spartanburg paper. As it happened, the owner of the *Journal* had an opportunity to join the Hearst publications and was willing to sell for $25,000.[19] It was Ball's plan to raise $12,000 of this amount by selling stock in the company in Spartanburg.

14. Not long after he joined *The News and Courier*, however, he rejected an offer to return to the *Greenville News* as editor (Vice President of the *Daily News* Company for President J. P. Caldwell to W. W. Ball, Nov. 11, 1905, Ball Papers).
15. W. W. Ball to John S. Bryan, March 18, 1908, Ball Papers.
16. J. S. Bryan to W. W. Ball, March 24, 1908, Ball Papers.
17. W. W. Ball to Fitz Hugh McMaster, May 27, 1908, Ball Papers.
18. A. E. Gonzales to H. L. Bomar, Feb. 27, 1909, Ball Papers.
19. H. L. Bomar to W. W. Ball, March 3, 1909, Ball Papers.

This, his attorney informed him, would be very difficult to arrange; there were too many other avenues for investment and people did not realize the importance of supporting a good newspaper.[20] Meanwhile, Ball pressed Ambrose Gonzales for a deal to share ownership of the *Herald*. He offered $14,000 for half interest or $15,000 for a majority of one share.[21] Gonzales passed over that proposition, but offered an alternative:

> When you were here the other day you admonished me that I had better not offer you $50.00 a wk. to come back to The State. Well, I do. . . . I believe the men in the office have almost an affection for you, even in the composing room. So, its [*sic*] up to you.[22]

Ball had not wanted to live in Columbia. He had so informed Fitz McMaster the year before when his friend suggested the two try to gain control of the *Record* there.[23] But now everything was changed. The possibility of his becoming a publisher in Spartanburg was slim. Aside from the financial troubles he had encountered, he confessed that the "mental anguish" which accompanied conducting a property and paying its bills appealed to him less and less.[24] When Ball replied to Gonzales's invitation, he said:

> I'll have to ask for time. Personally, I am very eager to accept your offer; I would not hesitate a second. Apart from the advantages of the offer, the News and Courier doesn't care anything about me, Hemphill does, but he is no better off than I am. I thoroughly like Hemphill but both he and I are the hired men of persons who don't make newspapers. If I can persuade Mrs. Ball I shall accept, but I am very much afraid I can't persuade her. I fear that the making of the change rather appalls her. Of course if I should pick up and come, so would she, but that I can't do—it wouldn't be right to do it. But I know that if I could come I would be easy and comfortable and I believe I could earn the money.[25]

Fay Ball's consent was won and a few days later Ball requested Hemphill to relieve him of his duties as of June 1, 1909, so that he could

20. H. L. Bomar to W. W. Ball, April 1, 1909, Ball Papers.
21. W. W. Ball to A. E. Gonzales, March 23, 1909, Ball Papers.
22. A. E. Gonzales to W. W. Ball, March 31, 1909, Ball Papers.
23. W. W. Ball to Fitz Hugh McMaster, May 27, 1908, Ball Papers.
24. W. W. Ball to Mr. Burnet of Spartanburg, April 3, 1909, Ball Papers.
25. W. W. Ball to A. E. Gonzales, April 2, 1909, Ball Papers.

take a post with *The State*. He quit *The News and Courier* reluctantly, because to him the paper had a unique place in American journalism. She was a "grand dame": old, steady, conservative, proud. He left, or so he told his chief, because

> I want to go forward and here I am too much at rest. The largely increased salary that I shall get is an object in itself of course but it is equally important to me as signifying progress. I thought when I came here that I would [be] satisfied to stop; three or four years taught me that I never could be. If I declined this Columbia post I would feel that I had capitulated in the prime of my newspaper life to a frail inclination towards ease and freedom from responsibility.[26]

Thus Ball joined *The State* as managing editor, answerable only to publisher Ambrose Gonzales and his brother William Elliott Gonzales, the paper's editor.[27]

Ball's decision to move to *The State* was contingent upon the assurance of Ambrose Gonzales that he would not be called upon to perform duties which were physical or routine but be allowed instead to concentrate on writing editorials and developing news features. In the last two years at *The News and Courier*, he had been removed from "drudgery" and he was careful to see that in Columbia there would be no retrogression. For a month after Ball became managing editor of *The State*, that paper and *The News and Courier* waged a good-natured tug-of-war for his services. Hemphill, instead of printing the expected resignation notice, announced that Ball was "visiting Columbia for 30 days."[28] Ball did not, however, return to Charleston. One reason he stayed at *The State* was his respect and admiration for the Gonzales brothers, survivors of one of South Carolina's illustrious families. Their father was General Ambrosio José Gonzales, exiled Cuban patriot and Confederate war hero. In 1891 his sons organized *The State* in the capital to oppose the Tillman Democracy. Narciso, murdered in 1903 by Jim Tillman, has been called "one of the half dozen leading editors in the history of South Carolina."[29] The growth of the paper continued under his broth-

26. W. W. Ball to J. C. Hemphill, April 12, 1909, Ball Papers.

27. Apparently, Hemphill was dissatisfied also with conditions at *The News and Courier*. There are indications that Ball and other friends tried to have Hemphill appointed President of the University of South Carolina. See Fitz Hugh McMaster to W. W. Ball, April 17, 1908, and W. W. Ball to August Kohn, May 14, 1908, Ball Papers.

28. *The News and Courier*, June 2, 1909.

29. Wallace, *South Carolina*, p. 651.

ers, Ambrose and William, and when Ball rejoined the staff in 1909, *The State*, not yet twenty years old, enjoyed the largest circulation of the eighteen dailies published in South Carolina.[30]

W. W. Ball was forty years old when he became managing editor of *The State*, the father of a growing family which began to take more of his time and attention. Mrs. Ball and the five children, waiting for a suitable house to be provided, remained in Charleston more than a year before they came to the home Ball bought for them at 1720 Pendleton Street in Columbia. By the time the Balls had become settled in their new house, the eldest daughter had reached teen-age. Katharine was a difficult child who caused her father deep concern. While they were separated, Katharine had admonished her father, "You write to all of the other children and never to me."[31] Immediately after her arrival in Columbia she enrolled for courses at the College for Women, where her grades were good and bad, utterly unpredictable.[32] Two years later she matriculated at Chatham Episcopal Institute, a Virginia boarding school, where she was regarded as an interesting challenge. Headstrong, self-willed, quick-tempered and impulsive, her troubles were more be-havioral than academic. Ball exercised all the patience with Katty that a loving and sympathetic parent could muster. To her charges of discrimi-nation and intolerable treatment at school, he would reply affectionately, if somewhat wearily, that he would come to talk with the principal if it would help, but that everyone had problems and she must stay at Chatham.[33]

Family affairs, however, were but one of the non-professional activi-ties crowding Ball's day. His interest in real-estate dealings intensified; he had a propensity, almost a compulsion, to collect property. Ball became a stockholder in the Jasper Development Company created to develop land in Jasper County, South Carolina. He was also a partner in several holding companies dedicated to accumulating quick profits through speculation.[34] He was often joined in these ventures by his friend and brother-in-law,[35] Thomas R. Waring, once Ball's protégé and now

30. Figures from *N. W. Ayer & Son's Directory, Newspapers and Periodicals* (Philadelphia, 1910).
31. Katharine Ball to W. W. Ball, Nov. 18, 1909, Ball Papers.
32. Euphemia McClintock to W. W. Ball, Dec. 10, 1910, Ball Papers.
33. W. W. Ball to Katharine Ball, Jan. 18, 1913, Ball Papers.
34. W. W. Ball to T. R. Waring, Nov. 4, 1912; W. W. Ball to T. R. Waring, Feb. 10, 1913; T. R. Waring to W. W. Ball, March 13, 1913; Ball Papers.
35. Waring was married to Fay Ball's sister Laura, the youngest of the Witte girls.

editor of the *Charleston Evening Post*. Through another friend, Yates Snowden, a professor at the University, he became interested in history. In 1912 Ball and Snowden attended the annual meeting of the American Historical Association in Boston; soon afterward Ball was elected to membership in the Association.

Ball also continued to be active in the Alumni Association of the University of South Carolina, and in 1912 he was chosen president and chairman of the committee of the Richland County chapter. During his term of office he arranged to bring Charles Francis Adams to address the Founder's Day gathering in January of 1913. Adams, economist, historian, and grandson of John Quincy Adams, was seventy-seven years old when he came to Columbia; he talked about Robert E. Lee; and he greatly impressed Ball, who remarked a few years later:

> I spent three or four hours in the company of Mr. Adams when he was here in 1913. . . . Of all Northern men I have known he was in the South the least self-conscious. I went with the old gentleman (carrying him in my car) to call on Mrs. J. C. Haskell and the Misses Hampton, the latter the aged sisters of the late General Wade Hampton. Mr. Adams was a most interesting person, a man of alert mentality and great energy and vigor. . . . He was a Yankee of wholly different type from any other I have seen.[36]

Perhaps Ball's major concern at this time was the textile industry; indeed, cotton mill affairs, together with real-estate negotiations, comprised the bulk of his correspondence. The expansion of the cotton mills beginning about 1880 had provided impetus for the entire Southern industrial development which included important gains especially in the manufacture of iron and tobacco products. With the social stability that followed the end of Reconstruction, dozens of mills sprang up along the Piedmont in an arc that stretched from Southern Virginia to Georgia and into northern Alabama. Prophets of the "New South"[37] called for progress in education and industry in order to provide the diversified economy that would lead the poor South to prosperity. Because capital was scarce, thousands of Southerners of modest resources pooled money as part of a regional crusade. It was not uncommon for a single mill to have a thousand stockholders; Ball, for example, held stock in at least

36. Ball, Diary, I, 26–27, May 1, 1916.
37. Among the exponents of a "New South" were Henry Grady of the *Atlanta Constitution* and Capt. F. W. Dawson, editor of the Charleston *News and Courier*.

three mills and was for a time a member of the executive committee of the Watts Mills of Laurens.

Now reports that came to Ball from the mills read like a catalogue of distress: the difficulty in obtaining immigrant workers,[38] falling prices, passed dividends, and mills operating at a loss. The Walhalla Mills, in which Ball had an interest, were working a five-day week of eleven hours a day but paying the operatives for ten hours a day and contemplating another small cut in wages already drastically low by national standards.[39] Stockholders who wanted to sell found few buyers. The management of the mills, furthermore, was often crippled by rival factions struggling for control. The wry Eliza Ball wrote her son from Laurens, "The two mills located here have furnished for the past three years, as much excitement as the red shirt campaign."[40] Tom Waring remarked that they seemed about to lose everything they had invested in the mills. Was the textile industry in South Carolina going completely to the devil?[41]

Ball and his confidants, exercising their privileges as Southerners, ignored basic causes of difficulties in the textile industry. The chief advantages of the Southern mills were the availability of cheap labor, fuel, and power. The anticipated benefit from accessibility to raw materials provided illusory. Raw cotton had to be shifted within the region and material transported to the East to be marketed. For reasons of necessary economy, secondhand, obsolete machinery had initially been purchased; hence, the cloth produced was coarse and required finishing in Northern mills. It seemed the South could not yet overcome her colonial status, and an otherwise remarkable development was partially sapped. Ball's reaction, though superficial, was unusually casual. "You can't prevent a period of depression in textiles," he concluded, "or make the women quit wearing three yards of cotton underclothes when they ought to wear fifteen."[42]

Ball, as a newspaperman, was more distressed by the political situation in the state, a state of affairs sharply affected by the growing cotton mill establishment. Two new classes joined Southern society: mill owners who often exceeded older merchants in wealth and rivaled "old families" for prestige; and workers who flocked to mill villages established in the countryside or on the outskirts of existing towns. Food,

38. W. E. Lucas to W. W. Ball, Nov. 20, 1906, Ball Papers.
39. E. R. Lucas to W. W. Ball, Aug. 5, 1908, Ball Papers.
40. Eliza Ball to W. W. Ball, March 29, 1908, Ball Papers.
41. T. R. Waring to W. W. Ball, March 18, 1912, Ball Papers.
42. W. W. Ball to T. R. Waring, Nov. 25, 1912, Ball Papers.

clothing, shelter, and sundry minor necessities were all provided by mill owners. Jobs were reserved for poor country whites; Negroes were generally excluded both to enhance white opportunities and to prevent disruptive racial conflict. In the mill villages, often within sight of the new pillared mansions of the owners, the operatives developed a class consciousness both anti-intellectual and anti-conservative. In 1911 Coleman L. Blease assumed the governorship of South Carolina, the first chief executive to be elected primarily because of his appeal to the "lintheads."

Blease became the new mass leader replacing Ben Tillman, whose authority in the state gradually declined after he entered the Senate. Whereas the one-eyed Tillman had been startling in appearance, Blease was handsome and smooth. In an age when demagoguery was at its height in the South, Blease was perhaps the Dixie demagogue supreme. He stimulated class and race antagonism, while according to Southern historian Francis Butler Simkins, "His administration was almost entirely devoid of constructive legislation for the benefit of the poorer people who voted for him."[43] V. O. Key remarked that Blease "mesmerized" the mill workers, tenant farmers, and poor whites and at the same time opposed governmental programs that would benefit them.[44] He fought affiliation of textile unions with national labor organizations because he did not want Yankee interference, and consequently drew "quiet and effective support from mill owners"; yet by appealing to race prejudice he got "cheers and votes" from the white workers who virtually monopolized the mill jobs.[45] Thus the new cotton mill classes in their response to Blease rendered politics even more complex.

Blease's tactics, together with his personal vulgarity and his use of the pardoning power to release hundreds of convicts, horrified traditionalists. In full fury, Ball charged with characteristic overstatement: "I think it not impossible that every decent person in South Carolina may be driven to flee to North Carolina."[46] To David F. Houston, his college friend who had just become President Wilson's Secretary of Agriculture, he confided:

> You have gotten out of South Carolina, while the rest of us have to confront a wretched condition in morals and politics—the let down in South Carolina affairs was bad enough in the nineties but we did

43. Francis B. Simkins, *A History of the South* (New York, 1953), p. 543.
44. V. O. Key, *Southern Politics in State and Nation* (New York, 1949), p. 144.
45. *Ibid.*
46. W. W. Ball to M. L. Copeland, Sept. 4, 1912, Ball Papers.

not for[e]see the degradation to which it was a mere curtain raiser. Did I not have multifarious interests, business and social, I think, for the sake of my family I would even at this late day leave South Carolina for a land uncurst by the heritage of ignorance that is the South's as a by product of the slavery institution.[47]

Ball's cure for Bleasism was to put "somebody" in the penitentiary and to restrict the ballot, but as Tom Waring reminded him, "The penitentiary has no bolts while Blease is governor and your much boasted 'sturdy yeomanry' will not hear of any restriction upon the suffrage."[48]

Because Ball was only assistant to the editor of *The State*, he took a secondary role in the overwhelming press criticism of Blease in which *The State* played a leading part. He was not, however, sheltered entirely. Ben L. Abney, Blease's cousin and an attorney for the Southern Railway, had been drawn into the controversy; his name had appeared in the editorial columns of *The State*, sometimes in paragraphs written by Ball. On the Saturday before Christmas, 1912, Ball and Abney met at the Columbia Club. Abney, who, according to Ball, had been drinking, attacked *The State* and Ball personally. Ball considered the affront so challenging that he must resist the insult or leave the club and the city. They grappled, Abney with a cane, and fell to the floor, where the brawl ended.[49] Ball, a person of gentle nature, was mortified at having been involved in such an episode, but Abney assumed all responsibility for the incident and the Columbia Club advised Ball that he had been exonerated from a charge of improper conduct.[50]

The Abney affair, though it was a minor altercation, depressed Ball and contributed to his restlessness. His sporadic attempts to relocate again, to better his position, had begun, however, soon after his arrival at *The State*. His Laurens weekly, still managed by members of the family, had been in a precarious financial position for some time, and in 1910 he sold the *Advertiser* and removed himself from the ranks of independent publishers.[51] But he had not yet given up the idea of owning a daily. Ball and Waring for a time considered purchasing a paper and conducting it as partners. Yet, when an opportunity arose for him to purchase the Spartanburg *Journal*, he backed away. His explanation

47. W. W. Ball to D. F. Houston, March 15, 1913, Ball Papers.
48. T. R. Waring to W. W. Ball, Sept. 16, 1912, Ball Papers.
49. W. W. Ball to T. R. Waring, Jan. 2, 1913, Ball Papers.
50. Columbia Club to W. W. Ball, March 10, 1913, Ball Papers.
51. The purchasers were Arthur and Allison Lee.

conveys an inertia heightened by lack of confidence: "I conclude that it will be impracticable for me to leave my post here, to give up a safe and comfortable berth to undertake the severe work and responsibility of owning and conducting a newspaper."[52] The Spartanburg opportunity, he claimed, required a careful businessman as well as a capable newspaperman, and he did not pretend to be both. In this personal estimate, Ball was not being modest; his business accountings, like his office desk, were cluttered and confused.

Ball's aspirations and his actions seemed never to meet; the frustration was equally apparent in his attempts to secure a more responsible editorial position. Ironically, had he chosen not to accept the job on *The State* he probably would soon have become the editor of *The News and Courier*. Within a year after Ball left Charleston, Hemphill resigned to become editor of the Richmond *Times-Dispatch* and Robert Lathan, who had worked under Ball, was appointed in his place. Lathan was quick to acknowledge his debt to Ball for his technical knowledge and for hours spent on "lessons in perspective, in poise and in purpose."[53] Hemphill lighted briefly in Richmond; before a year had passed he had taken a post in Charlotte. When Ball learned that Hemphill was about to move, he again wrote to publisher John Bryan in Richmond suggesting that they confer about the possibility of Ball's coming to the *Times-Dispatch*. "I am placed exactly as I was in Charleston," he said, "except as to salary—I am where I cannot advance."[54] Bryan's reply was polite but inconclusive.[55] The speed with which Ball notified Bryan that he wished to withdraw his name from consideration revealed his sensitivity to the tepid response to his proposal, but he added:

My relations to Mr. A. E. Gonzales are of a nature rather unusual between employed and employer and he is doing for me more than most men would dare expect. I suppose he has had me under sort of a mesmeric spell for the last twenty years and it is a pleasant bondage.[56]

Two years later, Ball terminated negotiations on an offer to go to Pittsburgh:

52. W. W. Ball to H. L. Bomar, March 13, 1912, Ball Papers.
53. Robert Lathan to W. W. Ball, June 2, 1909, Ball Papers.
54. W. W. Ball to J. S. Bryan, Oct. 6, 1911, Ball Papers.
55. J. S. Bryan to W. W. Ball, Oct. 12, 1911, Ball Papers.
56. W. W. Ball to J. S. Bryan, Oct. 14, 1911, Ball Papers.

> Long ago I heard Ben Tillman (whom I fervently dislike) in a speech tell the story, from "The Sentimental Journey," of the caged starling that cried continually, "I can't get away!" Then when the cage door was left open, it did not escape but continued to cry its sorrow. It had lost capacity to enjoy liberty. I don't think I have reached that point but—"I can't get away."[57]

Ball never again seriously considered leaving South Carolina. He was her victim; he knew her towns and families—and her faults. He could use his energy to criticize but not to leave. He was an upcountryman tied to his land.

While Ball remained under the Gonzales shadow he nevertheless enhanced his reputation through the platform and the press. He made the usual number of speeches at college commencements, before Rotary Clubs, and beside the familiar obelisks erected by the United Daughters of the Confederacy. Another convenient forum was the Kosmos Club of Columbia. The Kosmos was organized on October 14, 1905, as a literary, scientific, and social club with Ball's cronies Yates Snowden and Fitz McMaster as charter members.[58] Ball was voted a member soon after he moved to Columbia. The makeup of the Kosmos was "town and gown" with its membership distributed between University of South Carolina professors and Columbia professional men, mostly newspapermen and lawyers. During the academic year the club met twice a month; members alternated in presenting papers after which there would be discussion and, on a good night, argument. Ball adopted the practice of having some of his addresses to the Kosmos privately printed and distributed to his friends. The first of Ball's pamphlets to be so circulated was *A Boy's Recollections of the Red Shirt Campaign of 1876 in South Carolina*, printed in 1911. Ball also became a familiar speaker before the State Press Association. His address analyzing effects of the Industrial Revolution in South Carolina came to the attention of the *Sewanee Review* and at the invitation of the editor Ball adapted it for publication. His views reveal the impact of industrialization upon the philosophy of agrarian conservatism.

With the perspective of time, Ball at last understood the superficiality of the rivalries of the nineties. While the Tillman movement represented a democratic surge, both reform and conservative factions were an-

---

57. W. W. Ball to Mr. Ross, Dec. 18, 1911, Ball Papers.
58. Minutes of the Kosmos Club (in The South Caroliniana Library), I, 5.

chored by the same predominant class—the landowning farmer. Now in hundreds of mill villages lived an army of landless voters growing daily in numbers and political potency. A new cleavage had developed, between capital and labor. Real class conflict was at last possible because the disputes of the combatants were not muted by their mutual respect for the sanctity of the land. How could class warfare be prevented? Of course, the race issue might be expected to unite all whites in the end. But, for insurance, Ball urged that each wage-earner buy his own home and perhaps a plot of twenty-five acres. Financial institutions should be established to aid him. Then once again the land would become the great common denominator.[59]

Ball's essay was one of his numerous hymns to the sanctity of property. It had been a century and a half since American revolutionaries cried "Liberty and Property," but the inseparability of home ownership and good citizenship was still an article of his faith. In a commonwealth of home owners, Ball saw the stability that would insure the continuation of historic Southern traditions amidst the disputes inherent in industrial capitalism. His fears were those of a Southerner who saw evil example in the North; his reactions were those of an upcountryman who saw cherished values increasingly threatened.

Ball also saw land ownership as a protection against the triumph of political demagoguery. But the press, he urged, had a role to play too. A meeting of the Press Association in June, 1913, was the occasion for the presentation by a colleague on *The State* of Ball's paper "The Freedom of the Press in South Carolina and Its Limitations," which was printed the next day in *The News and Courier*. Written at a time when South Carolina had not yet adopted a compulsory education law, that thoughtful essay considered the relation between the ignorance of the people and the role of the newspaper. The press, according to Ball, must lead the people, but it cannot be too far in front. The press is sensitively responsible to the prevailing opinion of the people and it is held back as they are held back. In South Carolina many voters never saw a newspaper. The state was ruled by two separate classes: those to whom the written word appealed, and those who followed the spoken word. If that word was spoken by a demagogue, then there was danger. As a result of this condition, the press of South Carolina became elevated into a political issue per se and was often the object of haranguers. Ball doubted that

59. W. W. Ball, "The Industrial Revolution in South Carolina," *Sewanee Review*, XIX (April, 1911), 111–137.

any daily press was read more closely than that of South Carolina—by those who were able to read. The editorial page was more influential, perhaps, than in papers of other sections, and the whole paper was an educational agency hardly less important than the school or pulpit.

The state press therefore, must be truly free. Efforts to bring it under the control of politicians must be strenuously resisted. Bills, such as one recently introduced into the legislature, that would compel newspapers to print corrections offered by politicians to statements they allege to be erroneous or injurious, must not become law. Newspapers, he concluded, if they were to be free of legislative interference, must also be worthy of a position of respect and privilege. Secret newspaper ownership was bad; the ideal paper was one whose ownership and editorial control were one, without other important financial interest. The editor's responsibility was great: in public life he could mingle with those he could not reach with print and thus transcend the barriers of ignorance.[60]

Ball had a high conception of the role of the editor in American life, and he was soon to have the opportunity to apply his ideals. Two months after the Press Association at the Isle of Palms heard his theories, William Elliott Gonzales was appointed Ambassador to Cuba by Woodrow Wilson, and Ball advanced to editor-in-chief of *The State*. As in most other matters, Tom Waring of Charleston was among the first to know. To him Ball poured out all of his feelings about the promotion. The duration of political appointments was uncertain and some day Willie Gonzales would return. Ball felt a little like a "queen dowager with the powers of a regent."[61] His present position, he said, was easy and conducive to sleep at night (though Ball often complained of insomnia); from now on the abuse of Cole Blease previously reserved for Gonzales would be turned on him. But with it all there would come some "transient prestige" which would make it easier to retire from "this glorious trade."[62] Perhaps a sense of insecurity prevented him from speaking with candor; in truth, the departure of Gonzales for Havana brought Ball the chance for recognition he had been seeking through two decades of shift and disappointment. In August, 1913, when he was forty-four years old, William Watts Ball became the editor of the most important newspaper in South Carolina.

60. The essay is reprinted in Ball, *The Editor and the Republic*, pp. 12–27.
61. W. W. Ball to T. R. Waring, March 15, 1913, Ball Papers.
62. *Ibid.*

CHAPTER FIVE

BUILDING A REPUTATION

WHEN W. W. Ball assumed the editorship of *The State* he was cata-
pulted into the center of the South Carolina political milieu at a time
when factional hatred was intense. Cole Blease was in the midst of his
second term as governor. Blease, born in the same year as Ball, had
middle-class parents and a college education, though he was dropped
from the University of South Carolina for plagiarizing an essay. After
serving in the state legislature, he became almost a perennial candidate
for high state office. He was ever a candidate, but seldom a winner.[1]
Using his flamboyant oratory to play upon the rancor of the poor, Blease
first won notable success when he defeated conservative C. C. Featherstone for the governorship in 1910 and thus opened what was perhaps
the most hectic four years Columbia had seen since Reconstruction. His
usurpations of power and his despotic stubbornness almost immediately
alienated him from the Supreme Court. He refused to appoint special
judges legally nominated by the court and instead called upon the
legislature to invest him with the power of appointment. His dealings
with the legislature were equally chaotic; most of his many vetoes were
overridden.

One of the state's prominent historians has described Blease's aver-
sion to the press, a feeling which was, with a few exceptions, returned in
full:

> We must go back almost two hundred years . . . for such hostility
> as Governor Blease's to the press. In vetoing a bill to modify the
> severe libel law, he used the word "lie" thirty-three times, "liar"
> eight times, strewed along "cowardly," "slime," "scurrilous
> blackguard," "low down," attacked newspapers by name, branded
> the newspaper fraternity a dirty set of liars, and glorified Jim
> Tillman's murder of Editor Gonzales. The House expunged all but
> the essential parts of the message, as self-respect forbade such

1. Though Blease often ran for high office, he was elected only three times, each
by small majorities: elected governor in 1910; governor, 1912; U.S. senator,
1924.

language in its records. The Senate refused to record the accompanying exhibits, and The News and Courier felt restrained by court decisions from printing some of the passages.[2]

"Never before in the State's history," the same authority observed, "had there been an individual who so fully made his own personality and interests the center of politics."[3] Blease's election to the governorship in 1910 had been partly a result of the overwhelming majority he received in Charleston. Cosmopolitan to a degree that separated her from the rest of the state, Charleston recoiled from Featherstone's advocacy of prohibition and supported Blease. Two years later, however, as Blease ran for re-election, Charleston's mayor John P. Grace charged that the governor had not only broken his promise not to put liquor constables in Charleston, but had appointed men more corrupt than any in the long history of the Dispensary. Nevertheless, in a campaign reeking with personal abuse and obvious slander, and in spite of rejection by Ben Tillman, who had founded the movement Blease now pretended to lead, the governor won from the voters another two-year term.

Ball had long been smitten with Charleston; he enjoyed every moment in the "city of delicious contradiction."[4] He was well aware of the peculiarities of Charleston life that had contributed to the rise of Cole Blease, and of broad differences that for two centuries had set Charleston apart from the rest of the state. Rivalry and antagonism between upcountry and the older low country whose heart was Charleston has always been a factor in South Carolina. Perhaps sectional resentments reached their peak in 1767 when the backwoods Regulators rose against a colonial government, dominated by coastal interests, which offered them slight benefit or protection. Symptomatic of the growing strength of the upcountry was the removal of the capital from Charleston to Columbia in 1790. Although by the early twentieth century the outlines of sectional distinctiveness had faded, they had not disappeared. Charleston became static while the Piedmont, with its expanding textile interests, grew in wealth and population; yet she maintained a remarkable independence and in some respects remained what she had been in colonial days—the city-state of the old rice coast, pursuing her whims as diligently as possible and letting the rest of the state go by. She had liquor bars and horse racing during the periods when other cities in

2. Wallace, *South Carolina*, p. 659.   3. *Ibid.*
4. W. W. Ball to Yates Snowden, Dec. 10, 1909, Papers of Yates Snowden, The South Caroliniana Library.

South Carolina had neither. But did not her innate superiority justify her violating laws made in Columbia? From atop the spires of St. Philip's and St. Michael's she looked down with some detachment upon the state that sprawled beyond her bounds.

Ball regretted Charleston's isolation and, not long after he became editor of *The State*, he made the problem the subject of an address which he delivered in that city to the 184th anniversary dinner of St. Andrew's Society. As he took "A View of the State," he found Charleston aroused over the liquor question and the attempt of the upcountry to force its ways upon her through statewide prohibition. Liquor had always been a part of Charleston living and was not considered immoral. Ball charged:

> If you inquire whether this quarrel be reconcilable, I reply that it is, and that the settlement of the wretched whiskey question is but an item in the train of blessings to come to you and your city from the reconciliation. The solution is better acquaintance with your kin in this commonwealth. You do not know them, and they do not know you.[5]

In maturity, stability, the absence of self-consciousness, Ball continued, Charleston was the one city of South Carolina. Renowned for her hospitality, Charleston, in her new relations with the upcountry, should seek as well as give. Possessing important Catholic and Jewish elements and blessed with the gift of sophistication, she must strive to mellow the bigotry, narrowness, the hardened Scotch Puritanism that was a check not only to the advancement of Charleston, but to every section of South Carolina. "This Puritanism," he concluded, "must be broadened and softened, and given lines more graceful and colors more lovely."[6] The people of South Carolina needed a "nearer acquaintance with their historic metropolis."[7]

As the crucial campaign of 1914 approached, however, Ball was beset with problems which eclipsed his concern for the future role of Charleston. In the excitement of South Carolina politics, where strong language was common, one of Ball's incontrovertible tenets was "politeness of manner." It soon became apparent that, with Ball as editor, *The State* would be a prudish newspaper. Senator Tillman granted an interview to *The State* which, when it appeared in print, had one paragraph

5. W. W. Ball, *A View of the State* (Columbia, S. C., 1913), p. 7.
6. *Ibid.*, p. 11.   7. *Ibid.*

omitted. Tillman was furious; he threatened to give the Columbia paper no more news unless it would agree in advance to publish his disclosures verbatim.[8] Ball explained the deletions had been made because words had been too "expressive." The Senator's copy would always receive considerate treatment, but *The State* could not promise not to edit his remarks. In spite of continued protests from Tillman, Ball insisted that a newspaper had a responsibility to publish only what conformed to the standards of good taste and that the editor must be the final judge of what he should print.[9]

Early in 1914, with the election approaching, Ball began an editorial campaign in behalf of honesty in South Carolina primaries. Irregularities in the 1912 primary had produced persistent demands that the outmoded primary regulations be strengthened. New rules were adopted by the Democratic party in state convention in May, 1914, and became law in February, 1915. The registrant was required to list his age and occupation and to have been a resident of South Carolina for two years, of the county for six months, and of the precinct for sixty days. Since rules for party membership were not defined by law, the Democrats could exclude Negroes without technically violating the Fifteenth Amendment. Bleasite charges that new rules would discriminate against them were refuted when the party imposed no property or educational qualifications. Ben Tillman had earlier suggested that no man ought to participate in the primary who could not stand the test of registration for the general election, but he had abandoned that ambitious position by the time the state convention met. The revised primary rules "left criminals, lunatics, paupers, and illiterates eligible for the only elections that count."[10] The new regulations certainly did not satisfy Ball, who steadfastly believed an educated and property-holding electorate was the only key to good government and who said so in the columns of *The State*. He was reminded by an editor friend, however, of political realities in South Carolina and urged not to deceive himself.[11]

In the 1914 campaign Governor Blease, having reached the constitutional limit of two consecutive terms, sought election to the United States Senate. Chief among his opponents, in the first election after the Seventeenth Amendment had made senatorial elections subject to popu-

8. P. H. McGowan to W. W. Ball, Nov. 8, 1913, Ball Papers.
9. W. W. Ball to P. H. McGowan, Nov. 4, 1913, Ball Papers.
10. Wallace, *South Carolina*, p. 662.
11. N. Christensen to W. W. Ball, May 15, 1914, Ball Papers.

lar vote, was the incumbent, Ellison D., or "Cotton Ed," Smith. Tillman again condemned Cole Blease, but the Governor's abuse of the pardoning power was the chief charge made against him by his enemies. Estimates of the numbers of convicts pardoned by Blease range from fifteen hundred to more than seventeen hundred. D. D. Wallace, who extensively examined the cases, stated that while the record was bad, Blease was carrying to excess a common abuse of American governors, and that in some instances, he pardoned many who had already served terms longer than the law currently required.[12] Wallace added, however:

How serious was the situation was illustrated in connection with the pardon of a man who defiled a child relative in his home, a pardon for which Governor Blease was reproached during the 1914 campaign. Dr. James H. McIntosh, whose name was attached to the typed letter stating that the convict's health demanded release, declared the letter a forgery, for his letter was hand written and had stated the opposite. The Doctor was shot down (though not killed) after midnight on the day he was to confront the Governor at the Columbia meeting by a man who shouted as he fled, "Coley won't be bothered with you tomorrow."[13]

The State, along with almost all the other papers in South Carolina, urged the defeat of Blease. The Governor's misdeeds and scores of bitter, sometimes exaggerated, attacks upon them, combined with the press barrage, spelled his defeat. In the primary election, E. D. Smith was returned to Washington and Blease's senatorial ambitions temporarily thwarted.[14] While Ball and *The State* had made their distaste for Blease clear, they hesitated in choosing between the gubernatorial candidates, who included the Bleasite John G. Richards of Kershaw County, conservatives Richard I. Manning of Sumter and Robert A. Cooper of Laurens, and Professor John G. Clinkscales, who advocated compulsory education. Ball claimed to have little preference between Manning and Cooper except that the latter should be easier to elect, and that he knew Cooper better.[15] But Ball also had communication with Cooper's opponent; he had sent Manning a copy of a paper on taxation which he had

12. Wallace, *South Carolina*, p. 663.   13. *Ibid.*
14. The vote was Smith 72,266; Blease 56,913; L. D. Jennings 2,258; W. P. Pollock 1,364.
15. Ball, Diary, VI, 187, May 14, 1924.

delivered to the Kosmos Club. The principal thesis of the essay was that the exemption of dwellings and small amounts of personal property from taxation would encourage the wage earners of the state to own their own homes[16]—and to Ball the ownership of property was still the beginning of all political virtue. Manning replied with guarded thanks, saying "at first glance" the propositions set forth seemed to be of value in dealing with "this problem."[17]

As the date of the first primary approached, *The State* began receiving letters asking when it was going to take its stand. Ball went to his publisher, recommending that, if necessary, five or six days before the primary was to be held, *The State* should declare for Cooper. Ambrose Gonzales reached no decision, and Ball left his office in distress and disgust. Pressure on *The State* to announce its preference continued. On August 23, 1914, forty-eight hours before the primary, Ball, acting independently, announced in a front page editorial, "Unpledged Voters Trending to Cooper and to Manning." For the information of its readers and Democrats of South Carolina, Ball reported, *The State* gave its opinion based on telegrams, letters, and interviews. Unpledged supporters, anti-Bleasites, should cast their votes for the leaders: Cooper and Manning, in that order.[18] This vagary, hovering somewhere between endorsement and neutrality, was repeated in almost the same words the next day, and on election day itself.

No candidate won a majority in the August primary. Ball misjudged when he thought Cooper was leading Manning, because it was the latter who battled John G. Richards, the Blease administration's candidate in the September run-off. On the morning of the second primary, Ball's editorial comment was: "It wouldn't surprise The State, though we do not predict it, if Manning should carry each and every county."[19] Still the paper did not urge, "Vote for Manning!" He did indeed win, with 73,739 votes to Richards's 45,091, and all Bleasite congressional candidates were defeated. Ball heard later that Gonzales took credit for restraining him from printing the Cooper editorial and thereby committing a serious blunder. This remark, to Ball's mind, distorted the facts and he was resentful; he believed, to the contrary and for reasons difficult to comprehend, that *The State*'s handling of Cooper in 1914 was an indispensable factor in Manning's close victory over Blease in a

16. W. W. Ball to R. I. Manning, March 27, 1914, Ball Papers.
17. R. I. Manning to W. W. Ball, March 12, 1914, Ball Papers.
18. *The State*, Aug. 23, 1914.   19. *Ibid.*, Sept. 9, 1914.

later election.[20] More reasonable was his claim that the announcement by *The State* that Cooper and Manning were the leading anti-Blease candidates had, by eliminating Clinkscales, reduced the danger that the vote would be divided among so many adversaries as to give Richards a victory in the first primary.[21]

On the day when Manning's victory in the second primary assured his succession to the governorship, Ball complained to his old friend Hemphill that the state had had no clear-minded, honest, unselfish leadership since Tillman had knocked out the "old fellows" in 1890. Bleasism had been the natural development of Tillmanism on the one hand and the "educated puerility" on the other. The intelligentsia, of whom Ball was a "sorry" representative, were ignorant of conditions in the state. "If Manning doesn't give us a progressive administration," Ball warned, "if our leaders do not awake to the economic evils in South Carolina, if we do not get beyond the mere miserable play and byplay of politicians, we shall have more Bleasism."[22]

Richard Irvine Manning, a substantial farmer and banker with extensive business experience and the third member of his family to be governor of South Carolina, provided the sort of enlightened leadership for which Ball had hoped. Manning enjoyed exemplary co-operation from the legislature in initiating his program of economic and social reform, a local reflection, somewhat tardy and mild, of the national Progressive spirit. The Board of Charities and Corrections was created and the facilities of the State Hospital for the Insane were modernized and improved. The age limit for child labor was raised from twelve to fourteen years in factories and mines. Other benefits to laboring men included a workmen's compensation act. Appropriations for public education were increased markedly and the way opened for the first compulsory education law in the state, which was enacted in 1919. Under Manning's direction, the State Tax Commission was organized and began important work in supervising the collection of both the income tax, ineffective since the passage of the enabling act in 1897, and excise taxes necessary to support the enlarged activities of the state government.

In spite of his humanitarian efforts in behalf of the underprivileged, Manning was never able to capture their fancy. He was instilled with

20. Ball, Diary, VI, 188, May 14, 1924.
21. *Ibid.*, VI, 187, May 14, 1924.
22. W. W. Ball to J. C. Hemphill, Sept. 8, 1914, Ball Papers.

Bourbon reserve and appealed to the intellect rather than the emotions; he lacked a political personality. When he sought re-election in 1916, he faced Cole Blease in a long, harsh campaign. Ball had been one of those whom Manning first consulted. After his initial election, he and Ball discussed the Governor's future appointments.[23] Now, with another election ahead, Ball was invited to Manning's office at seven o'clock on June 17, 1916, to hear his opening campaign speech.[24]

That spring Ball began entering his thoughts in a journal which he kept for the rest of his life.[25] One of the first things he confessed to his diary was his growing weariness with political wrangle. "Heavens! how I *do* like praise . . . unquestionably, I do receive a great deal of praise for my editorial work,"[26] he admitted. But the work of editing a political newspaper in South Carolina, he complained, was a thankless chore. "The game is not worth the candle."[27] In any state but South Carolina or Mississippi, one could leave a bad political party for one less bad, but because of the masses of Negroes in those states, one-party government choked political life. "To devote a part of one's energies, of one's life, to public service in this state is to feed one's self to a Beast—a Beast that lives on prejudice, on hate, directed at Negroes."[28]

The Negro problem had for years caused Ball many hours of reflection. It was the subject of one of his speeches to the Kosmos Club, and of a letter he wrote to *The New York Times*. The Negro had been virtually disenfranchised by the white man's primary; those few Negroes who voted were constant prey for demagogues. "The prevailing attitude of the whites toward Negro education is one of aloofness and indifference. . . . The feeling of the average man in South Carolina is that the Negroes are better off without education, that if they must be [educated], training should be of the manual kind."[29] The Negroes'

23. R. I. Manning to W. W. Ball, Dec. 23, 1914, Ball Papers.
24. Ball, Diary, I, 132, June 17, 1916.
25. Ball discovered in 1935 that the first page of volume one of his diary had been torn away. He re-entered what he thought he had written on April 17, 1916: "Last night Gov. D. C. Heyward was at the house and we talked of past political incidents. When I recalled an incident Heyward said: 'Ball you have an uncommonly good memory; *you ought* to keep a diary.' 'Well, perhaps I shall,' I answered. Today I bought this book. How long will it be before it is filled or will it ever be filled?" (Ball, Diary, I, 00, Sept. 23, 1935). Almost devoid of personal detail, Ball's diary is a catalogue of political events, a vast commentary on public life. He intended that the journal should be read after his death and explain his relationship to important events of his time.
26. Ball, Diary, I, 131, June 16, 1916.
27. *Ibid.*, I, 43, May 9, 1916.   28. *Ibid.*
29. W. W. Ball to Albert Watkins, May 11, 1914, Ball Papers.

willingness to work for lower wages than the whites created a special economic problem and destroyed the effectiveness of unions. Ball held no brief for organized labor, but he accepted it as a fact of American social and industrial life. The Negro, he urged, must either be unionized or restricted from trades in which he was in direct competition with the white man.[30] "Are the Negroes free?" Ball had asked the members of the Kosmos Club one evening in 1914. The way to freedom, he suggested, was to train and school both the Negro and the poor white man, so that the Negro living standard would improve and with it his wages; the white man, by virtue of his native superiority, could be trusted to keep ahead of the black.[31]

Ball's racial attitudes were typical of those held by New South conservatives schooled in Old South aristocratic traditions. Though he hoped for improved political and economic conditions for the Negro, he entertained no thought that there should be a change in his social status. He was a believer in separate, equal facilities; he thought no crime was perpetrated by Jim Crow laws and abhorred any attempt to compel mixing as a violation of the freedom of the individual. As he explained to a newspaper friend in Hartford, Connecticut:

> My father was a slave-holder and a Confederate Officer. My grandfathers were slaveholders, one of them a member of the South Carolina Secession convention. In all of this I have pride. A chapter of the Daughters of the Confederacy bear my father's name. . . . No man has the instinct of social race separation more strongly developed that I have; I don't want any white servants about me but, to be "brutally frank," I only want the Negroes as servants. . . . I am not unaware that I am expressing a barbaric opinion but the truth.[32]

At that time South Carolina had approximately 900,000 Negroes and a few more than 700,000 whites. The amelioration of the state's troubles could come, Ball said, only with dispersion of the Negroes to be accomplished through the arrival in South Carolina of stronger and abler whites. So that immigrants would not be discouraged from coming, the living standard of the Negro must be raised. The fault, he admitted, was largely "our own," and he stressed that the 700,000

---

30. Letter of W. W. Ball, *The New York Times*, June 1, 1909.
31. Ball, *The Editor and the Republic*, p. 35.
32. W. W. Ball to Frederick C. Norton, March 11, 1916, Ball Papers.

whites must learn to meet the situation in a "spirit of enlightened justice."[33] The race question in South Carolina was an important contributor to Ball's settling pessimism. Though he talked of improving the state's backward economic and political life by helping the Negro, there were times when the magnitude of the task dismayed him. During one such moment he wrote, "The whole Negro question appalls me—I seriously think of taking my family and going to the North to get away from it—all our troubles are rooted in it."[34]

Ball, of course, did not leave the state, and in the summer of 1916 he plunged into another political campaign. Readers of *The State* would not have guessed his disillusion at being a political editor, for as the only regular editorial writer on the paper[35] he waged a vigorous campaign against Bleasism. From the beginning, Ball feared Manning's defeat, although he never admitted his worry in editorials or in public conversation. Blease was much more the popular figure, and Ball doubted whether the people of South Carolina really wanted good government. Blease was indeed an annoyance and menace to good government, Ball judged; a man whose "personality excites disgust but, after all, it excites one's sense of humor, too."[36] Ball expected that Blease would capitalize on Manning's appointment of twenty-two Negroes to the office of notary public. The governor had been ethically right, but he may have been politically wrong.[37] Only to his close friends did Ball express his concern for Manning's chances. To one, he confided: "Manning's friends are confident. Their reports are that Blease stands no chance whatsoever. . . . Nevertheless I am apprehensive."[38]

As in 1914, Manning and Cooper competed for the governorship and combatted the Bleasites, in 1916 represented by Cole Blease himself. The antagonism between partisans of Blease and Governor Manning was particularly acute. Two months before the first primary, an upcountry friend of Manning wrote to Ball charging collusion. Supporters of Blease and Cooper, the informant charged, had secretly combined, or would soon combine, for the election of Cooper. Ball, he urged, should expose the plot. The editor, however, refused. He would do nothing to embarrass Cooper in case the second primary should find Manning eliminated and Cooper the candidate of good government opposing the

33. *Ibid.*
34. W. W. Ball to Albert Watkins, May 11, 1914, Ball Papers.
35. W. W. Ball to Thomas F. McDow, June 1, 1916, Ball Papers.
36. Ball, Diary, I, 102, June 4, 1916.   37. *Ibid.*, I, 132, June 17, 1916.
38. W. W. Ball to T. F. McDow, Aug. 17, 1916, Ball Papers.

return of Bleasism. Revelation of the plot, if one actually existed, might, of course, work to the advantage of Manning, who Ball confidently believed deserved re-election. But Ball would not take the chance.[39]

A decade later, as the two men rode together to their old home town, Cooper gave Ball a full explanation. Before the first primary, Cooper received a letter issued from Manning's Columbia headquarters alleging that he was in the contest to split the conservative vote and thereby to aid Blease's candidacy. The charge was made in spite of the fact that Cooper had declared himself opposed to Blease's election under any circumstances. In South Carolina it is customary for rivals seeking the same office to tour the state together, each in turn speaking from the same platform to townspeople and countrymen gathered in the town square or on the courthouse lawns. These hours of oratory are an ancient state institution; the assembly serves both as a political camp meeting and a public entertainment. At the Bishopville meeting, according to Cooper, he informed Manning of the letter he had received charging his alliance with Blease. Manning disclaimed knowledge of the letter but said that, as it had been written by one of his friends, he could not denounce it. About the same time, Blease suggested to Cooper that he had been treated unfairly by Manning. A night or two later, when the candidates were in Bennettsville, Blease called Cooper to his room, and, from his bed, asked Cooper if he thought Manning could be elected. Cooper replied that he expected to beat both of them. Blease confessed that if it seemed likely Manning could be re-elected, he was prepared to withdraw from the contest immediately and let Cooper beat him. Cooper said that he would not consent to such an arrangement; he could not make a similar offer to Blease; and he preferred that Blease remain in the contest. "I might have written Blease's statement withdrawing from the race that night," Cooper told Ball.[40]

Blease continued to campaign actively, while Manning's friends worried about his ineffectiveness as a politician. During a conference with the Governor at the executive mansion in mid-July, Ball and others discussed the need for a more aggressive approach. A month later it was decided, at Ball's suggestion, that, in an attempt to enliven the campaign, a conference would be held to arrange speeches at various places throughout the state in Manning's behalf.[41]

On the night of the first primary in late August, Ball's office and other

39. Ball, Diary, I, 149, June 26, 1916.
40. *Ibid.*, VII, 66, July 4, 1926.   41. *Ibid.*, II, 66, Aug. 15, 1916.

rooms in *The State* building were crowded with people, all opposed to Blease, watching the election returns. As Blease's lead grew, everyone became discouraged. The final vote gave Blease about 50,000, Manning more than 33,000, and Cooper in excess of 25,000. Manning would stand against Blease in a second primary, but Ball feared the plurality of 23,000 votes could not be overcome. Only Ball and two others talked confidently. Ball's optimism belied his true feelings, but just after midnight he wrote an editorial for the next morning's paper. He emphasized that the Cooper and Manning vote together had exceeded the Blease vote by 8,000. To best him in the second primary, anti-Bleasites had but to hold the margin. It was written to give courage to opponents of Blease and to get them to work without delay. No other newspaper had an editorial on the election that morning, Ball discovered; *The State* had been twenty-four hours ahead. For that reason Ball believed that his comment on the results of the first primary of 1916 was "the most effective editorial I ever wrote."[42]

Ball appealed to the responsible citizens of the state: "To re-elect Mr. Manning will require a hard, steady, resolute campaign. It will be said that the Blease lead is too big to overcome. That is absurd. The good government Democrats can poll 75,000 or 80,000 votes in the next primary, and they will poll them, too."[43] Cooper urged his followers to support Manning, and the battle was on. In the two weeks between the first and second primary, Ball waged the sort of relentless editorial campaign for which he became famous. Almost every newspaper in the state opposed Blease, but no editor could equal Ball when it came to persistence. Day after day, a series of front page editorials blasted Blease from every side. Today Ball stressed his abuse of the pardoning power; tomorrow it was his violation of the two-term tradition for the governorship that drew the editor's attack. South Carolinians thoroughly enjoy their politics and the political editorial draws more attention there than in most other states. But what of the half of the electorate that does not read a newspaper? If Blease held his first vote and got 17 per cent of the Cooper vote, he would win. A week before the run-off, Ball hoped "God in his wisdom and mercy may prevent the election of Blease next Tuesday."[44]

W. E. Gonzales, in Cuba, guessed his pessimism. Ball's editorials made "a brave show of courage," but he imagined "that Ball did not

42. *Ibid.*, II, 82–84, Sept. 23, 1935.   43. *The State*, Aug. 31, 1916.
44. Ball, Diary, II, 80, Sept. 5, 1916.

have much more than hope for Manning."[45] He added, however, "I do not see how you could have done more or better for Manning."[46] In Ball's opinion, the Bleasites were a party bound together as tight as any group in the state. Two-thirds or three-fourths of them were honest and well-meaning; the rest voted for him because they expected him to let them sell whiskey—statewide prohibition had gone into effect in 1915—or because they hoped to get pardons through him. "If I had a son in the penitentiary," Ball once remarked, "I have no doubt I would be for Blease."[47] The opposition, he complained, was too often directed by individualists who quarreled among themselves about little questions. After the first primary, however, Ball saw a real campaign beginning as earnest citizens went to work. Gradually he became more optimistic; a few days before the second primary, he admitted to a friend, "I believe Blease will be defeated."[48]

Manning did, in fact, win a second term in a close election which defied easy analysis and contradicted the state's normal class-oriented voting patterns. The Governor's biographer found that "working quietly but vigorously against Manning, a banker and cotton mill director himself, were the cotton mill executives and the state's banking and other financial leaders."[49] The mill men had been offended by his policies toward labor and the financial interests alienated when he demanded strict accounting of tax returns. Charleston, in rebellion against Manning's anti-race-track and liquor-law enforcement policies, had given Blease a big majority; but the totals for the state read: Manning 71,460; Blease, 66,785. Letters of congratulations came to Ball from all over the state; some credited Manning's renomination to the editorials in *The State* and *The News and Courier*. Ball's professed feeling was one, not of exultation, but of relief. The cause of good government had prevailed; Ball did not see how Blease could ever again be elected to an important office in the state. Another harsh campaign ended. Ball's side had won, and to him belonged a major share of the credit.[50]

45. W. E. Gonzales to W. W. Ball, Sept. 4, 1916, Ball Papers.
46. *Ibid.*
47. W. W. Ball to A. F. McKissick, Sept. 4, 1916, Ball Papers.
48. *Ibid.*
49. Robert M. Burts, "The Public Career of Richard I. Manning," unpublished doctoral dissertation, Vanderbilt University, 1957, p. 313.
50. It was Ball's belief that an editor should not compromise himself by asking favors from politicians who had enjoyed his editorial support, and there were apparently few occasions when his actions contradicted his announced convictions. Two such departures occurred, however, after Manning's renomination when Ball

During Manning's second administration a legislature crowded with unfriendly Bleasites virtually blocked a continuation of his Progressive program. With the national Progressive tide at its peak, the politics of the state remained the same curious mixture it had become in 1890, a combination of dogged conservatism, anti-aristocratic prejudice, and acrimonious personal rivalry.

As domestic events were overshadowed by the coming of World War I, Ball hoped the United States could avoid actual participation in the war; yet he was openly sympathetic to the Allied cause. Most of the German-Americans in South Carolina, and the Irish-American element as well, had been friendly to the Central Powers; but after the American declaration in April, 1917, they loyally supported the war effort. In May, however, John P. Grace, the editor of *The Charleston American*, condemned Congress for declaring war and was enthusiastically supported by Cole Blease. Blease, in speeches made that summer, not only attacked American entrance into the war but denounced Woodrow Wilson and Richard I. Manning for their parts in committing American men to a foreign war. The war issue was already building as the dominant question for the elections of 1918.

At the same time, a full year before the coming campaign, speculation grew about the plans of Ben Tillman. Senator Tillman was completing his fourth term in Washington, but it was well known that he was ill. By September, 1917, Tillman had announced that he would not be a candidate for re-election the next year, but would run if the people he had served for twenty-seven years demanded it. Among critics of Tillman, Ball must be considered one of the severest judges, not withstanding the Senator's consistently conservative voting record in Washington. Ball simply could not forgive him for upending the Bourbons in 1890, and now, in 1917, he doubted the sincerity of his statement. At that point Ball regarded Tillman as having no organization, being without political friends, but imagining that his following of the early nineties would be true to him. "The truth," he thought, "is that the old man doesn't want to let go."[51] Contrary to Ball's prediction, Blease had all

---

first asked the Governor, as a favor, to appoint his friend, P. H. Gadsden of Charleston, to the next vacancy on the Board of Trustees of the University of South Carolina (W. W. Ball to P. H. Gadsden, Sept. 30, 1916, Ball Papers); and when he inquired of Manning the possibilities for obtaining a commission for Ambrose Gonzales's son Robert, then serving with a South Carolina regiment on the Texas border (Ball, Diary, II, 117, Nov. 4, 1916).

51. W. W. Ball to W. E. Gonzales, Sept. 13, 1917, Ball Papers.

but declared himself a candidate, and Tillman's wavering attitude hindered attempts to organize against Blease. Ball saw Blease, through speeches and the editorials in *The Charleston American*, trying to bring Tillman out to meet him and him alone. The result would, he predicted, be a disaster. "From what I can learn," Ball revealed, "Tillman would be unable to take the stump and would not expect to do so."[52]

It is doubtful that Tillman was as weak politically as Ball imagined, but his appeal for the voters was the secondary issue. Because he understood that Tillman's poor health had rendered him utterly incompetent, Ball was incensed at newspapers which pushed his candidacy. He was particularly bewildered by the attitude of *The Columbia Record*. A few days after one of the principal directors of *Record* policy had expressed doubt that Tillman would live to open the campaign, that paper announced itself for Tillman. By doing so, Ball concluded, the *Record* was playing into the hands of Blease, "sacrificing public interest in order to retain possession of this old man for some immediate purpose of their own."[53] What the game was, or if indeed there was one, Ball did not discover.

The State would, of course, support Tillman if necessary, but Ball hoped that Representative A. F. Lever would oppose Blease for the Senate. Lever was not afraid of Blease and would fight him, but he would not run against Tillman, and the veteran Senator would not withdraw. *The State* might try to stop the Blease-directed campaign to project Tillman as the candidate, but Ball was not optimistic about its chances for success. He informed Lever that he was convinced the systematic effort underway would persuade Tillman to run and that the Senator was "busy persuading himself in the same way."[54] Lever replied, agreeing.[55]

The next spring Blease and N. B. Dial, a Laurens businessman, declared openly their candidacy for Tillman's Senate seat. Dial was a staunch supporter of President Wilson, and even Blease advocated full support of the war effort while criticizing his enemies for attempting to use patriotism for political purposes. Governor Manning, however, anxious to guarantee the President the strongest possible support, warned Senator Tillman, who had suffered a paralytic stroke, that his precarious

52. *Ibid.*
53. W. W. Ball to A. E. Gonzales, Oct. 20, 1917, Ball Papers.
54. W. W. Ball to A. F. Lever, Sept. 27, 1917, Ball Papers.
55. A. F. Lever to W. W. Ball, Oct. 1, 1917, Ball Papers.

health provided the crux of a serious political dilemma. When Tillman failed to respond, Manning asked Woodrow Wilson to intercede in securing Tillman's withdrawal in favor of A. F. Lever. The President, however, believing Blease could not win, insisted that Lever continue as chairman of the House Agricultural Committee.

D. F. Houston, Wilson's Secretary of Agriculture and a South Carolinian, helped effect Lever's withdrawal from contention. Houston, observing that all of the candidates could be expected to support the war effort and stressing Lever's importance in his present position, hoped that he was not taking an "unwarranted liberty" in suggesting that Lever not press his candidacy.[56]

In the end, Tillman accommodated those who sought his elimination from the race. By the time the summer campaign was barely underway, he was dead. N. B. Dial now opposed Blease for the Senate. To Governor Manning fell the duty of choosing someone to fill Tillman's unexpired term. In early July he summoned Ball to his office, where he announced that he had appointed Christie Benet, Columbia attorney, to fill the vacancy caused by Tillman's death. Benet would also enter the special election, which would be held at the same time as the Blease-Dial contest, to determine who should serve the final months of the unexpired term. Ball commended the Governor's action. A few days later Senator Benet called on Ball and together they discussed his campaign. Ball recommended that Benet attack Blease's past utterances against the Wilson administration and suggested that the election of Blease would present South Carolina as being in opposition to the war.[57] During the campaign Benet and his opponent for the short term, W. P. Pollock, though neither was running against Blease, attacked him rather than each other. There is no better testimony to the remarkable role Blease played in South Carolina politics.

When the campaign opened officially on June 15, Ball's most important work had already been accomplished. *The State* was the first newspaper opposed to Blease which concentrated on his anti-war speeches of the previous summer. In late April precinct clubs met to elect delegates to county conventions which in turn elected delegates to the state convention. By making Blease's disloyalty the issue, Ball hoped to pack the convention with delegates who were solidly behind Wilson

56. D. F. Houston to A. F. Lever, n. d., 1918, David F. Houston Papers, Harvard University Library.
57. Ball, Diary, IV, 65, July 15, 1918.

and the war while rejecting Blease in spite of his current co-operative attitude. The precinct clubs were to meet April 27. Two days before, *The State* reprinted the speech made by Blease at Pomaria in his home county of Newberry. Ball dramatically scored two points at once by reproducing the account of the speech which had appeared on July 27, 1917, in *The Charleston American*, one of the papers presently supporting Blease for the Senate.[58] The next day, across from the editorial page, *The State* reprinted an address Blease delivered at Filbert in York County on August 3, 1917. Once again Ball used the Bleasite press as his source, this time going to the weekly *Yorkville Enquirer*, the other paper then busily praising Blease. The theme of the Filbert speech was peace: we could and should have peace with Germany now. Blease saw no reason why the United States should fight, but he struck out at those who impugned his loyalty. Men who said that he had ever in word or deed been a traitor were liars and puppies. The conservative press came under his attack:

> It has been published of late in the anti-Reform press that I and the party to which I belong are outcasts in the political world just now, but I want to say to you so far as I am personally concerned, that I would rather be an outcast in the eyes of Woodrow Wilson and a follower of Jesus Christ than be a follower of Woodrow Wilson and be an outcast from Jesus Christ.[59]

Other papers followed the lead of *The State* in attacking the wartime statements of Cole Blease. John Gary Evans, Democratic Party Chairman in South Carolina, approved Ball's course and urged him to continue the agitation. When the anti-Blease forces captured forty-two of the forty-five county delegations to the state Democratic convention, Ball attributed the major part of that success to the publicity given to the Filbert and Pomaria speeches. Again in July, Ball reprinted *The Charleston American*'s account of the Pomaria address wherein Blease restated his opposition to American entrance into the war. If he had been in the Senate, Blease said, he would have voted against it, but:

> Do not misunderstand me. We are now in this war and it must be pushed to a successful conclusion. . . . We are in the fight, and we must fight it to the finish with all the power of our great nation. . . . So far as the war is concerned, I offered my services, once we

58. *The State*, April 25, 1918.   59. *Ibid.*, April 26, 1918.

were in it and offered to raise a regiment or a brigade and would have done so had I been permitted. But that kind of regiment or brigade with officers elected by those whom they were to command was not desired by the powers that be in South Carolina. . . . Today in South Carolina we live under a limited monarchy, selfish and self-seeking in which the people have no voice.[60]

Goaded by consistent attacks of hostile editors, Blease fought back through one of the few newspapers available to him—*The Charleston American*, a paper with a small circulation founded by Mayor Grace in 1916. A front-page news story, titled "Blease Exposes the Dial Press," reported Blease's speech to a gathering at the Olympia mill village in Columbia. Blease presented his opponent as a servant of the corporations and proceeded to a scathing indictment of his press critics. Charles R. Wright, editor of *The Columbia Record*, he charged, was the secretary of Ed Robertson, whose father had laid the foundation of his fortune while United States senator by grace of a Negro and scalawag legislature in Reconstruction days. Wright was merely a tool whose personal reputation could be sized up in the statement that he had been expelled from a Columbia Club for cheating at cards. Ball was also smeared in a manner extreme even for Blease:

> He pointed out that W. W. Ball, the editor of the Columbia State, a man who is now questioning the loyalty of other people, had married a daughter of Mr. Witte, the German consul in Charleston, at that time, and that the money which Mr. Ball was now parading around the streets of Columbia via automobiles, was money straight from Germany; that Mr. Ball's children had blood in their veins half German: and yet that was the man questioning the loyalty of Blease and others in this critical time of the nation's career.[61]

Whether or not affected by the mud Blease had splattered upon him and his family, Ball displayed more than ordinary editorial concern for the outcome of the Blease-Dial contest, whereas it had been his custom to declare his immunity from personal involvement. Several nights before the first primary, he talked after midnight with cronies and was not able to sleep until four o'clock in the morning. "The sleeplessness is

60. *Ibid.*, July 23, 1918.
61. *The Charleston American*, July 28, 1918. Thomas R. Waring, editor of the Charleston *Post* and husband of Laura Witte, was therefore also discredited as an authority on patriotic duty.

due," he explained, "to tense interest in the political contest and my work in relation to it plus too much smoking of tobacco."[62] Ball need not have worried; Blease had committed perhaps the largest blunder of his career when he misjudged the feelings of South Carolinians and attacked Woodrow Wilson and the war. N. B. Dial won by a substantial majority, and Robert A. Cooper easily defeated John G. Richards, Bleasite candidate for governor.[63] On election night Ball was once again among the anxious who gathered late at the offices of *The State* to follow the election returns. When the result was definitely known, at about 1:30 A.M., Ambrose Gonzales called Ball into his office. There Ball had a drink as he watched the crowd in Main Street milling near the screen on which the returns were being flashed by *The State*. Hundreds of people lingered until shortly after 2 A.M., when the display ended.[64]

The next day a letter arrived for Ball from N. B. Dial:

I desire to thank you most heartily for the great interest you took in my race and for the magnificent service you and The State rendered the cause. Many of your Editorials made me feel that I was unworthy of the kind words that you were saying and I shall ever remember the assistance, you, the paper, and your force gave me.[65]

A few days later Ball met Dial in the street and he advised the senator-elect to study hard until his term began in March, to try to know as much as he could, but to know more than anyone else about any two subjects. Dial did not say he would follow his advice, and Ball chided, "You won't do this—you never have been a student any more than I have been."[66]

Though he repeatedly denied it, Ball found politics fascinating; yet he never sought office. Two months before, former Governor D. C. Heyward and a member of the staff of *The State* told Ball that they intended to ask Governor Manning to give Ball the appointment which ultimately went to Christie Benet. Ball refused to allow his name to be suggested for the unexpired term of Senator Tillman. Manning would not select him, Ball reasoned, so why should he let Manning think that he wanted the post? Even if the job were offered to him, he thought that he would refuse it—but he could not be sure.[67] Perhaps his decision to forego a

62. Ball, Diary, IV, 147, Aug. 25, 1918.
63. Since Ball, Dial, and Cooper were all natives of Laurens, the county enjoyed unusual political prominence that year.
64. Ball, Diary, IV, 150, Aug. 28, 1918.
65. N. B. Dial to W. W. Ball, Aug. 28, 1918, Ball Papers.
66. Ball, Diary, IV, 157, Sept. 3, 1918.
67. W. W. Ball to Eliza Ball, July 3, 1918.

political career was that of a proud man who would not risk defeat; perhaps he knew that a man of his ultraconservative views would not win elections; or perhaps, as he so often said, he preferred being a free man aloof from the political scramble. But, like all his ideas, his view of politics and politicians had roots which were deep in his youth. Many years later, when Ball was an old man, he wrote, with more than a trace of bitterness:

> I was deeply interested in my father's political ambitions, in which he was not successful. He was successful when his services were needed, in 1876, but of the tricks and wiles of office-holders he was as innocent as a babe. Almost he was nominated for congressman in a convention in 1884. As I grew up I perceived not only the futility of a political career in South Carolina but that success in it would be at the cost of one's intellectual integrity—and from my mother too I acquired the dislike for it. She saw the emptiness of it. So, all my life, I have been active in politics, as a newspaper man, but I have never asked for an office or held one, except notary public and one or two trusteeships. Relatively, at least, I have been independent, no man's man.[68]

At another time he summarized his position much more succinctly: "To refuse to participate in politics in a democratic country is snobbish; ergo —I am a snob."[69]

A career in politics might have brought Ball fame which is beyond the grasp of most editors, and he would have liked that. He was a sensitive man and he had his share of human vanity. In 1917 he received permission from W. E. Gonzales to change his official title from "managing editor" to "editor" during the Ambassador's absence from Columbia. The public did not make the distinction, he admitted, and the only thing involved was his own self-satisfaction.[70] Still, his name was hardly an obscurity. In 1918 he was appointed by the national chairman to the Southeastern Committee of the War Work Council of the Y.M.C.A., whose aim it was to bring before the public the requirements of the American Expeditionary Force and the Allied armies.[71] At the invitation

68. Ball, Diary, XII, 106, April 26, 1941.
69. *Ibid.*, I, 52, May 16, 1916.
70. W. W. Ball to W. E. Gonzales, May 12, 1917; W. E. Gonzales to W. W. Ball, May 18, 1917; Ball Papers.
71. George W. Parkins to W. W. Ball, June 23, 1918, Ball Papers. Members of the National Committee included Rockefeller, Ford, Mellon, and Carter Glass.

of editor Mark Sullivan, Ball had agreed to write for *Collier's* an occasional paragraph on Southern problems. One such contribution, appearing without by-line, stressed the need for diversification of agriculture to improve the South's backward economic condition. Resourcefulness was not one of the South's natural resources; the farmers, as a group, were ignorant and must be educated in modern agricultural philosophies. Diversify knowledge, he said, and the crops will diversify themselves.[72] With Southern industry expanding daily, Ball the romantic called for remedies offered nearly a century before by ante-bellum reformers. Still, after three campaigns during which he and *The State* had led the fight against Cole Blease, Ball had surely become a political power in the state.

Finally, in 1919, there came to Ball an honor which he interpreted as demonstrating at last that he was an individual of importance. The trustees of the University of South Carolina voted him an honorary degree, and, on June 11, his alma mater conferred upon him the title "Doctor of Laws." Ball admitted that the compliment "tickled his vanity."[73] In his part of the world it was difficult for a man to obtain recognition except by going into politics. Now, he noted with pleasure, "the University tells the public that I am somebody."[74]

72. *Collier's*, LV, No. 16 (July 3, 1915), 14.
73. W. W. Ball to E. M. Blanding, July 29, 1919, Ball Papers.
74. Ball, Diary, V, 2, June 11, 1919.

CHAPTER SIX

A POWER IN POLITICS

W. W. BALL was fifty years old when he received the honorary Doctor of Laws degree from the University of South Carolina; the occasion also marked the passing of ten years since the Balls had come to Columbia. By the end of the decade the elder Ball children had reached college age. Eleanor represented the fourth generation of Balls at the University. Her twin, Margaret, entered Winthrop, the women's college of South Carolina, and Ball discovered that he was not altogether a snob because he rather liked the idea of her being one of a thousand girls in a democratic state school.[1] Before long William, Jr., would be at The Citadel. Ten-year old Fay, from all accounts a charming youngster, was already displaying the interest in becoming an actress that her mother had never been able to satisfy. Katharine, the eldest, ever impulsive and volatile, had survived a series of educational crises and in June, 1919, married an Army captain she had met while he was stationed in Columbia during the war. The bridegroom was Clements Ripley, whose parents were Vermonters. Ball reported himself "entirely pleased" by the prospect of family association with New Englanders, because, though he was a sentimental Rebel, he was glad that the Union had been saved.[2]

The departure of Katty reduced the ranks of the strong side in a household dominated by women. The house at 1720 Pendleton Street was filled with women's voices—taking sides on current issues, talking about the theater, and arguing an extensive range of topics both personal and academic. Often at dinner there were several concurrent conversations while "Papa" talked without an audience. Throughout the female fluster, Ball maintained a virtually imperturbable façade. His hours of quiet conversation were spent with Fitz McMaster or over a drink with former Governor Heyward and Professor Snowden. These exchanges were, throughout his life, a valued source of entertainment to Ball, sprinkled as they were with politics and genealogy. The idea of "family" was very important to him; he and his sister once paid a professional

1. W. W. Ball to Eliza Ball, Jan. 10, 1920, Ball Papers.
2. W. W. Ball to F. C. Norton, March 18, 1919, Ball Papers.

genealogist for conducting months of research to prove that their antecedents were families of English nationality who had lived in Virginia before the Revolution.[3] He seemed to know the family connections of every notable figure in the state, including his grandparents on both sides.

Tracing, and talking about, the lineage of the new editor in Orangeburg or that ambitious young lawyer in Sumter, was, for Ball, a diversion, for he had no conventional hobbies unless his interest in history could be so considered. One of his friends was Professor J. G. de Roulhac Hamilton of the University of North Carolina, to whom Ball sometimes sent his privately printed speeches. Ball was also in touch with the eminent Southern historian Ulrich B. Phillips; the two exchanged information about slavery and plantation holdings. For a time, too, Ball fancied himself an inventor; he contemplated, but later abandoned, plans to secure a patent for a checkerboard game he had devised. Of course, his cotton mill and real-estate affairs took a substantial portion of what might otherwise have been leisure time. Ball's income as editor was not sufficient to support and educate his family. The money that kept the Balls in "comfortable" circumstances came from dividends, from the buying, selling, and trading of mill stocks and properties belonging both to him and to his wife. Ball speculated, as he had done for thirty years, and there were good years and bad. In 1914 he complained that he must borrow money to live on. In 1918 he and Fay Ball lost more than eighteen hundred dollars in the failure of the Jasper Land Development Company.[4] But in two weeks during January, 1920, he made two profitable trades for profits greater than his annual salary from *The State*.[5] Over the years, Ball neither made nor lost a large amount of money, for he was a cautious investor.

As Ball grew older his routine scarcely varied. The paper work which accompanied his editorial and business interests consumed many hours —hours lengthened by the perpetual disorder of his desk, confusion that his secretary could not completely rectify. Then, the frequent evening sessions with the same few close friends; one tall drink—except at parties, he usually took only one; often, after midnight, the entry of news into his diary; and then to bed.

3. W. W. Ball to J. C. Underwood, Jan. 24, 1911; J. C. Underwood to W. W. Ball, Feb. 12, 1912; W. W. Ball to J. C. Underwood, March 16, 1912; J. C. Underwood to W. W. Ball, March 24, 1912; Ball Papers.
4. W. W. Ball to D. C. Heyward, March 13, 1919, Ball Papers.
5. W. W. Ball, Diary, V, 55, Jan. 29, 1920.

If his habits did not change, neither did his ideas. At a time when most political thought centered upon the idea that the wealth of the country must not be allowed to accumulate in the hands of big business and that, as a remedy, an enlarged federal government must be created and brought closer to popular control, Ball's thinking ran strongly in the opposite direction. The Progressive Movement had reached its crescendo, but Ball could not see how its democratizing features (popular election of senators, initiative, referendum, recall, municipal government reforms, and so on) had made government any less corrupt, any more efficient; and prohibition had violated the personal liberty of the individual. What the country needed was not more democracy but less. The notion that men were equal was fallacious; the very nature of democracy was dooming the United States to the level of the commonplace; rule by "all the people" was the sure road to mediocrity.

Ball, though he was moving against the tide, was sure and steadfast in his reaction. In 1917, and again in 1919, he expressed his disillusion with the democratic dogma in essays read to the Kosmos Club and printed a few years later under the title *Essays in Reaction*. In the earlier tract, "Back to Calhoun," he chastened South Carolina to heed the words of her great leader on suffrage, representation, and the concurrent majority. In his *Disquisition on Government*, Calhoun had outlined these theories. The right of suffrage by itself could do no more than give to those who elect complete control over the conduct of those they have elected. If everyone in the community had the same interests, there would be no problem, but such was not the case. Each faction strove to obtain possession of the powers of government as the means to protect itself or to advance its own respective course regardless of the interests of others. If the numerical majority ruled, the domination of the community by one group was possible, even probable. But through government by the concurrent majority, each interest group would possess a veto over any action which was detrimental to its well-being. Only bills on which each interest group could concur would become law. This, said Calhoun, was in the true spirit of democracy.

Government by the concurrent majority, Calhoun added, would make possible an enlargement of the electorate: among the other advantages which governments of the concurrent majority had over those of the numerical majority—and which strongly illustrated their more popular character—was that they admitted with safety a much greater extension of the right of suffrage. It might be safely extended in such governments to universal suffrage: that is, to every male citizen of mature age, with few ordinary exceptions; but it could not be far extended in those of the numerical majority, without placing government ultimately under the control of the more ignorant and dependent portions of the community.[6]

In governments of the concurrent majority, Calhoun said, "Mere numbers have not the absolute control; and the wealthy and intelligent being identified in interest with the poor and ignorant of their respective community, become their leaders and protectors."[7] This was Ball's conception of the duty of the aristocracy. He always believed that the masses of common people were not fit to rule themselves. That they were capable of choosing directly all state officers was utter nonsense. What did they know of qualifications of candidates for welfare, education, agriculture, labor, or financial posts? Such choices could be safely made only by the General Assembly, as had been the case in the days of Calhoun.

In "Back to Aristocracy," Ball described the class which should lead the state back to standards of a less-liberal era. His "aristocrat," however, need not be wealthy or name-proud; potentially every man was a political aristocrat. The terms "aristocrat" and "voter" would be synonymous, but the suffrage would be sharply curtailed. Educated intelligence and property ownership, either or both, were to entitle the citizen to participate in government. But, of the two, Ball considered the latter the more important. A man must possess something of tangible value to give him a practical stake in the preservation of honest, orderly government; furthermore, literacy was no bar to socialism.[8]

Ball's theories of aristocracy and government were unmistakably influenced by his consistent Anglophilism. He said of the state constitution which had been devised after the United States had separated from Britain: "From 1790 to 1865, three-quarters of a century, South Carolina had a government of English begettal and its essential life-principle was the blending of manhood suffrage and property-holding as the basis of representation. Therein lay is health, its safety. . . ."[9]

Moreover, he had an abundant respect for the English ruling classes. The British Parliament, Ball maintained, had the wisdom to see that universal enfranchisement of an ignorant people was incompatible with

6. R. K. Cralle, ed., *The Works of John C. Calhoun* (6 vols.; New York, 1857), I, 45–46.   7. *Ibid.*, I, 46.
8. W. W. Ball, *Essays in Reaction* (Columbia, S. C., 1923), p. 52.
9. Ball, *The State That Forgot*, p. 285.

the perpetuation of civilized government. The privilege had been extended gradually as the masses acquired education and property; as they became ready, they had been admitted into the electoral body. The impressive truth of this story of popular aggrandizement, Ball felt was

> . . . that the British upper classes could be trusted to deal justly with the people, that they held the government as trustees for the people, that they did not misuse their power, that they distributed it liberally, if prudently, not gripping and hugging it to themselves as a divine endowment.[10]

That Ball's interpretations of English political history were open to criticism is a point almost too obvious to mention. But he was convinced of their rightness no less than he was sure of the justness of the Confederate cause or of the everlasting value of Jeffersonian self-reliance. And, together, these pillars sustained him during countless onslaughts from modernists. It is a mistake, however, to imagine Ball as a total reactionary busily pursuing the worship of his ancestors. He was not against all "progress"; he wrote editorials espousing *state* action leading to an eight-hour work law, the building of good roads, the abolition of the county chain gang, and the continuance of humanitarian agencies like the Board of Charities and Corrections.

Discernible at the time, however, was his growing rigidity of opinion on racial issues. The post-World War I period was one of mounting tension marked by race riots, rumors of Negro uprisings, and the rebirth of the Ku Klux Klan. Despite the decline in lynching which accompanied the growth of towns and public education facilities, fear and hatred of the Negro began to intensify for the first time since white superiority had been re-established. The causes were several and they combined to produce an atmosphere of insecurity. In part, of course, growing anti-Negro feeling in the South was a regional reflection of national tendencies toward nativism and xenophobia during the twenties. But there were local causes as well. Negroes began their migration north during the war in search of job opportunities. Their journeying back and forth, its effect on the cheap labor supply in the South, and the presence in the area of recruiting agents from the North created the first real signs of Negro mobility since Reconstruction. The Negro's experience during

10. Ball, *Essays in Reaction*, p. 43.

World War I also contributed to his restlessness. While he served in the armed forces he experienced more liberal treatment both in the North and in Europe; consequently, he was less inclined to resume the countless obligations of caste.

At home, the number of Negro farm owners increased slowly but steadily, as did the number of those engaged in business. Negroes also received their small share of benefit from a continuing Southern emphasis in public education. Careful pressure for the ballot began to appear. More important, the first notes of militancy had been struck by W. E. B. Du Bois and other officers of the National Association for the Advancement of Colored People, then hardly a decade old. The Association's demands for immediate civil rights were disturbing to a society which had entertained with sufferance Booker T. Washington's patient philosophy of Negro progress through vocational advancement. Was the black man ripe for conversion to communist revolutionary?

Ball shared the uneasiness of the great majority of Southern whites as he stressed with increasing regularity the necessity for keeping the South a white man's country. More and more, his decisions on important issues seemed to be dictated by the effect each had upon the Negro problem. For example, the 1920 census had shown that though the percentage of Negroes was shrinking, South Carolina still had a few more blacks than whites. Ball's idea was that the poverty of the state could be reduced by encouraging the immigration of thousands of white farmers, thereby redressing the racial balance. It was preferable, though not essential, that the immigrants be Western Europeans. The Anglo-Saxon homogeneity of the South had been overemphasized, he asserted, and it might be wise to stir up the blood by the injection of a foreign strain.[11] He applauded Senator Dial's efforts to bring Italian laborers to the state in order to offset losses in population growth brought about by a steady Negro migration to the North.[12] And yet, in a comment-provoking editorial, Ball declared that if rumors were true and Southern congressmen were changing their attitude on immigration, they were following a policy detrimental to the interests of the state. If they were becoming more lenient about restrictions because they hoped that the beneficiaries of their generosity would work the Southern fields aban-

11. W. W. Ball to Moss E. Penn, editor of the Memphis *News Scimitar*, April 6, 1922, Ball Papers.
12. W. W. Ball to G. R. De Saussure, April 26, 1923, Ball Papers.

doned by departed Negroes, their plans would boomerang. Immigrants would flock to Northern jobs, Ball predicted, and cut off the flow of Negroes to the North, the migration which the South so badly needed.[13]

Ball opposed the ratification by South Carolina of the women's suffrage amendment also for reasons that were partially racial. In 1919 he seemed not to be concerned with racial restrictions on voting; if the suffrage were restricted to the "aristocracy" of both races, the whites would continue to exercise control by virtue of their natural superiority.[14] It was stupidity to indulge the notion that race discrimination in political affairs would at any time be lawful, he said, "nor will sex discrimination anywhere long be tolerated."[15] But early in 1920, as the General Assembly considered the amendment, Ball urged its rejection. He apparently felt that its passage would be a relatively greater gain for Negroes than whites; not more than 5,000 of the 190,000 white women in the state, he guessed, had given the matter a passing thought.[16] A young South Carolina Representative in Congress named James F. Byrnes agreed with the editor that colored women would vote if given the opportunity, whereas many white women would not.[17] Ball's basic objection, however, was that suffrage was a matter for state rather than federal determination:

> The State is not opposed to woman suffrage—though it is opposed to any and all suffrage laws enacted for South Carolina by the voters of Oregon, Kansas, Texas, and Wisconsin. When the women of South Carolina (not a few thousand signing petitions, but a hundred thousand speaking in a clear voice after serious consideration) demand the ballot they should have it.[18]

Although the discussion of the Nineteenth Amendment did not otherwise engender much excitement in the South Carolina press, Ball pursued the subject relentlessly, as if the national outcome depended on what happened in Columbia. The "Anthony" amendment, as he termed it in deference to Susan B., was battered by a typical Ball campaign as *The State* proclaimed a time for conservatism. Another day, another editorial; in one particular issue, four different editorials appeared, all

13. *The State*, May 2, 1923.
14. Ball, *The Editor and the Republic*, p. 63.
15. *Ibid.*, p. 62.
16. W. W. Ball to Mrs. J. S. Pinckard, Nov. 7, 1919, Ball Papers.
17. J. F. Byrnes to W. W. Ball, Jan. 18, 1920, Ball Papers.
18. *The State*, Jan. 12, 1920.

urging its defeat.[19] The House refused to ratify the amendment; the vote was 94 to 20.

In Ball's mind, however, the most important issue of the early postwar years was neither women's suffrage nor immigration, but the need for a new state constitution. He believed that now, during the enlightened administration of Governor Cooper, while the spirit of wartime purpose still lingered, the people would be in a state of mind to send to a constitutional convention only the best and ablest men. In educational facilities and in per capita income, South Carolina ranked among the lowest in the nation. Now was the time for the development of a constitution less democratic, more capable of serving as the basis for the creation of a revitalized commonwealth.[20] Such a convention, of course, did not meet in 1920, nor has it ever met; it would have represented an "undemocratic" trend in the state. Such a movement was unlikely in South Carolina or anywhere else in the United States. But Ball was not deterred. Seldom has an idea of a public man been so long sustained by sheer fancy.

The year 1920 was singular in one important respect: a temporary political calm had settled over the state. Governor Robert A. Cooper was re-elected without opposition. Ball remarked: "No one is interested in state politics except a few candidates."[21] It is a phenomenon indeed when South Carolinians are not eager to talk politics. But the reason for the quiet in 1920 was all too apparent: Cole Blease, for a change, had chosen not to run. The unpredictable Mr. Blease, still smarting from his humiliating defeat in 1918, spoke against Wilson and the League of Nations, and publicly hoped that Cox would not be successful on the national Democratic ticket. Ball's informants heard that Blease would not vote in the primary that year, that he did not consider himself a member of the Democratic party; still, he urged his followers to support "Cotton Ed" Smith for re-election to the Senate. One of Smith's friends accounted for Blease's unexpected generosity by theorizing that, if Harding defeated Cox, Blease would seek from the Republicans an appointment as federal district attorney and that he wanted Smith favorable to his confirmation.[22] But Senator Smith, visiting at Ball's office, claimed never to have heard that explanation and seemed unable to

19. *Ibid.*, Jan. 16, 1920.
20. W. W. Ball to Dr. W. M. Riggs, President of Clemson College, Jan. 21, 1919, Ball Papers.
21. W. W. Ball to D. F. Houston, Aug. 5, 1920, Ball Papers.
22. Ball, Diary, V, 112, Aug. 27, 1920.

explain Blease's conduct.[23] The Blease-Smith mystery could not enliven a dull campaign, and Ball wrote, "For the first election summer in ten years I am having a comfortable experience."[24]

In the next two years there were other pleasant surprises. In the spring of 1921 Ball became a grandfather when Katharine and Clements Ripley became the parents of a son. Also, Governor Cooper appointed him member of the board of commissioners of the state Institute for the Education of the Deaf, Dumb, and Blind at Cedar Spring. In accepting, Ball informed the Governor that he would have accepted perhaps no other public appointment for fear of embarrassing his position as editor.[25] A few weeks before, at the invitation of Cooper, Ball dined with the Governor in order to meet Bernard Baruch, the wealthy South Carolinian who had already assumed his perennial role as economic adviser to the government, having served as chairman of the War Industries Board in 1918–1919. The meeting in Columbia marked the beginning of a long friendship between Ball and the Kershaw County man he described as "a striking example of the upper class Semite."[26]

During his long career Ball met many celebrities, and he usually recorded detailed physical descriptions of them in his journal. Vachel Lindsay once came to Columbia to read some of his poems at the Town Theatre, a project in which the Ball ladies were closely interested. The next day the poet had dinner with the Balls, after which he made pen-and-ink drawings for the children, autographing them with verse. Late that night, as he made his journal entries, Ball recalled that Lindsay was above average in size, and though not fat, awkward in appearance and ugly. His light brown hair grew far back on his narrow, retreating forehead. His nose was straight, his upper lip long and convex, his lower lip thick. His most striking feature was the frontal bone, which protruded above his eyes and from which his forehead slanted backwards, the line of his nose making a "mighty angle" with that of his forehead.[27] It was entirely customary for Ball to observe and record such data; moreover, dozens of diary notations reveal his addiction to details of the most trivial nature. He recorded, for instance, that

23. *Ibid.*, V, 115, Sept. 4, 1920.
24. W. W. Ball to D. F. Houston, Aug. 5, 1920, Ball Papers.
25. Ball, Diary, V, 166, April 25, 1921.
26. *Ibid.*, V, 157, March 4, 1921.
27. *Ibid.*, V, 238–239, April 30, 1922.

while a trip to Laurens from Columbia consumed two hours, thirty-four minutes, the ride back took two hours, thirty-five minutes.[28]

In 1922 Ball made one of his rare trips outside the borders of South Carolina when he accepted an invitation to be one of the speakers during Journalism Week at the University of Missouri. Before the session sponsored by the School of Journalism there, Ball delivered a plea for the survival of the country weekly. The rural press, he complained, was dying in South Carolina. Young newspapermen were deserting, as he had, the field of independent weekly publication in exchange for salary and servitude on the urban dailies. As a result, they were underestimating the value of the weekly press and robbing the state of one of its important institutions.[29]

At the same time Ball espoused his theories for an audience in Missouri, he faced practical journalistic problems of his own, one of them involving fundamental policy. In May, 1922, M. Goode Homes, head of the School of Engineering at the University of South Carolina, was shot and killed in an office in De Saussure Hall by Benjamin Haile, Superintendent of Buildings and Grounds. A few minutes later, Haile went to an adjoining office where he turned the gun on himself. There were no witnesses to either shooting and the coroner's inquest attributed the deaths to Haile's temporary insanity. The president announced, "There had long been bitter feeling between the two growing out of their conflicting duties at the university."[30] The double tragedy caused a sensation on campus and in the town. Rumors of graft circulated widely but the most consistent impression was that trouble had begun with the criticism of the late Professor Homes in connection with building operations of the University which, the previous winter, had brought an investigation by the Board of Trustees, an auditing of the books, and a complete approbation of Homes's conduct.[31] According to Ball's information the matter was closed, and *The State* would do nothing that might help to perpetate a scandal.

Ball's coverage of the murder-suicide story was as conservative as was possible under the circumstances. After the first account of the crime, nothing appeared but the usual funeral notices. At the inquest, however, there had been introduced a letter written by Haile, which Ball

28. *Ibid.*, VI, 84, May 16, 1923.
29. W. W. Ball, "Country Journalism," May, 1922, Ball Papers.
30. *The State*, May 7, 1922.
31. W. W. Ball to T. W. Law, May 15, 1922, Ball Papers.

decided not to print. A group of interested men prominent in Columbia
met in Ball's office to discuss the best way to treat the letter. Ex-Senator
Christie Benet, who had consulted with the Haile family, seemed to
favor the publication of the letter. Ball rejected the suggestion and
believed that he was successful in convincing Benet that it would be
wiser to repress the letter.[32] It contained references to four prominent
men and would have stirred bitter controversy; to have printed it would
have been an infraction of good newspaper practice. Many times before,
Ball had been asked to suppress news pertaining to crimes, tragedies,
and scandals; but never in his thirty-two years as a newspaperman could
he recall an instance when there had been no objection to the release of
such a story.[33] Ball's refusal to print the Haile letter, and the resulting
suppression of the document, served notice once again of his deep sense
of the duty of the press to pursue a policy that was responsible, discrimi-
nating, and discreet. To Ball a newspaperman without judgment and
good taste was no newspaperman at all.

Much closer to Ball, however, was the agonizing problem of his
relationship with his publisher, Ambrose Gonzales. In 1916 Ball had
declined a confidential offer to buy into the *Greenville News* and assume
the office of president and general manager of the company. Willie
Gonzales was in Cuba and "Mr. Ambrose" was an old man in poor
health. Though Ball admitted it would be to his advantage to accept the
Greenville offer, and though he did not regard himself as indispensable
to the operations of *The State*, his refusal was not easy for him to explain
except that "There is an unusual bond between Mr. Gonzales and his
men."[34] But four years later there began a sequence of events that, as far
as Ball was concerned, was to place a heavy strain upon those ties of
loyalty.

In December, 1920, some unpleasantness resulted from the failure of
Ball's part-time stenographer to report to Gonzales for work to keep her
busy while the editor was absent from the office. Ball explained to his
superior that the nature of his work meant incessant interruptions, and
although he did not have need for a full-time secretary, he must have a
stenographer ready when he had either the time or the inspiration to
compose.[35] A few days after the trouble on *The State* began, Ball poured

32. Ball, Diary, V, 241, May 5, 1922.
33. *Ibid.*, V, 241, May 8, 1922.
34. W. W. Ball to E. A. Smyth, Feb. 11, 1916, Ball Papers.
35. W. W. Ball to A. E. Gonzales, Dec. 22, 1920, Ball Papers.

all of his resentments and fears into his diary. Ambrose Gonzales, he conceded, was the most gifted man with whom he had ever been associated—a man of vision, energy, and inexhaustible sympathies. He could have been a great writer, Ball judged, but he never had been a complete businessman. He could not delegate authority, even to his own brothers. Though he was overgenerous, he had not always been just. Willing to share his last crust with his employees, he often did not pay them enough, because he liked having dependents and beneficiaries about him. He was *too* proud that he had deprived himself of luxuries and comforts. Possessed of great tenderness of heart, he was excessively emotional, moved in an instant to laughter or tears. As an editor, Ball charged, he would have been a certain failure; he had always lacked political insight. Now he was not competent to direct the affairs of the paper. His will and judgment had been failing for years; anyone who chose could, with a little skill, impose upon him. Ball concluded:

I think it impossible for him (and this may have been his greatest crime) to dissuade himself that a gentleman of the coast of South Carolina is not made of a finer clay than an up-countryman. That notion lingers in many of the coast people. . . . All impulsiveness, of mighty impulses, and 90 per cent of them good—that is he.[36]

Soon afterward, Ball wrote to W. E. Gonzales, who was then in Lima,[37] warning him that his brother's failing health was affecting the conduct of the newspaper. Among Ball's complaints were his employer's exaggerated sense of responsibility for details, his stubbornness, and his reluctance to delegate authority. But, more important, he feared that Ambrose Gonzales's judgment and power to resist persuasion had been so weakened that he might commit an error which could be damaging, particularly financially, to *The State*.[38] Willie Gonzales replied, though not immediately, that there was very little he could do, and advised Ball to keep in close touch with his elder brother.[39]

Once again, as in previous periods when Ball, for one reason or another, had become disturbed, his lamenting of the trials of being an editor became more pronounced. This time, however, there was double reason for anxiety. The coming to power of the Republican administra-

36. Ball, Diary, V, 149–151, Jan. 30, 1921.
37. William E. Gonzales served as Ambassador to Cuba until 1919, when he was appointed Ambassador to Peru.
38. W. W. Ball to W. E. Gonzales, Feb. 3, 1921, Ball Papers.
39. W. E. Gonzales to W. W. Ball, March 11, 1921, Ball Papers.

tion in 1921 would soon put an end to the diplomatic career of Willie Gonzales. Did that mean that Ball, upon the return of Gonzales, would have to step down as editor of *The State* or seek another post? Ball had an alternative plan, which he revealed to T. R. Waring of the *Charleston Evening Post*: a chair in journalism, possibly at the University of Georgia, where a Henry W. Grady Professorship was to be created, or at the University of Virginia. Waring promised that he and Ben Hagood would do what they could to get Ball the Georgia appointment and relief from "daily contact with the things you loathe."[40]

In April, 1922, W. E. Gonzales arrived in the country from abroad and "Mr. Ambrose" directed Ball to have no correspondence with the former ambassador about the future disposition of the editor's chair because that matter only the publisher was competent to discuss. His brother, Ambrose Gonzales revealed, did not want to return to Columbia permanently except as a last resort; but if he did, Ball was assured, the staff of the paper would be reorganized in a way that would do Ball no injustice.[41]

A month later tension at *The State* began to mount. Ball received a communication from Ambrose Gonzales reminding him that when he had become editor nine years before, the clear understanding had been that all authority would come from the president of the company. But, he accused, "You have at times shown a singular indisposition—as tho' 'twould compromise the dignity of your position—to confer with me about the work of your Department, or to ask approval of certain editorial policies before they were given to the types."[42] Gonzales assumed that Ball's course, and that of another department chief, was prompted by desire to save him trouble or annoyance, but the exceeding of their authority by the heads of the editorial and business departments, he charged, had the opposite effect, causing him many sleepless nights.[43]

That criticism Ball could overlook or charge to Gonzales's declining health, but the next attack was one he could not ignore. Two weeks after the first missive, Ball received a second letter from Gonzales which deprecated his abilities as an editor. *The State*, Gonzales claimed, until the last five or six years, had enjoyed the reputation of standing out strongly and unequivocally. Since that time *The State* had not side-

40. T. R. Waring to W. W. Ball, June 9, 1921, Ball Papers.
41. A. E. Gonzales to W. W. Ball, April 8, 1922, Ball Papers.
42. A. E. Gonzales to W. W. Ball, May 15, 1922, Ball Papers.
43. *Ibid.*

stepped but a "rather unfortunate indefinition of expression" had given substance to charges of ambiguity.[44] These allegations Gonzales claimed to have foreseen; as he had read Ball's editorials, he knew "about" what he had meant. He concluded, "If you hit straight from the shoulder as *you can do*, you will serve yourself as the state."[45]

The same day, a second interoffice memorandum arrived which made the other seem mild by comparison. His brothers, Ambrose Gonzales insisted, had found interest in many things; but Ball seemed to find savor in little save state politics, good roads, cotton mill stocks, the University of South Carolina, and the punitive taxation of underdeveloped city lots.[46] Ball seldom gave consideration to the great agricultural and livestock industry upon which rested the prosperity of the state. "Broaden your interests," Gonzales urged. "I don't know when you read the paper, but I recall that upon several occasions I've called your attention to A. P. dispatches which you have not read up to two o'clock . . . and abate, if you can, your predisposition to gloom. . . . The State . . . *must* be hopeful."[47]

The criticisms made by Gonzales were not the ramblings of a man losing his competency; the truth is that he had scored valid, albeit exaggerated, observations of Ball's weaknesses as an editor. His writing was not the terse editorial prose which has become popular; his style was old-fashioned, circuitous, "country courthouse."[48] His paragraphs were long, his syntax involved, and it was sometimes necessary for the reader to examine his editorials twice to discover his precise meaning. Furthermore, he was given to haranguing repeatedly on a few favorite topics, sometimes pressing repetition far beyond the point of usefulness. And it was not unreasonable for Gonzales to accuse him of undue pessimism; every few years, it seemed, he reported political conditions in the state as being the most serious in history.

Of course Ball did not think the criticisms just, and he was both shocked and hurt. He typed a letter of resignation in which he said that

44. A. E. Gonzales to W. W. Ball, June 1, 1922, Ball Papers.
45. *Ibid.*
46. *Ibid.* "The punitive taxation of underdeveloped city lots" refers to a pet theory of Ball's that the state might help solve her revenue problems by placing a tax on lands held for speculative purposes, although such a levy would have added to his own tax burden. Ball had long been an admirer of Henry George and his single tax.   47. *Ibid.*
48. The term "country courthouse" was used to describe Ball's style by Mrs. Margaret Meriwether, a friend of the Ball family whose husband was Professor of History at the University of South Carolina.

if he believed the charges, his faith in himself would be so impaired that his future exertions would be worthless.[49] Ball did not mail that letter; according to an inked notation on the bottom, he showed it first to Willie Gonzales, who advised him to withhold it until he could speak to his brother. The younger Gonzales stated further, or so Ball noted, that his brother would be astonished at Ball's resignation. Willie believed that someone had injected into Ambrose Gonzales's mind the suspicion that Ball considered himself primarily responsible for the success of *The State*, and that his brother was making a "tremendous" effort to maintain himself as the directing power of the newspaper.[50]

A reconciliation between Ball and his employer took place the next day when Gonzales sent him "a rather pathetic note" expressing regret if Ball had been wounded.[51] Ball replied with equal generosity:

> Your note has given me the greatest relief. I have been profoundly distressed. It may be that I am over sensitive. I have not doubted your regard for me. Nothing can interefere with the affection in which I hold you but I can think of nothing that would so hurt me as that you would allow your affection for me to stand in the way of The State.[52]

That day Ball submitted a letter to Ambrose Gonzales stating an editorial problem. Gonzales, in return, gave him advice on how the editorial might be written. The two had avoided each other the day before; now they met, shook hands, and professed their mutual admiration. On the surface, everything was normal again.[53]

But Ball did not forget. For the present he had been relieved of annoyance, but his position was "not satisfactory."[54] He tried to tell himself that Gonzales was old and infirm, that he did not mean what he had said; and yet, the man wrote "infernally well."[55] To his mother he confided his most private feelings. He had been "kept down" by *The State*. What honors he had received had searched him out behind the walls of the newspaper building. *The State* did not send him to conventions as other papers did. Not one-tenth of the readers of *The State* knew the name of its editor. During the last ten years he had put aside all

49. W. W. Ball to A. E. Gonzales, June 2, 1922, Ball Papers.
50. *Ibid.*
51. W. W. Ball to T. R. Waring, June 6, 1922, Ball Papers.
52. W. W. Ball to A. E. Gonzales, June 2, 1922, Ball Papers.
53. W. W. Ball to T. R. Waring, June 6, 1922, Ball Papers.
54. *Ibid.*   55. *Ibid.*

ambition but the good of *The State*. "I have borne a great share of abuse that was leveled at the Gonzales family and I have never been overpaid," he complained, "and rough treatment from the head of the family, though an extremely ill man, is a strain on what Christian fortitude I may have."[56] All was calm now, but the next thing Ball expected was that, "He will gently tell me that I am doing better by reason of his lectures and that will infuriate me."[57]

For a month the offenses against him simmered in his mind and at the end he decided that he was not capable of giving vigorous editorial direction to *The State*. He went to Ambrose Gonzales and once again stated his desire to retire as editor, offering to stay on in a subordinate position. But Gonzales refused to accept Ball's resignation, asked him to forget the criticism, and stressed that his confidence in his editor was unimpaired.[58] Ball was persuaded, and the period of uneasy truce lengthened.[59]

The melodrama played in the halls of *The State* building in the spring of 1922 was particularly distracting to Ball because it coincided with the opening of another political campaign. Although Ball had once said, "When no matter of principle is at stake and the race is between good men and competent, I think it is the business of the Editor of the newspaper to keep his mouth shut,"[60] he was not permitted the luxury of silence in 1922. Cole Blease returned for another try at becoming a three-term governor. Ball regarded another Blease campaign as a nightmare, not because of the extra work it entailed for him, but, he protested, it was "the vile nastiness of our politics in which I am not interested"[61] that troubled him. He determined, nevertheless, not to shirk his responsibility.

As in every other recent campaign, the influence of *The State* became quickly apparent. Former Governor John Gary Evans[62] early consulted Ball about the possibility of his seeking the office again. Ball replied that

56. W. W. Ball to Eliza Ball, June 8, 1922, Ball Papers.
57. *Ibid.*   58. Ball, Diary, V, 253, July 9, 1922.
59. Ambrose Gonzales suffered a stroke in 1922 which reduced his strength and affected his speech. After this attack he compiled four volumes of stories in the unusual dialect of the low-country or Gullah Negroes: *The Black Border* (1922); *With Aesop along the Black Border* (1924); *The Captain* (1924); *Laguerre, a Gascon of the Black Border* (1924). Ball was one of many who admired Gonzales as a philologist.
60. W. W. Ball to J. H. McLure, July 15, 1919, Ball Papers.
61. W. W. Ball to A. E. Gonzales, March 30, 1922, Ball Papers.
62. Evans had been governor from December, 1894, to January, 1897.

though *The State* would not bring him out as a candidate, it would support him against Blease and give him a fair showing against any other candidate.[63] Ball hoped for an Evans-Blease campaign, but Evans was reluctant to declare unless the opposition to Blease would unite behind his candidacy.[64] The inability of those forces to consolidate was a chronic problem in South Carolina and a perpetual source of irritation to Ball. Again in 1922 he lamented, "The unfortunate circumstance is that people in opposition to Blease cannot get together and concentrate on a single candidate."[65]

By mid-July, with the first primary scarcely more than a month away, Ball became concerned that, except for a minor aspirant for the office of governor, no one except *The State* was attacking Blease's record. "You may think me an alarmist," he told Senator Dial, "when I say I believe the situation of the Democratic party in this state is rather more critical now than it has been since 1877."[66] He had been told, furthermore, that the Republicans in at least two counties had secretly obtained lists of all Negroes who paid taxes on property assessed at $300, and who therefore, under the state constitution, could not be denied registration certificates.[67] Dial agreed that lack of interest in the campaign meant emphasis must be placed on stimulating registration, particularly of women, and on restating the perils of Bleasism.[68]

Ball met with Richard I. Manning and out of the conference came a plan. More than a year before, *The Charleston American*, the loyal Blease paper, had published a letter from Cole Blease to Joseph Tolbert, leader of that branch of the state Republican party which enlisted Negro support. The letter expressed jubilation at the election of Warren Harding and suggested that the Tolbert group, rather than the opposing all-white faction, build up the Republican party in South Carolina. Now in the summer of 1922 the confirmation of Tolbert to a federal appointment was being argued in the Congress. It would not help Tolbert with some Republicans to have Blease advertised as his backer. Also, the cause of "good government" in South Carolina might be helped if Blease's affiliation with Tolbert (his "Republican flirtations") could be brought before the voters. The story could have great value, if the

63. Ball, Diary, V, 232, March 18, 1922.
64. W. W. Ball to T. R. Waring, April 15, 1922, Ball Papers.
65. W. W. Ball to C. P. Hodges, May 20, 1922, Ball Papers.
66. W. W. Ball to N. B. Dial, July 17, 1922, Ball Papers.
67. *Ibid.*
68. N. B. Dial to W. W. Ball, July 20, 1922, Ball Papers.

Blease-Tolbert letter were introduced into the confirmation debate, included in the *Congressional Record*, and released to the press outside South Carolina. *The State* would then act. The scheme to make political capital of the Blease-Tolbert letter was submitted to Senator Dial in Washington.[69]

P. H. McGowan, Dial's associate, replied that steps would be taken immediately to put the plan into operation. He agreed, furthermore, that if the letter were released first in South Carolina newspapers, Blease could cry "persecution." The matter had been taken, McGowan said, to the Democratic National Committee and its publicity director had promised to get the story to several newspapers which circulated in South Carolina.[70] Several days later Ball was advised that *The Columbia Record* and *The Charlotte Observer* had carried the Blease-Tolbert letter;[71] it also appeared in the *Asheville Citizen*.

The article in *The Charlotte Observer* was entitled "Cole Blease and Democracy." Democratic leaders, it said, who were very interested in the fight Blease was making for the governorship of South Carolina on the way to another try for the Senate, would prefer a man of a different type in Washington. Commenting on the Blease-Tolbert affair, the *Observer* noted that, though Tolbert had been Republican boss in South Carolina for a long time, in 1920 the national organization attempted a reorganization. There had been whispers that Blease might lead a new state party, but in a letter to Tolbert, the former governor made clear his position. He characterized himself as a "Jeffersonian Democrat who rejoiced over the election of Harding."[72] That letter, the *Observer* predicted, would be used against Blease in the coming campaign because "The people of South Carolina do not like for their Democratic statesmen to get too gay or be too happy over the success of the Republicans."[73]

The next day *The State* reprinted the article which had appeared in the North Carolina press, and with it began the familiar avalanche of anti-Blease reminders, some old and some new. On the day after the publication of the reprint, under the title "The Boys That Fought for Us," Ball asked: "Do the Democrats of South Carolina believe that it was an unholy, an unrighteous and wicked war that the Congress

69. W. W. Ball to P. H. McGowan, July 20, 1922, Ball Papers.
70. P. H. McGowan to W. W. Ball, July 21, 1922, Ball Papers.
71. P. H. McGowan to W. W. Ball, July 24, 1922, Ball Papers.
72. *The Charlotte Observer*, July 24, 1922.
73. *Ibid.*

declared against Germany, April 6, 1917? Are the people fast repudiating those who carried on that war for the defense of their country?"[74] On the following day, in "What Republicans Would Do," he charged: "If ever the Republicans obtain a foothold in South Carolina their effort will be to abolish the laws that separate the races in the industries. Their endeavor will be to bring about a condition in which negroes [sic] can obtain employment in the Southern cotton mills."[75] Ball did not hesitate to manipulate race prejudice to serve his cause:

> It should not be forgotten that Joe Tolbert is not the head of a lily white or white man's Republican faction in South Carolina. Under the Tolbert leadership, negroes [sic] are invariably sent along with white men to the national Republican convention and placed on the national electoral tickets. When Mr. Harding was nominated for president by the Republicans he received large support in the convention from negro [sic] delegates.[76]

Ball privately described Tolbert as "the wretched little boss of the Republican machine in this state" who controlled the Negro vote and who "wears no necktie and, I believe, sometimes no collar."[77]

During the month of August, the columns of *The State* were filled with references to Blease and "Tieless Joe" Tolbert. The celebrated letter became Ball's special fixation; as other papers in the state would publish and editorialize upon the letter, *The State* would reprint their comments. The article copied from *The Spartanburg Journal* left little doubt who was behind the drive to publicize the Blease-Tolbert letter. The *Journal* reported that it had received from the Washington correspondent of *The State* the text of a letter that should make a profound impression on all true Democratic voters at the primary.[78] By the middle of August, Ball saw the outlook improving daily; there never had been, he decided, any good reason to fear that Blease would be elected. He had failed to wage the sort of destructive campaign which was his only chance.[79]

When the voting in the first primary was over, Blease had a plurality of about 11,000 votes, while the combined majority of the anti-Blease candidates was more than 19,000. In the second primary, Blease would be opposed by Thomas G. McLeod, a man who had, in Ball's estimation,

74. *The State*, July 26, 1922.   75. *Ibid.*, July 27, 1922.
76. *Ibid.*, July 29, 1922.
77. W. W. Ball to Samuel F. Adams, Sept. 18, 1922, Ball Papers.
78. *The State*, Aug. 5, 1922.
79. W. W. Ball to August Kohn, Aug. 19, 1922, Ball Papers.

made a "pitifully weak" showing, telling traveling salesmen's jokes and saying nothing.[80] But the next day, *The State*, which up until now had declared only *against* a candidate, carried on its front page a positive endorsement: "Yesterday The State had no candidate for governor. It follows the lead this morning of the majority of the people of South Carolina in choosing as the candidate to win in the second primary THOMAS G. MCLEOD."[81]

After the first primary, Ball continued his attack, and as he had in 1918, Blease sought personal revenge through *The Charleston American*. Five days before the second primary, on September 7, 1922, the *American* printed a page advertisement which recalled Ball's support of Palmer against Bryan in the election of 1896, quoted extracts from editorials he had written for the *Charleston Evening Post*, and suggested that Ball had no right to criticize other Democrats for failing to support the national presidential nominee. Other papers reported the attack of the Bleasites, and at the same time, posters appeared throughout the state bearing the printed signature of Reverend Baxter McLendon attacking *The State* and its "hireling editor." Ball took editorial cognizance of these events,[82] but he did not yield. On the morning of the second primary, he again printed in full the Blease-Tolbert letter.[83]

Assisting Blease's candidacy in 1922 were the prevailing agricultural distress, partially induced by the boll weevil, and discontent following the collapse of wartime prosperity. But Blease, who had promised the abolition of the Tax Commission and the Board of Public Welfare, suffered in September, 1922, his eighth loss in ten state contests, when McLeod defeated him for the governorship.[84] At least two out-of-state papers commended South Carolina for her wisdom.[85]

Governor McLeod, a modestly capable if not outstanding statesman, not only held office during a period of agricultural depression but inherited from his predecessors a chronic revenue problem. This fact Ball fully realized, and as the General Assembly convened early in January

80. Ball, Diary, V, 264, Sept. 1, 1922.

81. *The State*, Aug. 30, 1922. Ball could be provokingly literal. His editorial support of McLeod represented *The State* as accepting a popular mandate. Hence, he was later able to reply with technical accuracy to a critic who charged he had attacked Blease too severely, that *The State* had no candidate for governor (W. W. Ball to G. W. Gardner, Sr., Sept. 1, 1922, Ball Papers).

82. *The State*, Sept. 10, 1922.   83. *Ibid.*, Sept. 12, 1922.

84. The vote: McLeod 100,114; Blease 85,834.

85. *Lynchburg* (Va.) *News*, Sept. 14, 1922; Richmond (Va.) *Times-Dispatch*, Sept. 13, 1922.

he urged the legislature to find a solution that would assist both farmers and manufacturers. The next day he called for a sales tax,[86] and for the next two months the need for a new taxation program became his particular editorial project. Before the election Ball "never had altogether twenty minutes conversation" with the new governor and did not see him during the campaign except on the nights of the primaries.[87] But two weeks after Ball opened his latest editorial campaign, McLeod summoned him to his office to discuss a prospective tax program for the General Assembly. Governor McLeod opposed raising the property tax, but favored a luxury sales tax and Ball agreed.[88] Ball warned in *The State* that if the legislature failed to enact a sales tax, preferably on non-essential commodities, thereby raising increased revenues without increasing the property taxes, it would have to cut appropriations to the bone, though it starved the public schools, benevolences, and colleges. The property tax, moreover, should be *reduced*. The way was clear: the General Assembly should select certain objects, impose a sales tax on them, and raise $2,000,000 or $2,500,000—as the last legislature had done with its tax on gasoline.[89]

Ball's tax advice attracted a new sort of criticism. One of the state's prominent men remarked to a friend of the editor: "Ball is a menace to South Carolina! What is the matter with Ball? Why this sales tax that he is advocating now—it will cost me $25,000 a year more than I am paying now." "Well," replied Ball's informant, "I guess that is why Ball is advocating it." The story delighted Ball; he remarked facetiously that it was the first genuine recognition to come to him. Before he had been cursed by the Bleasites, the roughnecks. But now, if the malefactors of great wealth were taking notice, he must be making progress.[90]

When, in March, the General Assembly approved a sales-luxury tax bill affecting candy, ammunition, tobacco, amusement admissions, stocks and bonds, mortgages, and the gross sales of manufacturing plants, Ball's reaction was mixed. The bill might have been worse, but the legislature could not be excused for failing to place a tax on soft drinks.[91]

As it happened, the successfully concluded revenue campaign was the last Ball was to conduct for *The State*. Behind the scenes interested

86. *The State*, Jan. 11, 1923.
87. W. W. Ball to C. P. Hodges, Sept. 18, 1922, Ball Papers.
88. Ball, Diary, VI, 41, Jan. 27, 1923.   89. *The State*, March 17, 1923.
90. Ball, Diary, VI, 53, March 18, 1923.
91. *The State*, March 24, 1923.

friends were working to provide the change that he had so often told them he needed. In the spring of 1923 the legislature established a new School of Journalism at the University of South Carolina.[92] Ball coveted the deanship, but he did nothing. It seemed that another would receive the chair when Fay Ball set in motion the forces necessary to procure the appointment for her husband. Ball's own reticence was in part unavoidable, in part a result of his reluctance to seek favors which would make him "beholden." But Mrs. Ball alerted Ben Hagood and August Kohn, both trustees of the University, to Ball's desires, and they were instrumental in making known their friend's "availability."[93]

On June 12 Ball was informed by telegram that the trustees of the University had elected him Dean of Journalism. His friends had done for him what he could not or would not do for himself; they had rescued him from an unsatisfactory situation. Though his relations with his publisher had improved and he was quick to praise Ambrose Gonzales, especially for the large measure of editorial independence he had enjoyed, he never really forgave the attacks of the previous year. And Willie Gonzales's return to *The State* meant that the paper now had "two editors." Ambrose Gonzales in accepting Ball's resignation, however, assured him that he was about to propose a plan for Ball to become associate editor, with the same salary as his brother Willie. Gonzales informed Ball:

> I want to make it clear that your position on The State, whatever it might have been called, was as permanent as life itself, for I expected that, at my death, Willie would become President, and that you would become editor of the paper for your lifetime, or as long as you wished to stay.[94]

92. W. W. Ball to T. H. Dreher, July 20, 1923, Ball Papers. A year before the School was created, E. L. Green commented on a paper read by Ball to the Kosmos Club in which Ball urged that a School of Journalism be instituted at the University. Green assured Ball that such a school was also desired by the general press and urged him to write an editorial making public his views (E. L. Green to W. W. Ball, April 12, 1922, Ball Papers). Ball refused Green's request, declaring that the time was not right (W. W. Ball to E. L. Green, April 15, 1922, Ball Papers).

93. Ball, Diary, VI, 95, June 12, 1923; T. R. Waring to W. W. Ball, June 15, 1923, Ball Papers. The small circle of devoted friends to which Ball belonged often pooled influence in attempts to advance the career of one of its members. In 1911, for example, Ball and Waring had tried to get Ben Hagood appointed to the bench of the United States District Court (W. W. Ball to U. S. Rep. George S. Legare, April 5, 1911; T. R. Waring to W. W. Ball, April 15, 1911; Ball Papers).

94. A. E. Gonzales to W. W. Ball, July 7, 1923, Ball Papers.

And although Ball professed that weariness of responsibility would have caused him to welcome a position secondary to Willie Gonzales, it seems unlikely that after ten years as editor he would have long been satisfied with less.

Ball's acceptance of the University chair at considerable financial sacrifice gave credence, at last, to his protest that he had become saturated with the tasks that fall to a political editor. He had complained before of the confinements of newspaper routine, but then admitted, "I can't stay away from it altogether though it be Christmas and no paper planned for tomorrow."[95] South Carolina politics was a "cheap, sordid game,"[96] one which gave him no satisfaction, yet each campaign found him back in the battle with undiminished vigor.

When Ball surrendered his editorship, he left the position that had brought him to prominence in South Carolina. *The State*, of course, offered him the opportunity; with its central geographic location and wide distribution, its proximity to the capitol, the Columbia paper had advantages to offer an ambitious editor that no other state newspaper could boast. But Ball made the most of his chances. Members of the informed public might not agree with Ball, but they knew who he was.

Politicians, especially, were keenly aware of his existence. Ball once asked Senator N. B. Dial to use his influence to get his son-in-law, Clements Ripley, an appointment for study in China. Dial's secretary informed Ball that they were working cautiously toward that end, that the Senator was anxious to serve him in any way possible.[97] When Ripley failed to receive the grant, Ball assured him that a strong effort had been made in his behalf, because, "Dial is a man who 'goes after what he wants,' and he is under more political obligation to me than to any other man and well knows it."[98] Later, Ball spoke to Dial about a West Point appointment for his son; though William Jr. declined it, the next vacancy assigned to Dial was offered to him. Tom Waring chided Ball that Dial was his personally owned senator.

Rising young politicians, too, often discovered reasons to correspond with Ball. James F. Byrnes found Ball's editorial page "a constant source of pleasure."[99] One of the letters congratulating Ball on his appointment as Dean came from Congressman Byrnes, recalling valued

95. W. W. Ball to Julian Mitchell, Dec. 25, 1921, Ball Papers.
96. W. W. Ball to P. H. Gadsden, June 29, 1923, Ball Papers.
97. McDavid Horton to W. W. Ball, June 17, 1920, Ball Papers.
98. W. W. Ball to Clements Ripley, July 13, 1920, Ball Papers.
99. J. F. Byrnes to W. W. Ball, Jan. 18, 1920, Ball Papers.

advice from Ball in 1906 when Byrnes worked on a paper in Aiken. The best experience for a newspaperman, Ball had said, was service on a country weekly, where shortage of newspaper space and lack of time to set type challenge the editor to question the right of every sentence to remain in every paragraph.[100]

Now Ball was leaving actual newspaper work for an opportunity to impart scholastic advice gleaned from thirty-three years experience on the press. It seemed that newspaper readers would not again experience his dogged reiteration or receive his benevolent scoldings. At the request of Ambrose Gonzales, Ball remained at *The State* until autumn, but on September 18, 1923, his active connection with *The State* came to an end. On that last afternoon, Ball wrote two brief paragraphs, made out the editorial schedule, and was presented by "Mr. Ambrose" with a handsome silver pitcher on which was to be engraved "William Watts Ball with The State's appreciation of Loyal and Unselfish Service." Then, without farewells, he returned to Pendleton Street for eight o'clock supper.[101]

100. J. F. Byrnes to W. W. Ball, June 18, 1923, Ball Papers.
101. Ball, Diary, VI, 135, Sept. 18, 1923.

CHAPTER SEVEN

DEAN BALL

BALL'S APPOINTMENT as Dean of the School of Journalism was greeted in the state with something less than universal acclaim. Criticism came mostly from sources where unfavorable comment might have been anticipated: the pro-Blease newspapers. Taking the lead was the weekly *Saluda Standard*. When the trustees decided that William D. Melton should replace President Currell as head of the University, the *Standard* claimed that an office had been created to save Currell the embarrassment of looking for employment. A doctorate program was established, the Graduate School reorganized, and Currell made Dean. In the same year, W. E. Gonzales returned from Peru to *The State* and consequently jeopardized the position of W. W. Ball. The result: Ball was selected as Dean of a new School of Journalism, which was in reality a sham, intended to be nothing more than a propaganda factory for the University. These developments, the *Standard* attributed to the "Columbia ring," that nebulous group whose interests coincided roughly with those of *The State*.[1]

The charge that the School of Journalism had been created to accommodate Ball was, of course, ridiculous; for one thing, in the preliminary catalogue of the school, the new courses were listed as being taught by the man Ball eventually defeated for the deanship. President Melton had chosen for the appointment Mr. Stanhope Sams, another of the editors of *The State*. Sams, he informed the trustees, read French, German, Spanish and Italian; had a colloquial knowledge of Japanese, Malay, and Dutch; and had studied "for literary purposes" Persian, Arabic, Latin, and Greek. His candidate, Melton noted, was not a politician and, therefore, not as subject to bias or prejudice as most journalists were. Already, at the president's direction, Sams had undertaken a study of various journalism schools and prepared an outline for a program at South Carolina. But the trustees in their meeting rejected Sams, despite his imposing linguistic accomplishments, in favor of Ball, whose name was placed in nomination by Ben Hagood. The board simultaneously

1. Hollis, *University of South Carolina*, II, 306.

noted that a sum, the amount to be determined by Melton, should be paid to Sams for services rendered in connection with the establishment of the School of Journalism.[2]

The *Saluda Standard*, moreover, was not the only paper to suggest collusion; the equally unfriendly *Yorkville Enquirer* not only maligned Ball[3] but attacked the entire University. In a sustained campaign, the *Enquirer* branded Carolina as a useless institution with no academic standing and little chance of attaining any. To support the University was to put money into "a rat hole."[4] Clemson, the Citadel, and Winthrop, all state schools, were doing useful work, editor Grist observed; the University might well be abolished.[5] Ball was shocked by the attack on Carolina. He regarded it as one of the state's preservative institutions; and he would not have believed in 1924 that within a few years he would also turn his scorn upon the old school.

Disparagements notwithstanding, Ball began his career as teacher and administrator with the announced aim that, if he held his position for ten years, he hoped to see his work reflected in thirty or fifty small weekly or daily newspapers that would recognize their opportunity to become a medium of independent expression in an age of consolidation.[6] Ball had expected to spend the summer at the Pulitzer School of Columbia University or some other School of Journalism, but he abandoned his plans when he agreed to stay with *The State* until the beginning of the fall semester. As a result, he began his academic duties with no training save experience. But then, most other professors of journalism had begun in the same way; fifteen years before there had been no such position.[7] Ball had, besides, written several papers on journalism and spoken during a recent Journalism Week at the University of Missouri. Throughout the past five years, he had been collecting a journalism library which by now had reached about one hundred and sixty volumes.[8] During the summer, when he found time, he studied in his own books and considered suggestions made at his request by the Journalism Departments at the universities of Missouri and Wisconsin.

It was Ball's responsibility as Dean, first of all, to co-ordinate the

2. Minutes of the University of South Carolina Board of Trustees, June 12, 1923.
3. T. F. McDow to W. W. Ball, Oct. 10, 1923, Ball Papers.
4. *The Yorkville Enquirer*, Dec. 23, 1923.
5. *Ibid.*
6. W. W. Ball to P. H. Gadsden, June 29, 1923, Ball Papers.
7. The first School of Journalism in the United States was established in 1908 at the University of Missouri.
8. W. W. Ball to P. H. Gadsden, June 29, 1923, Ball Papers.

other departments so far as newspaper students were concerned. Professor Yates Snowden, for example, would see that prospective journalism students received in their freshman and sophomore years instruction in the historical development of the press. Then in the junior and senior years Ball would instruct Bachelor of Arts candidates majoring in journalism in such practical skills as reporting, news writing, criticism, feature writing, editorial writing, advertising, the psychology of news and human interest, and management of the county newspaper. As the new school's first semester began, Ball outlined a wide future program for a small staff. His greatest need was for printing office like the one that had cost the University of Missouri $140,000.[9] But since the University of South Carolina had no mechanical plant, its School of Journalism would use the facilities of the Columbia papers.

After the first month Ball found that he was getting to like his work and to find it interesting. His classes grew and by early October he had eighteen or nineteen students in "his school."[10] He was comfortable in familiar surroundings, although the place had changed since the day he had entered as a freshman, when only Rutledge, Legaré, Harper, and De Saussure Halls faced the lawn inside the old horseshoe. In some respects, Ball simply adapted his newspaper routine to academic life. On Sundays, instead of going to the editorial rooms, he went to his office on the campus, two hours in the morning and two hours in the afternoon. The hold of the working press upon him was still strong, and his academic duties did not prevent him from writing occasional editorial articles for *The State*.

There was also evidence that though Ball had departed the political scene, he had not been forgotten. In 1924 N. B. Dial, preparing to run for re-election to the Senate, asked Ball to help him select a good campaign manager.[11] Later Ball refused Dial's suggestion that he himself take the job.[12] In May of that year Josephus Daniels, Secretary of the Navy under Wilson and still a power in national politics, asked Ball to make suggestions for the Democratic platform.[13] Ball did, indeed,

9. *Ibid.*   10. Ball, Diary, VI, 142, Oct. 6, 1923.
11. N. B. Dial to W. W. Ball, Jan. 4, 1924, Ball Papers.
12. N. B. Dial to W. W. Ball, May 28, 1924, Ball Papers.
13. Josephus Daniels to W. W. Ball, May 26, 1924, Ball Papers. Daniels, editor of the Raleigh, N. C., *News and Observer*, suggested to Ball a platform consisting of two planks: (1) thou shalt not steal (the Naval Oil Reserves, bread from the mouths of labor, fair profits from the farmers by denying them the world market); and (2) thou shalt not kill—the Republican party had failed to do anything worthwhile to restore stability to the world and was therefore responsible for the continued militarism, standing armies and navies.

have ideas on the national elections and they did not coincide with those of Willie Gonzales and *The State*. Ball and Waring of the Charleston *Post* agreed that Gonzales was making a mistake in driving for the nomination of his friend William G. McAdoo, who had been Woodrow Wilson's Secretary of the Treasury. But Gonzales was playing at high statesmanship; Ball guessed that it would mean a cabinet post for him if McAdoo won.[14] In Ball's estimation, neither McAdoo nor John W. Davis, the eventual nominee, nor Virginia Senator Carter Glass could beat the Republicans. His choice was Alfred E. Smith. If Smith were nominated, Ball judged, he could win, because he would carry the South (with the possible exception of North Carolina and Tennessee), and the states having foreign, Roman Catholic, and "wet" populations. "But," Ball added, "Smith will most assuredly not be nominated."[15]

As the time for the national nominating conventions approached, Ball received letters suggesting David F. Houston for the Democratic presidential nomination. One urged Ball to get *The State* to advise that the South Carolina delegation support him if McAdoo could not be nominated.[16] Houston, like McAdoo, had served in Wilson's cabinet, and it would have pleased Ball to see his old friend and fellow South Carolinian chosen, but he was convinced Houston had no chance. Every opportunity he had he "talked Houston"; but everywhere he was rebuffed.[17] Besides, Ball told Houston supporters, his opinion had no weight whatsoever, and he added the anecdote of the old newspaper man in Mississippi who wrote of an editor who had retired, "After that he didn't have the influence of a capon in a barnyard."[18]

Such political power as Ball retained, however, he exercised in behalf of N. B. Dial in the 1924 race. Among Dial's opponents were Cole Blease, again, and Representative James F. Byrnes, in his first senatorial contest. By mid-August the incumbent had become involved in the sort of tastless brawl which was all too familiar in South Carolina politics. In campaign competition on the stump at Greenwood, John J. McMahon, State Commissioner of Insurance and a senatorial aspirant himself, charged that Senator Dial had employed members of his family in his Washington office; specifically, Dial had used one of his daughters as a messenger "in violation of Southern chivalry."[19] Dial lunged at the

14. W. W. Ball to S. N. Evins, June 12, 1924, Ball Papers.
15. W. W. Ball to H. L. Watson, June 28, 1924, Ball Papers.
16. S. N. Evins to W. W. Ball, June 7, 1924, Ball Papers.
17. W. W. Ball to S. N. Evins, June 12, 1924, Ball Papers.
18. *Ibid.*
19. *The New York Times*, Aug. 9, 1924.

speaker, but the two were separated and persuaded to return to their seats, with Blease among the peacemakers.

Less than two weeks later another clash occurred, this time at Gaffney. McMahon had been attacking Dial's record, repeating the charge of nepotism and accusing the Senator of gambling in cotton and trading in oil stocks. Dial replied that he had been trading in cotton for twenty-five years and that the composition of his office force was his own personal business. Continuing, Dial branded McMahon a "stalking horse," who ran not in his own interest but who had set out to harass Dial in the hope that the chances of Byrnes would be enhanced. McMahon demanded that Dial withdraw the accusation and when he refused, McMahon called him a "dirty liar."[20] Dial, aroused, then swung a chair at McMahon's head and the battle was on. Both combatants were arrested for disorderly conduct but released on bond after a hearing before the mayor of Gaffney.

At this point, although Ball was dissatisfied with the complexion that the campaign had taken, he was concerned over matters more serious than Dial-McMahon fisticuffs. *The State* was silent; Blease was remarkably subdued. Neither Dial nor Byrnes attacked Blease because, Ball guessed, they both had their eye on the second primary and did not want to offend his supporters. No candidate had dared mention the latter-day Ku Klux Klan. They were all "pussy-footing."[21] In a meeting of some of Dial's advisers, Ball and the others agreed that Dial's supporters in all parts of the state must be notified to increase their efforts for the Senator. On the Sunday before the primary of August 26, Ball had an article in *The State* complimentary to Senator Dial, but when the results of the voting were known, Dial had been eliminated and Byrnes left to face Blease in the decisive second primary.

The defeat of Dial could scarcely be considered a political surprise. Ultraconservative in his approach to government, he had offended veterans by opposing liberal pensions. Worse perhaps, in ultrapartisan South Carolina, he was put on the defensive for saying that Calvin Coolidge was a better Democrat than many claiming the name. Even Ball, who had been his consistent supporter, considered him a politician of no more than ordinary abilities. He had endorsed Dial not because he saw in him the qualities of a statesman, but because he seemed the best man available at the time. In the past Ball had helped Dial; in Ball's judgment, he had been more helpful, perhaps, then any other man in the state. This

20. *Ibid.*, Aug. 20, 1924.
21. Ball, Diary, VI, 216, Aug. 11, 1924.

Dial "knew and admitted."[22] Dial "owed" him, and now Ball called to collect.

The day after the first primary, Ball had offered by letter his services to Mr. Byrnes, an invitation accepted only once during the course of the second campaign.[23] Ball's principal effort for Byrnes, however, though indirect, was designed to be conclusive. Ball reminded Dial that, although he was a member of the faculty of a state institution and perhaps should have remained neutral, he had actively supported the Senator for re-election.[24] He asked Dial to recall the 1918 election when, after the death of Ben Tillman in mid-campaign, *The News and Courier* asked that the entries for senatorial candidates be reopened. *The States*'s opposition to opening the lists, Ball boasted, had ended the matter and saved Dial from defeat.[25] Ball recalled also Woodrow Wilson's telegram in 1918, asking all his friends in South Carolina to vote against Blease, thus assisting Dial.[26] Now, in 1924, Ball asked that Dial do his part to insure that Blease would not be elected. Instruct your supporters, Ball urged, to back Mr. Byrnes! To Ball's "immense disgust,"[27] Senator Dial refused.[28] Ambrose Gonzales also wrote to Dial asking him to declare for Byrnes.[29] But the Senator would not be moved.

Dial's wrath was mighty and it would not be soothed. He believed that Byrnes, then serving his seventh term in Congress, had not yet earned the right to aspire to the Senate, that he should remain in the House of Representatives for at least another two years. Dial, moreover, was not alone among the state's influential politicians in his conviction that, as incumbent, he should have been spared conservative competition in the continuing battle against Blease. Edgar A. Brown of Barnwell, then a representative in the State Assembly, although he characterized Byrnes as both a personal and political friend, assured Dial that he had done what he could to convince Byrnes to stay out of the contest.[30]

22. W. W. Ball to William Egleston, Sept. 12, 1924, Ball Papers.
23. W. W. Ball to Col. J. M. Johnson, Sept. 13, 1924, Ball Papers.
24. W. W. Ball to William Egleston, Sept. 12, 1924, Ball Papers.
25. Ball, Diary, VI, 220, Sept. 3, 1924. Potentially strong candidates like A. F. Lever had not entered the contest in 1918 because of their respect for the aging Senator Tillman.   26. *Ibid.*
27. W. W. Ball to Col. J. M. Johnson, Sept. 13, 1924, Ball Papers.
28. W. W. Ball to William Egleston, Sept. 12, 1924, Ball Papers; Ball, Diary, VI, 220, Sept. 3, 1924. At the time Dial refused Ball's request, the two were on different sides of an argument over the management of the Lucas cotton mills in Laurens (Beaufort Copeland, in interview with author, June 5, 1957).
29. Ball, Diary, VI, 220, Sept. 3, 1924.
30. Edgar A. Brown to N. B. Dial, April 19, 1924, N. B. Dial Papers, Duke University Library.

Governor Manning "deplored the entrance into the race of candidates who, he believed, polled votes that would ordinarily have gone to Dial."[31]

To Dial, however, Byrnes's challenge was but the first of the injuries he had suffered. He believed that McMahon had played an ignoble part in his campaign and privately boasted that he could convict Byrnes and McMahon of conspiracy before any unbiased jury in South Carolina.[32] The full range of his indignation was revealed when, to a correspondent, he wailed:

> I thought our people wanted service and I tried to give it to them and believed they would take care of me at the polls. As a matter of fact, Blease has over forty per cent of the votes in any race and then when Byrnes went in that divided up the other vote, and at the same time hiring a thug to lie on me, and besides using my anti-bonus vote against me, it is not surprising at the result [sic]. In addition to this, many outside influences were worked, and some of these influences are the worst in the United States. I have circulars verifying the statement. Our people do not realize how near we are in the hands of the Bolsheviks.[33]

While Dial and his followers sulked, Ball smoldered. He felt that in the Dial-Byrnes quarrel the fault was about equally divided;[34] but in the end there could be no other consideration but the defeat of Blease. Dial's stubbornness was unforgivable, and Ball was determined that it would not go unnoticed. He would not let it; he would not keep his mouth shut. His anger was heightened, of course, by Dial's presumed ingratitude. "It makes me sick that I was instrumental in making Dial," he complained, "only for him to use his dying political energies for the making of Blease, I cannot say that I was taken wholly by surprise. I knew my man."[35] But Ball reserved for his letters to the aging but astute Eliza Ball the full measure of his contempt. To his mother he wrote, "Dial occupies the position of a man who was invited by accident to a dinner party and when he was denied a second helping of soup spat in his neighbor's plate in the hope of breaking up the party—"[36]

31. Burts, "The Public Career of Richard I. Manning," p. 505.
32. N. B. Dial to Allan Johnstone, Sept. 12, 1924, Dial Papers.
33. N. B. Dial to Charles A. Douglas, Sept. 6, 1924, Dial Papers.
34. Ball, Diary, X, 175, April 25, 1937.
35. W. W. Ball to T. R. Waring, Sept. 10, 1924, Ball Papers.
36. W. W. Ball to Eliza W. Ball, Sept. 3, 1924, Ball Papers.

Even without the endorsement of Dial, Ball believed that Byrnes would be elected by 15,000 votes.[37] But on September 9 Byrnes suffered his only defeat in an election when he lost to Blease by approximately 2,200 out of 200,000 votes. The reasons for Blease's victory are not easily decided. Was Byrnes's approval by the American Federation of Labor a factor? Labor support was no boon to a politician in a South where Jeffersonian individualism and toleration of social stratification still retarded the growth of unionism. How active was the Klan in Blease's behalf? He had been advertised as 100 per cent American. And how important was the role played by Senator Dial? Blease called upon him; he was urged by many to declare for Byrnes; but he refused both sides. Did his silence swing his supporters to Blease? State Senator Edwin McCravy, who was delegated by a Greenville caucus to approach Dial in behalf of Byrnes, judged that Dial's friends in Greenville and Laurens counties voted all but solidly for Blease. During his talk with McCravy in Laurens, Dial had little to say in favor of Blease except that he was by no means all bad. But as McCravy drove through the streets of the town, he saw stretched across the street, from the window of an office which he presumed had been used by the Senator as his headquarters, a red lettered sign which read, "We are for Blease."[38] Was this a calculated silence? Apparently it was, because after the defeat of Byrnes, Dial wrote to Blease, "The election turned out as we expected it. . . . If I can be of any assistance here or in Washington, please feel at liberty."[39]

Many people, including T. R. Waring, believed that Byrnes was a victim of religious bigotry. Byrnes had been born a Roman Catholic, but as a young man became an Episcopalian. On the afternoon before the second primary, thousands of circulars purporting to endorse the candidacy of Byrnes were distributed throughout the state, particularly in the areas where the Ku Klux Klan was strong and active. Signed by ten persons, the announcement stated that, in his childhood, Byrnes had attended the Sunday School of a Roman Catholic church in Charleston and had served as an altar boy. Byrnes has described his own reaction to the incident:

It was a blatant effort to arouse the religious prejudice of anti-Catholic voters. I could recall only two or three of the persons whose

37. W. W. Ball to W. D. Douglass, Sept. 8, 1924, Ball Papers.
38. McCravy, *Memories*, pp. 47–48.
39. N. B. Dial to Cole L. Blease, Sept. 12, 1924, Dial Papers.

names were signed to the circular, and those I had known only casually in my boyhood and had not seen for more than twenty-five years. Upon inquiry that night, I learned that they were my bitter political opponents. . . . I saw no point in investigating who perpetrated the trick.[40]

Most observers, including Ball and Waring, agreed that the conspirators were "ten little altar boys," Roman Catholics who were bitter because Byrnes had left the church.[41] They hoped to retaliate by publicizing his early Catholicism and thereby to contribute to his defeat in a heavily Protestant state. Resentful Catholics, as Tom Waring said, had "put the knife under Jimmy Byrnes' fifth rib"; "the tribute of his colleagues who served 'on the altar' of St. Patrick's Church with him was deadly poison in the Klaverns up the State."[42] When Catholics attacked him as a renegade, they set in motion a political phenomenon whereby prejudice from two sides trapped Byrnes in the middle.

While Ball believed that the religious issue had been a factor he was convinced that Blease had been elected by former anti-Blease voters because of the "pitiable bankruptcy in leadership" of the opposing faction. South Carolina was the loser in the "miserable squabbles of men who, as the event proves, have themselves rather than the state as the first consideration." There could be no respectable politics in the state until responsible elements organized and stayed organized. Under the present system with its multiplicity of candidates, individuals ran, financed their own campaigns, and were responsible to nobody.[43]

From the shelter of the university campus, Ball could not blame *The State* for staying in the background. He recalled:

When I was editor, year after year, the task was placed upon me of carrying most of the offense—for candidates in the choosing of whom I had not the slightest voice. They nominated themselves—it was left to The State to provide them with the records, the direction, the material for their campaigns. I became weary of it, and I cannot blame my successor for allowing candidates to do as they wished.[44]

40. James F. Byrnes, *All In One Lifetime* (New York, 1958), p. 53.
41. W. W. Ball to William Egleston, Sept. 12, 1924; T. R. Waring to W. W. Ball, Sept. 15, 1924; Ball Papers.
42. T. R. Waring to W. W. Ball, Sept. 15, 1924, Ball Papers.
43. W. W. Ball to William Egleston, Sept. 12, 1924, Ball Papers.
44. *Ibid.*

Still, he confessed, if he had been editor of *The State* he could not have remained silent, though he might have lost his reputation as a political editor.[45]

Ball did not boast that if he had been editor of a major paper, Blease would have been defeated. But the fact is that while he held an important editorial post, Blease did not win. In any case, the United States Senate had a new member from South Carolina. Politicians of all stripes had warned against his election. Ben Tillman, an older mass leader, had remarked before his death:

> Blease is such a slippery duck you never can tell where he will turn up. With all, he is unscrupulous and has to be watched all the time. Those of our citizens who consider his election to the Senate as a disgrace to the State must realize that it is everybody's business to see that he is defeated. I will do all I can towards that object by letter writing and distribution of documents and printing. . . .
> It would be a great disgrace to South Carolina to have Blease elected to the Senate, and I simply can't bring myself to the idea of such a thing happening. It ought to be impossible and, therefore, I believe it will not come about.[46]

But now, after years of denial, Coleman L. Blease, the man Ambrose Gonzales had described as the "worst public man" in the United States,[47] was being sent to Washington.

The particulars of the election of 1924 aside, one can only wonder how Blease was able to hold his supporters throughout decades of broken promises. Perhaps because Blease, like Tillman, had instilled in stagnant whites—at the expense of Negroes and whites of "good family" —the notion of their own innocence and virtue. And in a society where change was slow to come no matter which faction held power, the emotional reassurance that Blease gave to the poor proved to be their consolation.

By the mid-twenties Ball had become as much concerned with the state's financial condition as with her political health. Although Ambrose Gonzales had, in one of his temperamental outbursts, accused him of monotonous pessimism, Ball could not resist confiding his fears to Gonzales. The people, he observed sadly, were demoralized; 50 per cent

45. Ball, Diary, VI, 226, Sept. 12, 1924.
46. Benjamin R. Tillman to H. W. Woodward, June 25, 1918, Ball Papers.
47. A. E. Gonzales to W. W. Ball, Oct. 10, 1917, Ball Papers.

of those in Columbia who owned automobiles could not look their credi-
tors in the eye. "Perhaps it was too much to expect the average man to
take the rejected advice of The State in 1917, 1918, and 1919—to buy
for cash only . . . and pay debts with it," but "wanton, regardless,
reckless" prodigality was the cause of bankruptcies and other common
misfortunes.[48] The American people were living improvidently and
wealthier states might soon experience the hard times which had prevailed in South Carolina since the autumn of 1920.

In a commencement address at the College of Charleston in May,
1925, Ball charged that South Carolina and the nation were drifting on
tides of materialism; the respect of the community for virtue, honesty,
and obedience to law had declined. To say that the state suffered from
too much democracy, he admitted, was unpopular; but the state needed
unpopular leaders, especially in politics—men and women who would
speak and write the "hard, biting truth."[49]

The next election produced no encouraging signs. John G. Richards,
a member of the Blease faction, was elected as the first governor to serve
the new four-year term. D. D. Wallace has observed:

> The campaign of 1926 illustrated the vacuity to which politics had
> been reduced. A candidate for the United States Senate who almost
> unseated E. D. Smith asserted (on the strength, when he was
> called down, of somebody's having told him) that three judges of
> the World Court were Negroes, and huge excitement raged against
> the one-cent tax on soft drinks—a device raising a large revenue, an
> appreciable amount being from persons who escape almost all other
> contribution to the State which protects them.[50]

To Ball, the real issue in South Carolina at the time was "one of
common honesty."[51] A legislator whom Ball regarded as one of the most
reliable men in the state had told him that public officials had shortages
in a majority or at least a large proportion of the counties of the state.[52]
To an editor friend in Greenwood, Ball revealed:

> In six counties fiscal officers appointed by a Democratic governor
> by and with the advice of the senate nominated in the primaries,

---

48. W. W. Ball to A. E. Gonzales, Nov. 7, 1924, Ball Papers.
49. Ball, *The Editor and the Republic*, pp. 91–92.
50. Wallace, *South Carolina*, p. 679.
51. W. W. Ball to T. F. McDow, April 12, 1926, Ball Papers.
52. *Ibid.*

have defaulted in an aggregate sum of $1,250,000. A state officer is under indictment. A sheriff is under indictment. So are several constables. . . . In a word, corruption is far greater in this state now than in dispensary days; it is worse than at any time, since 1876.[53]

No one, Ball lamented, seemed to care.

In all, South Carolina was a "paradise of nitwits";[54] but Ball had his own problems at the university. His teaching load was usually nineteen semester hours. During the course of a year, he tried to offer seven different courses, not including laboratories. Returning from a meeting of the Association of Schools of Journalism and the Association of Teachers of Journalism, Ball concluded that it was a mistake to maintain a school under the present circumstances. Ball was not only Dean, he was the entire school. "One chair and nominal physical equipment," he informed President Melton, "simply cannot be a 'school of journalism.' "[55] The University now had a "department"; the addition of one full-time instructor would give it a "school." He repeatedly urged the journalism staff be increased to two, so at least they could become eligible to join the association of Schools of Journalism.

But Ball did not despair. His little school was growing; after eighteen months he had thirty students, and counting duplicates, fifty-five in all classes.[56] There were other gratifications, too. Ball was pleased when the university chapter of Phi Beta Kappa elected him to faculty membership, citing him as one of the university's most distinguished alumni. He accepted, of course, adding that he would want to purchase a key. The long summer vacations, furthermore, gave him the leisure to do a little reading and writing, and to travel about in the state and in North Carolina; but mostly, he "idled a great deal and talked a great deal."[57] On the other hand, Ball and Yates Snowden, "the man with the cloak," inimitable with his white hair and pincenez, were skeptical about signs of "progress" at Carolina. They engaged in a half-serious protest over the increasing emphasis being placed on a doctor's degree as the badge of competence.[58] Professor Snowden, using his nom de plume "Smelfungus," wrote in *The State*:

53. W. W. Ball to H. L. Watson, Oct. 8, 1926, Ball Papers.
54. Ball, Diary, VII, 67, July 4, 1926.
55. W. W. Ball to President W. D. Melton, Jan. 4, 1926, Ball Papers.
56. *Ibid.*
57. Ball, Diary, VII, 23, Sept. 14, 1925.
58. Hollis, *University of South Carolina*, II, 307.

God bless my old professors; how far they all surpassed
Your pedagogues with gig lamps and little mental grasp!
Our prodigies of learning, each one a Socrates
Was worth at least a cartload of your modern Ph.D.'s.[59]

Much later, Ball confided to his colleague, "The practice of sardining universities and colleges with oafs, upstarts, and anile asses because they are 'doctors' is uncivilized."[60]

In the spring of 1926 the university community was shocked by the death of President Melton. In the search for his replacement, Ball's name was one of those prominently mentioned for the presidency. Among the half-dozen papers supporting him for the office were the Charleston *News and Courier*, the Greenwood *Index-Journal*, and the *Fort Mill Times*. But to all their editors, and to Thomas McLeod, the former governor, he replied that he should not be president and would not accept the post if it were offered to him.[61] Meantime, he confided to Ben Hagood, "These things tickle me; they inflate me immensely."[62] And to Hagood's suggestion that he would support him for president of the University of South Carolina or for Pope, Ball responded:

I thank you heartily for the suggestion in reference to the Papacy. I could fill that job more completely than a college presidency. It would be pleasant to be a member of the College of Cardinals. So far as I know, in these democratic times it is the . . . only exclusive social organization.[63]

During the time he was in the midst of squelching any attempts to advance him as a candidate for president, Ball reluctantly accepted responsibility of a different sort. He agreed to be editor of the proposed "South Carolina Handbook," a publication sponsored jointly by the State Agricultural Department and Clemson College. The book would publicize the state's natural resources, be an advertiser for the state, but would be "free of braggadocio."[64] Ball did not find the prospect of

59. *The State*, Jan. 4, 1925. Quoted in Hollis, *University of South Carolina*, II, 307.

60. W. W. Ball to Yates Snowden, Sept. 20, 1932, Snowden Papers. Quoted in Hollis, *University of South Carolina*, II, 307–308.

61. W. W. Ball to T. F. McLeod, May 14, 1926; W. W. Ball to Robert Lathan, May 14, 1926; W. W. Ball to H. L. Watson, May 14, 1926; W. W. Ball to W. B. Bradford, May 7, 1926; Ball Papers.

62. W. W. Ball to B. A. Hagood, May 14, 1926, Ball Papers.

63. *Ibid.*

64. W. W. Ball to D. F. Houston, May 3, 1926, Ball Papers.

editing the handbook very inviting. No agreement had yet been reached on his salary and he was unwilling to name it himself; he feared that there would be criticism from politicians because he already drew a state salary as professor in the university. He did not like the job, but he took it because he needed the money.[65]

In 1926 the university designated Ball to appear as visiting lecturer at Vanderbilt University. Before a small audience in Nashville on May 11, he suggested that some university should conduct a survey to reveal to newspapers how they are regarded by their readers. There must be rapport, he cautioned, because "nothing is so dear or near to the people" as the press.[66]

Ball was careful to preserve his own ties with the working press. One summer he toured New Hampshire with other newspapermen from the state. It was while Ball was away on the press trip that Ambrose Gonzales died, and while he could not attend the funeral, he contributed a eulogy to *The State* which Josephus Daniels described as "perfect."[67]

Once again Ball thought about purchasing a newspaper. He was not discontented at the university, he said. He would like to control a paper so that his children could have employment near him; hence, he would only invest in an arrangement that would give control of the stock to him or his family. Indeed, Ball's children seemed to be developing a family newspaper tradition. Eleanor had attended the Pulitzer School at Columbia University, and was now looking for employment. Ball wished that she could follow her career but still return home and be an "old fashioned girl." Her twin, Margaret, had worked on college publications; in April, 1926, she married Harry Hickey, a reporter for the Associated Press.[68] Although he was not a newspaper man, Katharine's husband, Clements Ripley, having failed as a peach farmer in North Carolina, had become successful as a writer of adventure novels. Only William and Fay seemed not to be heading toward a future which would, in one way or another, involve them with professional writing. And these were the children that Ball worried about most.

65. Ball, Diary, VII, 60, June 2, 1926, Ball Papers.
66. Ball, *The Editor and the Republic*, p. 106.
67. Josephus Daniels to W. W. Ball, July 13, 1926, Ball Papers.
68. Harry Hickey was a Roman Catholic. His wedding to Margaret Ball took place on the night before a mayoralty election in Columbia in which the Ku Klux Klan was an important issue. To his good friend Tom Waring, Ball remarked not very seriously, "To be sure, I had some apprehensions about the KKK. . . . I suppose it was comparatively safe to have good Father Murphy at 1720 Pendleton Street last evening" (W. W. Ball to T. R. Waring, April 27, 1926, Ball Papers).

His only son, undecided about a career, had gone from The Citadel to the Wharton School of the University of Pennsylvania and then to work for Ball's friend Philip Gadsden at the Philadelphia Gas Company. Ball feared the boy lacked a sense of direction, and he wanted to help, but the two were not close. He wrote to William, "I am handicapped; I know so little about you, and I am so eager to be your friend, to have your confidence."[69] When Fay was sixteen, she left for New York, chaperoned by her mother, to spend a summer at the Theatre Guild School. As autumn approached, she begged her father to allow her to stay in dramatic school. Mrs. Ball was willing; her husband's attitude was the same as her father's had been a generation before. Ball was as conservative in manners as he was in politics and, to him, actresses were not quite "respectable." He disapproved; but he was powerless when the women of his household were united. Fay remained in New York and, for a time, her mother stayed with her.

Although Ball insisted that his interest in owning a newspaper was solely for the benefit of his family, there were other signs that he was becoming restive on the campus. As early as September, 1925, Hagood suspected that Ball was tiring of the quiet life. On hearing that Ball contemplated a move, he admonished: "Now Billy, don't you think of that! You have a great work before you. A work which *no other man* in South Carolina can do. I hear from a great many people that you are doing it remarkably well."[70] A year later, to his nephew at Sewanee, Ball wrote, "As a former, a retired, a shelved editor, an editor emeritus, I envy you in your active service."[71] When Ball decided it would be well for him to control a paper, his first thought was to negotiate for *The Spartanburg Journal*. But later he heard that Tom Waring might be interested in purchasing *The News and Courier*. Ball offered to help by subscribing to some of the stock. One might like to own *The News and Courier*'s interest in the past, he conceded, and live in Charleston. But a man ambitious for power could no longer have it through the "N. & C." Influence in national politics was usually built upon influence in state affairs, and *The News and Courier* was a low-country, not a state, newspaper.[72]

Six months later, Waring informed Ball that a group of Charlesto-

69. W. W. Ball to W. W. Ball, Jr., April 28, 1927, Ball Papers.
70. B. A. Hagood to W. W. Ball, Sept. 5, 1925, Ball Papers.
71. W. W. Ball to T. R. Waring, Jr., Oct. 29, 1926, Ball Papers.
72. W. W. Ball to T. R. Waring, April 16, 1926, Ball Papers.

nians, who included owners of the rival *Evening Post*, had purchased *The News and Courier*. The paper would be owned and virtually controlled by the *Post*, but there would be no merger. Robert Lathan, a recent Pulitzer Prize winner,[73] would be asked to continue as editor, but he was badly shaken and apparently dissatisfied with the change in ownership. The new owners, who held 95 per cent of the common stock, included besides Waring, B. A. Hagood, and Julian Mitchell.[74] All three were Ball's intimates; two were his brothers-in-law.

After the remarkable turn of events in Charleston, Ball made no secret of his boredom. In January, 1927, he remarked to a friend of the new owners of *The News and Courier*: "When I was editor of *The State* I tired of political controversy, the monotonous and cheap campaigns to beat Blease—there was so little in them. Now I long for a 'scrap.' I am not content without a fight on my hands."[75] After Robert Lathan had resigned as editor of *The News and Courier* to accept a post in Asheville, Waring came to Columbia. He offered Ball the vacant editorship and the Dean accepted. Ball's appointment was to remain secret for two weeks, but rumors circulated widely,[76] and when the announcement was made in mid-April, it was no surprise in South Carolina newspaper circles.

Ironically, the same day that *The State* carried the account of Ball's coming departure from Columbia, it also reported that he had been criticized on the floor of the legislature. Senator D. A. G. Ouzts protested the lack of progress reports on the new "State Handbook."[77] The coincidence prompted a friend to jest that the threat of an investigation of his "Handbook" appropriation had forced Ball to "leave town."[78] By the end of May, Ball had read the last of the page proofs, and his work on the "Handbook" was all but finished. On June 1, Ball submitted in writing his official resignation to the university.

A dozen newspapers in South Carolina were enthusiastic in welcoming Ball back into the fold, but perhaps the most gratifying tribute was one that came from outside the state. Douglas Southall Freeman sent Ball a copy of an article he wrote for the Richmond *News Leader*, with

73. Lathan received the Pulitzer Prize for an editorial entitled "The Plight of the South," which appeared in *The News and Courier* on Nov. 4, 1924.
74. T. R. Waring to W. W. Ball, Nov. 5, 1926, Ball Papers.
75. Ball, Diary, VII, 105, Jan. 7, 1927.
76. T. R. Waring to W. W. Ball, April 2, 1927, Ball Papers.
77. *The State*, April 15, 1927.
78. Wilson Harvey to W. W. Ball, April 15, 1927, Ball Papers.

the comment: "The enclosed lacks much of being a good editorial, but it has the virtue of expressing, however imperfectly, my admiration of your great work and my interest in your move."[79]

The nearly two decades that Ball spent in Columbia came to an end in one important sense when, one night in early June, his friends in the Kosmos Club invited him to a testimonial dinner at the Jefferson Hotel. When Ball departed Columbia, he left behind a handful of men whom he cherished, but at the same time, he was going to *The News and Courier* because others of his closest friends were calling him there. To Tom Waring, Ball revealed:

> I exult at the prospect of the realization of a yearning that has been with me 18 years. The yearning was not so much to be the editor of The News and Courier as to be back in Charleston and I was never more than 'domiciled' . . . in 1720 Pendleton street. I have been a denizen in this capital.[80]

Charleston was "one of the few communities retaining civilization."[81] There were signs that rich outsiders would go down and buy from the natives, but he supposed, "the civilization will last as long as I do."[82] When Ball became editor of *The News and Courier* in June, 1927, a long-postponed but somehow inevitable natural alliance was at last completed.

79. D. S. Freeman to W. W. Ball, April 23, 1927, Ball Papers.
80. W. W. Ball to T. R. Waring, April 14, 1927, Ball Papers.
81. W. W. Ball to E. D. Sompayrac, April 25, 1927, Ball Papers.
82. *Ibid.*

CHAPTER EIGHT

CHARLESTON EDITOR AND AUTHOR

The News and Courier was known in Charleston as "the Old Lady of Broad Street." Claiming to be the oldest daily newspaper in the South, she traced her origin to the *Charleston Courier*, founded in 1803. *The News and Courier* was formed from the merger of the *Courier* and the *Daily News* in 1873. Seemingly as permanent as the city itself, she survived war, depression, and pestilence. *The News and Courier* had an issue on the streets the night of the great earthquake of 1886.[1] Preserver of traditional Southern attitudes, she ranked among those American newspapers possessing a distinctive personality. But steadily, she had been losing ground both in the Charleston area and in the state. In 1910 her average daily circulation, in South Carolina second only to *The State*, was 8,919; the rival *Charleston Evening Post* was selling 5,074 copies. In 1927, when Ball became editor,[2] *The News and Courier* had dropped to sixth position among the state's papers. Of course, the Charleston area had not kept pace with the rest of the state in population increase. But even in Charleston, *The News and Courier* had fallen behind the upstart *Post*.[3]

If a lively argumentative editorial page could improve her standing (and Ball believed that it would), *The News and Courier* found a rejuvenator in her new editor. Immediately after his arrival in Charleston, Ball contracted to buy the early Georgian house at 14 Water Street, well to the south of Broad Street in the "right" part of town. The house, believed to have been built in 1769,[4] sat in the part of Water Street that forces Church Street to bend around as it winds its course north from the Battery. The typical English single house in Charleston has its "end" on the street and broad piazzas on the side to catch the ocean breeze. But

1. Herbert Ravenel Sass, *Outspoken: 150 years of The News and Courier* (Columbia, S. C., 1953), p. 119.
2. Ball was only the fourth editor of *The News and Courier*. His predesessors were Francis Warrington Dawson, 1873–1889; James C. Hemphill, 1889–1910; and Robert Lathan, 1910–1927.
3. Daily circulation average for 1927; *Post* 14,737; *The News and Courier* 10,424. Figures from *N. W. Ayer & Son's Directory, Newspapers and Periodicals.*
4. W. W. Ball, Jr., in interview with author, May 11, 1959.

the Ball house sat flush in the bend of Church Street and looked toward the sea. To Ball, the most delightful feature of the house was his library —a large room on the second floor, with fourteen windows, a fireplace, and a stairway to the street. There he worked, and late at night, wrote in his diary. By the time the Balls had settled in the house on Water Street, Ball had begun his controversial six-year campaign against prohibition.

In 1914, when Ball was editor of *The State*, he had refused to print letters from prohibitionists. But state prohibition came the next year, and in 1919, federal prohibition. Though he opposed the Eighteenth Amendment, partly because he maintained that liquor laws were a matter for state deliberation, he consistently urged that, since it was the law, it should be enforced. While he was Dean, he saw that enforcement was impossible and violations of the law were having a corruptive influence in the state. Stories from around the state alarmed him. One friend reported that in Berkeley County in 1923 there were five hundred illicit distributors, large and small, although Ball thought the figure exaggerated. One farmer two years before owed seven hundred dollars on his farm and six hundred dollars on his livestock. Now, according to Ball's informant, bootlegging profits had enabled him to pay his debts, improve his home, and send his daughter to boarding school; he no longer made whiskey. One woman moonshiner had four cars: a Cadillac, a Ford, and two trucks. When she went first to market, she drove her Ford. If searching officers stopped her, they found nothing. The whiskey came in later in the other cars. There were many new houses in Berkeley, paid for by money made in illegal liquor. But whiskey was then so common that profits were small; it could be bought for three dollars a gallon.[5] In 1926 when Ball spoke out in favor of Governor Alfred E. Smith and against prohibition, the St. Matthews, S. C., *Times* criticized him sharply because, in its estimation, a professor in a state college should not do such things.[6] But now Ball was an editor given wide freedom by his publishers; and he made the issue of repeal his first business.

From the time Ball launched his campaign in 1927 until the repeal of the Eighteenth Amendment, he was, most of the time, alone outside of Charleston, for "dry" sentiment was high in South Carolina. *The News*

5. Ball, Diary, VI, 116, July 30, 1923.
6. *Ibid.*, VII, 103, Dec. 31, 1926.

and Courier attacked prohibition from every conceivable angle, but at the heart of Ball's criticism was the often repeated charge of hypocrisy. Liquor interests did not complain of business depression, he remarked in the summer of 1928, as did manufacturers and the sellers of lawful commodities.[7] When Ball had last lived in Charleston, drinking was incidental to entertaining; now the "drinking party" was itself a form of entertainment. All who wanted whiskey had it; Ball was offered it in all the houses he visited. "The Scotch and other liquor is of good quality," he reported, "and I hear no complaints about the corn. Old Snowden is here and he and I drank gin rickies last night and we feel fine."[8] Wherever a town was large enough, there was a "smart set"—a group of young people who gave cocktail parties.

All signs indicated a steady spreading of the liquor habit in South Carolina; bootleggers were taken for granted. The clergy, their followers, and Governor Richards shut their eyes to the truth. Ball said, in a letter to *The New York Times*:

> These people think they have done their full duty, their consciences are easy when they have voted dry. They declare in a church convention that prohibition is a 'glorious success,' and yet a Federal agent in Greenville says in interviews that about 1,500 persons in and around that town of 30,000 inhabitants are engaged in the liquor business and that 3,000 gallons a week are distributed from it. Apparently most of the prohibitionists do not worry about the facts—and the homicide rate does not decrease in these parts.[9]

Ball gave facetious editorial approval to Governor Richards's proposal that buyers and sellers of intoxicating liquors be punished alike. The Governor, Ball observed:

> . . . has hit upon a policy that would make him illustrious, that would send his name ringing down the ages, if he should succeed in having it written into law. . . . [It] would fill the jails with officers of the law, the entrancing spectacle of an occasional sheriff, judge, or state officer on a chain gang breaking rock would halt the motorist speeding from Quebec to Miami.[10]

7. *The News and Courier*, July 8, 1928.
8. W. W. Ball to James C. Derieux, Oct. 25, 1928, Ball Papers.
9. *The New York Times*, Nov. 25, 1928.
10. *The News and Courier*, Jan. 11, 1928.

Ball's position, stated briefly, was that, while "all of us favor temperance,"[11] prohibition was neither right nor feasible. Naturally enough, he
was one of the earliest supporters of Alfred E. Smith for the Democratic
presidential nominee in 1928. A year before the nominating convention,
Ball sent telegrams to Senator Blease and Governor Richards. He asked
for their comments on an article in the *Christian Index* which stated that
if Smith were nominated, Blease and Richards would bolt the party,
taking with them an overwhelming majority of the state's voters in
support of an independent candidate.[12] Both men assured *The News
and Courier* that they were loyal Democrats.[13]

In the spring of 1928 Ball began his editorial drive in behalf of
Smith, an effort which the New York Governor acknowledged in early
May.[14] For the Democrats to nominate any other man, Ball said in his
editorials, would be to "carry on a shadow campaign." While the
delegates were meeting in Houston to select their candidates, Ball directed his editorials against the efforts of clergymen, especially Bishop
James Cannon, Jr., of the Methodist Episcopal Church, South, to inject
prohibition into politics as a religious question, to "drape it in sanctity."[15] The terms "dry" and "Protestant" were not synonymous, he
reminded his readers and invited them to look to Europe.

Immediately after Smith's nomination, Ball thought he stood an excel-
lent chance of election. Throughout the summer, Ball urged the voters
not to reject Smith because he was a Roman Catholic. Some critics
suggested that he devoted too much time to the Catholic issue, but he
felt strongly that Smith's nomination had been a good thing, a victory
for religious freedom. As the elections approached, however, and the
campaign in the South against Smith both as a "wet" and as a Catholic
took on the proportions of a crusade, Ball lost hope. By September he
saw no chance for the election of Smith, but he maintained:

> I am writing every day to prevent the division of the white party in
> South Carolina, to check the desertion of anti-Catholic and "dry"
> democrats to Hoover. This is the right course for me and the
> N. & C.; I'm pressing for it with all vigor. . . . In my secret heart

11. *The New York Times*, Nov. 25, 1928.
12. *The News and Courier* to C. L. Blease, July 14, 1927; *The News and
Courier* to J. G. Richards, July 14, 1927; Ball Papers.
13. C. L. Blease to *The News and Courier*, July 15, 1927; J. G. Richards to
The News and Courier, July 15, 1927; Ball Papers.
14. Alfred E. Smith to W. W. Ball, May 5, 1928, Ball Papers.
15. *The News and Courier*, June 29, 1928.

I do not greatly care, if I care at all, if these silly bigots smash the Democratic party in the South. It would mean a degree of intellectual emancipation.[16]

Yet in *The News and Courier*, in the few hours after the polls had closed but before the results of the election were known, there appeared an editorial reminding the electorate that prohibition, religious differences, and tariff policies were trifles compared with the necessity of preserving the white man's party in South Carolina.[17]

After the defeat of Smith, Ball continued his war on prohibition, in spite of the admonishments of his close friend Fitz McMaster that his attitudes encouraged the violation of the laws. Wild tales spurred him on while other papers were silent. Ball claimed that Olin Johnston of Spartanburg, then a member of the House of Representatives, told him one day when Governor Richards had come to the State House to confer with a committee of legislators, two fruit jars of whiskey were on the floor of the room, bottles of liquor were in the water cooler, and other containers were visible in a rolltop desk.[18]

Ball's drive for repeal was typical of his editorial campaigns: many editorials, several approaches, varied styles (ranging from the fiercely direct to the devious and coy). Editorials which appeared two days apart in 1930 provide illustration:

Fifty-two Cases in Horry

Fifty-two cases of violations of the prohibition laws are before the [state] court for trial in Conway, county of Horry. Horry is a county in which three-fourths of the population are white people, most of them small farmers. It is a coastal county, containing seaside resorts and two or three villages.

Never in the history of the "old barroom system" were fifty-two persons, perhaps never as many as a dozen in one year, engaged in the liquor business. When barrooms were open, they were in the policed town.

Whiskey-making is now for the most part a countryman's business, in South Carolina. Probably most of the bootleggers, too, in Horry are countrymen.

No one advocates return to barrooms, but barrooms are less evil

16. Ball, Diary, VII, 204–205, Sept. 10, 1928.
17. *The News and Courier*, Nov. 7, 1928.
18. Ball, Diary, VII, 319, April 15, 1930.

than unlawful distilleries and bootlegging. The barkeepers are not law-breakers. It was never necessary for law officers to hold them up or to shoot them, nor was it necessary for an undercover man to buy from them under false pretense to obtain evidence.

Between 1907 and 1916 independent county dispensaries were operated in about fifteen counties, there were no scandals in connection with them, they produced revenues for the counties, and drinking and drunkenness were less common than at this time. The state, the counties, and the federal government were not paying out hundreds of thousands of dollars a year for law enforcement that does not enforce. The governor had no need for gubernatorial constabulary.

Drinking goes on now in all South Carolina communities where people wish to drink.

The principal thing accomplished by prohibition is to put a premium on whiskey high enough to tempt poor people to make and sell it.

The fifty-two cases in Horry, mark, are for one term of court.

If in the course of a year twenty stills are seized in Horry it is safe to assume that five times as many are operated part of the time. Whenever a still is set up scores of people must and do know something about it.[19]

The New Idolatry

The activities of the women and men who have been urging the judiciary committee of the national house of representatives that it exert itself to bring about the repeal of the Eighteenth amendment present a strange spectacle. They are asking the country to abolish what the constitution, the organic law of the republic, outlaws, so that what the Jones law, an act of Congress, calls a "felony," may also be abolished.

Think of people who count themselves respectable citizens wishing the congress to permit what is "felonious" to be done?

Supporting the Eighteenth amendment and the laws for its enforcement, including the definitions of "felony," are numerous good people. Assured perfectly that they are righteous, they have known a heinous deed when they see it, they have taken the selling

19. *The News and Courier*, March 4, 1930.

of liquor and converted it into a "felony." Given a perfect sense of righteousness and a majority, any deed may be converted into a felony—as, for instance, spitting on the sidewalk.

Yet we are confronted with ladies, and citizens who pass for gentlemen, including members of congress, boldly urging that certain felonies be abolished.

Were these same ladies—and gentlemen—to appear before Representative Graham and his committee urging that grand larceny or burglary be abolished as felonies, what would the country say? We think that it would say that they are "Reds." The cry would go up from every quarter that they are dangerous persons. Probably some of them would be mobbed, hanged.

The truth is, nevertheless, that grand larceny and burglary are, federally speaking, not unconstitutional, not felonies, unless the federal government be robbed.

The little state of South Carolina can reduce grand larceny or burglary to a misdemeanor without consulting the U. S., the congress, or the other state legislatures. It is none of their business. The English common law is by statute the law of South Carolina unless and until it shall be modified by statute, and if we South Carolinians wish to abolish crimes, it is only necessary that we elect a state legislature to do so. It is within our state sovereignty to define or abolish murder or any other offence according to our taste and fancy—but we cannot say that the sale of a pint of beer is not a "felony." The state of South Carolina can revolutionize its whole criminal code, we can set up a "Red" commonwealth if we choose, in respect of crime and felony, as long as we do not trespass on the narrowly limited laws of the republic (which do not interfere with our definitions of murder and arson) and the United States cannot themselves—or itself.

If the nature of the felony can be injected into the act of selling a pint of whiskey by the congress, either the congress or the state legislature are [sic] equally authorized to abolish burglary as a felony, and legislatures, national and state, speak with the voice of God. To our mind, to impute that power to a legislature is idolatrous. Now Paul and Barnabas "scarce . . . restrained the people, that they had not done sacrifice unto them," and those people were poor, ignorant fools—why should intelligent Americans attribute

godlike powers to human legislatures when they try to define
"morals?"[20]

Anti-prohibitionist organizations seeking a repeal referendum had
invited Ball to testify to the failure of the experiment in South Carolina.
Ball was one of many witnesses; he was hurried, but he knew what he
wanted to say. National prohibition, he informed the Congressional investigating committee, was worse than the old saloon at its worst.
Moonshining once had been confined to the mountain counties; now it was
all over the state. More than eight hundred stills had been captured in
one year. In the past, a host had served a little Madeira; now he staged
cocktail parties with "doctored" corn liquor. Ball claimed the right to
speak as an authority on that subject, because he came from a "cocktail
party country."[21]

Ball's statement that conditions were worse then than under the
saloon system incensed many of the "drys" in South Carolina. Criticism
came from press and private sources alike. *The Columbia Record*
said:

> Those who agree with him are wholly responsible for the condi-
> tions. . . . Editor Ball's judgment is essentially unsound. He has
> encouraged contempt for the prohibition law. . . . His judgment
> in respect to law observance being so unsound in that respect it is
> not to be expected that it is [sound], certainly not, in related
> subjects. There is the age old proverb: False in one, false in all.[22]

In the *Greenville County Observer* ("Friend of the Working People"),
the editor charged that Ball had displayed "unreasoning and bitter
prejudice" and "perverted use of his powers."[23] Charleston, furthermore, was depicted as "a place where drunkenness was rife among
society folks, who are giving lots of cocktail parties."[24] In Sumter, the
district meeting of the Women's Christian Temperance Union issued
the following statement: "We flatly deny the accuracy of Editor Ball's
statement. . . . That statement is either a reflection on Mr. Ball's
intelligence or honesty."[25] To scores of sincere abstainers, Ball was the
devil and Charleston the seat of debauchery. To make matters worse, the

20. *Ibid.*, March 6, 1930.   21. *Ibid.*
22. *The Columbia Record*, March 6, 1930.
23. *Greenville County Observer*, March 13, 1930.
24. *Ibid.*
25. Charles J. Epps to W. W. Ball (letter and clipping), March 10, 1930, Ball
Papers.

Greenville Piedmont had quoted him inaccurately. Ball had testified that perhaps 40,000 of 1,800,000 people in the state were engaged, at least part time, in the liquor business. According to an article in the *Piedmont*, Ball had accused 40 per cent of the state's people of being involved in illegal practices. After Ball's protest, the Greenville paper printed a correction, blaming the error on the dispatch from Washington.[26]

Caught in a fight, Ball always stood fast, though he did believe it necessary further to explain his statements before the investigating committee. Ball felt that the furor had arisen partly because his remarks had been misunderstood. When he said that conditions were worse now than before, the "drys" had inferred that he meant there was more drinking during prohibition than when the saloons were open. Actually, he was referring to the sum of present conditions. "What I was thinking of in the main," he explained to a friendly, though presently critical, editor "was that national prohibition compels this country to live under and in dense strata of hypocrisy, duplicity, bribery, and law-breaking."[27] "Bad laws ought to be defied," he advised the Columbia Kosmos Club, "*and* you gentlemen teaching in [a] *civilized* institution of *unmixed race* are doing so because you *are law-breakers*, as your fathers *were*."[28] In offering himself for dissection, Ball admitted to his old friends that he was now the most notorious "wet" in the state.[29]

Ball spoke for the majority of Southern whites, however, when he reacted to strikes, union organizational attempts, and other aspects of the growing labor unrest which accompanied the gradually advancing tide of regional industrialism. In a long editorial—and he wrote many long ones—Ball observed:

> So another "abolition movement" has been started, this time in New York, and "slavery" in the Southern cotton mills is to be ended. . . .
>
> If the mill workers in the South wish to form unions, it is their right to form them. Surely the N & C would not object. They will have no right to dictate to employers who shall and who shall not be employed, and that is the milk in the cocoanut [sic]. The union organizers look on unions as of no value unless shop is closed, and

26. *Greenville Piedmont*, March 11, 1930.
27. W. W. Ball to H. L. Watson, March 12, 1930, Ball Papers.
28. Ball, *The Editor and the Republic*, p. 115.
29. *Ibid.*, p. 107.

the employers would be not in the least apprehensive of unions if by them their right to "hire & fire" would not be interfered with.

The abstract right of organizing is not in question—it is the "hereafter" with which both sides to the controversy are concerned.

The N & C repeats that the industrial constitution of the Southern mill is artificial, exceptional, and that the benevolent Northern agitators . . . do not understand it—probably do not want to understand it.

The Southern cotton mill is an industrial device whereby white Southern labor is given employment separate from colored labor and partial relief from its competition. The result of it is wages and living conditions not so good as are those enjoyed by most Northern laborers and far better than farm laborers in the South enjoy. Most of the Southern farm laborers are Negroes, and most of the white men in the mills of their fathers ran away from Negro competition, "coolie" competition, which of course they were wise to do.

The farm laborer's wage in South Carolina is a dollar a day, a cabin, and a "garden spot."

The mill laborer's wage is twice as much, and his house and comfort are five times better. This is not saying that he is well paid; it is saying that his alternative is to "live like a Negro" on a farm unless he leave the South for a land where Negroes are few or none. Tens of thousands of poor whites are still scattered on the farms of the South—shall the Southern mills be closed to them? That would be the meaning of the "closed shop!"

Were these Northern "philanthropists" intelligently sincere, their sympathies would be aroused first by the plight of the one dollar, not the two dollar a day man. While they are trying to "liberate" half a million or three quarters of a million Southern mill workers from what they are pleased to call "slavery" they are trying to condemn two or three times as many poor whites to stay on the farms with five or six million negro [sic] farm laborers. These farmers are of course the tariff serfs—whose wages are soon to be reduced by raising the price of sugar $15 a year to the family.

These Northern agitators and lovers of their fellow creatures succeed in closing their eyes and ears to the real, the poignant, the enveloping, the suffocating poverty of the South. The only laborers who interest them are laborers whose condition is at worst incomparably better than the condition of the great majority.

To close the mill shop is to close the exit from the farm to the white farm laborer of the South. Give these people a chance on the farm and they would scorn the mill opportunity—and their brothers and cousins would flock back to the farms.

The American Federation of Labor harbors not the slightest intention or hope of breaking down the racial barriers in the Southern mills, to undertake that now would be to defeat the Southern mills invasion at its beginning, but theoretically at least, the Federation opposes racial separation in industry. The separation is, in fact, unnatural, and, considered in its broader aspects, destructive of labor's objects. We all know that. Last week the Journal and Guide, negro [sic] newspaper of Norfolk, was quoting President Green, of the Federation, as cordially inviting Negro cooperation in the Federation, and stating the Federation's denial of racial distinction. In a factory town of Ohio, with 5% of negro [sic] labor, it might be practical to ignore the "race question."

While the Federation would not consciously attempt to disrupt the existing arrangements in Southern mills, others would not hesitate to do so. The negro [sic] question is the thorn in the flesh of the American Socialists. To mention it soils them. Norman Thomas, the candidate of the Socialists for president last year . . . is a man of high character and intelligence. He knows perfectly that to admit the propriety of racial separation in labor would be to abandon the whole Socialistic program. He would be the last man to stultify himself by yielding the principle that labor should recognize no color line. Associated with Mr. Thomas in this campaign to "emancipate" the Southern mill "slaves" are many men and women in agreement with him—and they are the educated element, the writers, speakers, thinkers, enlisted for this "war." To them, to demolish the artificial industrial structure of the South seems not only practicable but highly desirable. It would be to win a decisive battle on that part of the far stretching front where opposition to Socialism is most stubborn and embarrassing. Not to lend all their energies and brain power to the Federation and the philanthropic allies would be to neglect a great opportunity. From their point of view they are right—we cannot expect them to betray Socialism, their cause, and if, marching with the American Federation into the Southern mill villages, they expect to infiltrate the workers with their notions, they are resorting to good strategy. Their plan (not the Federation's) is, in time, to let the negroes [sic] into the mills, and we think that so candid a man as Norman Thomas is would scarcely deny it.

To us Southerners Socialistic theories and campaigns are foreign. We are concerned with realities. We may be derided as opportunists. We want the Southern mills for Southern white labor. We want them to remain, as they have been, villages of refuge, isles of safety, for poor white families driven in flight from the farms. Therefore, the "closed shop" cannot be thought of.

The life in the mill is far from what it should be, we hope that it will improve—and it has improved marvelously in the last 30 years. The N & C looks forward to a 45 hour week—to be gained without legislation. Labor agitation would probably retard its coming. With the great majority of our population non-industrial, the chances of gaining it by legislation would be remote at best.

Between the closing of the gates by agitators to white families who would come from the farms to the mills stand the mill presidents, directors, owners. It is to their financial advantage, to be sure.

But it has been and still is the salvation of the despairing white farmers.[30]

That review of "cotton mill realities," dotted with those oddly placed prepositional phrases which helped give Ball's prose its unique flavor, was more than the statement of a conservative who owned cotton mill stocks. Certainly, principle and interest did complement each other here. Had he not been a shareholder, would the editor have spoken differently? It is not likely; for Ball voiced the South's overriding preoccupation with the race issue and its historic rejection of "outside interference."

Although Ball displayed a greater interest in national affairs after he moved to Charleston, *The News and Courier* did not neglect local politics. Ball played a politically significant role in the senatorial election of 1930. Cole Blease, ending his first term in the Senate, was seeking re-election. Though Blease may not have distinguished himself, he had not proved as irresponsible as his critics had feared. Conservatives were

30. *The News and Courier*, July 16, 1929.

forced to admit that many of his positions in the Senate "voiced his sound sense."[31] But early in 1929 he had defended Joe Tolbert, South Carolina Republican boss, against charges of selling postmasterships, whereas a few months before he had said, in effect, that every postmaster in South Carolina had paid Tolbert for his job. In the summer of 1930, when Ball once more undertook a prolonged editorial campaign against Blease, it seemed to him that other newspapers in the state were so mildly anti-Blease that they might as well not be classed as opposed to him. Eliza Ball was immensely proud of her son's accomplishments, but she could be critical when she thought his judgment had faltered. A month before the first primary, she urged him to let up on Blease: "It is time now to get a new subject."[32]

As a result of the first vote, Representative James F. Byrnes won the right to contest Blease in the second primary. A third candidate, Leon W. Harris, who had been eliminated by the first election, issued a statement announcing that he would not campaign for either Blease or Byrnes and suggesting that his followers decide for themselves which of the two men they would support.[33] A few days later, however, after a conversation with Ball, Harris told the editor that he would vote for "Jimmy," and gave Ball permission to say so in *The News and Courier*. Ball later composed the statement that appeared on the front page of the next day's paper—a statement carefully worded to avoid conflict with Harris's earlier announcement. Harris was not now telling readers how to vote, Ball stressed; Harris was simply saying that *he* would vote for James F. Byrnes.[34] For his own part, Ball urged all those opposed to Bleasism to get out and vote against Cole Blease and to remember that J. F. Byrnes was a son of Charleston.[35]

In the 1930 run-off Blease and Byrnes faced each other as they had six years before; but this time Byrnes was the winner. T. R. Waring claimed that credit for the defeat of Blease belonged to ex-mayor Grace.[36] Ball admitted that Grace's failure to support Blease had meant votes for Byrnes in Charleston; but to Ball's mind, Byrnes owed *him* for his election.[37] His bringing Harris out in support of Byrnes, Ball judged,

31. Wallace, *South Carolina*, p. 676.
32. Eliza W. Ball to W. W. Ball, July 30, 1930, Ball Papers.
33. *The News and Courier*, Sept. 1, 1930.
34. *Ibid.*, Sept. 7, 1930.   35. *Ibid.*, Sept. 8, 1930.
36. Ball, Diary, VIII, 16, Sept. 10, 1930.
37. *Ibid.*, X, 175, April 25, 1937.

had been crucial. In either case, the brief national career of Cole Blease came to an end. In 1932 he tried to unseat Senator Smith, but "Cotton Ed" won easily.

Ball "allowed himself" to become interested in the senatorial campaigns in which Blease was a candidate.[38] In spite of himself, he enjoyed playing the game. As a journalist, he could not help playing it—"trying to move these little politicians as pawns on a board."[39] He was all but disinterested, however, in the current gubernatorial election. Ibra C. Blackwood and Olin D. Johnston, both of Spartanburg County, were the contestants in the election of 1930. But *The News and Courier* had to choose between them, and Blackwood received the endorsement. Blackwood's unwillingness to declare himself to be anti-Blease had irked Ball. The editor chose him over Johnston, however, because he seemed more likely to allow the completion of the highway program, begun under retiring Governor Richards.[40] Although Ball was bored with the Blackwood-Johnston contest, he was nevertheless drawn into it. A few days before the deciding election, Blackwood phoned Ball to state that, if elected, he would be impartial in the administration of his office and would recognize no factional alignments. Ball questioned Blackwood about the rumor that, if he became governor, he would not allow John P. Grace to come to his office. Blackwood denied that he had made any such threat, and Ball reported his statement in the next day's newspaper, adding, "If Mr. Blackwood shall not be elected next Tuesday an immense surprise is coming to The News and Courier."[41] Ball's prediction was accurate, for Olin Johnston was defeated, the Democratic state executive committee refusing his request for a recount, particularly in Charleston County.

Perhaps no Americans, save Louisianians, have been so obsessed with politics as have South Carolinians. But in Charleston, politics was something unique even for South Carolina. If in the rest of the state campaigns resembled carnivals, in Charleston they became extravaganzas. Occasionally punctuated with shootings and ballot burnings, mayoralty elections customarily consumed the interest of the populace for months at a time. Long before he became editor of *The News and Courier*, Ball had passed his judgment on Charleston politics, branded it more or less accurately as a competition of personalities rather than ideas. Back in

38. *Ibid.*, VIII, 11, Sept. 7, 1930.   39. *Ibid.*, VIII, 264, June 15, 1932.
40. *The News and Courier*, Sept. 7, 1930.
41. *Ibid.*, Sept. 5, 1930.

1915, during an election in which disturbances appeared imminent, Governor Manning authorized the sheriff to swear in as many extra deputies as might be needed. He also placed under arms four companies of the national guard and four divisions of the naval militia which were to be held ready. On that occasion, none of the special reinforcements were employed; the election was peaceful, although the incumbent, Boss Grace, had apparently been defeated for the office of mayor by Tristram T. Hyde with a majority of only nineteen votes.[42] But a few days later, when the city Democratic executive committee met to canvass the returns, the antagonisms erupted in bloodshed. Hardly had the chairman declared the meeting open before a shot struck down a young reporter from the *Evening Post*, and in the general exchange of shots that followed, four men—all of the Grace faction—were wounded. During the affray two or three ballot boxes and several club books were hurled through the windows, and in the ensuing scramble in the street, two men were clubbed.[43]

As editor of *The State*, Ball could not resist commenting on the murder which had resulted from the bitter Grace-Hyde rivalry. There had been no real issues, he lamented; the killing had been caused by the "tragedy of egotism in Charleston politics."[44] Four years later, when Grace attempted to recapture his office, Waring of the Charleston *Post* asked Ball for an editorial in *The State* supporting Hyde against Grace.[45] The former mayor, Waring cautioned, was a capable and confirmed mob leader whose power over "roughnecks" was striking. He could set them to pillage, or he could keep them in check with a word. "There is fire and menace in the situation constantly," Waring warned.[46] Ball responded with the desired editorials, but Hyde was ousted from the mayor's office although Grace did not receive a majority of the votes. Grace's victory was made possible by party practices that permitted the faction which controlled the vote-counting committee to determine the outcome, though it might contradict the popular verdict. Thus the function of the primary was nullified. Ball deplored such conditions but he blamed them on the peculiarities of state politics which made Democratic nomination equivalent to election and on the necessity for retaining the racial primary.[47]

42. *The State*, Oct. 12–13, 1915.   43. *Ibid.*, Oct. 16, 1915.
44. *Ibid.*
45. T. R. Waring to W. W. Ball, Aug. 5, 1919, Ball Papers.
46. T. R. Waring to W. W. Ball, Aug. 24, 1919, Ball Papers.
47. W. W. Ball to Joseph W. Barnwell, Jan. 10, 1920, Ball Papers.

Later, when he became a local editor, Ball necessarily assumed a front seat for the Charleston political circus. Early in the mayoralty campaign of 1931, Burnet Maybank, with five of his supporters, called on Ball to inform him that, though Grace was not a candidate for mayor, Maybank desired to be regarded as the anti-Grace candidate.[48] Their strategy was obvious: Grace had in recent years been bitterly criticized by many Charlestonians, and by making an early declaration against Grace, Maybank sought by implication to associate any eventual rival with the controversial former mayor. Later, after Lawrence M. Pinckney entered the contest, the Maybank forces took advertisements in the papers claiming that he was running a "Grace" campaign and boasting that there were no would-be dictators behind Maybank.[49]

A few days before the election, a committee of Pinckney supporters also visited Ball. They brought with them a letter addressed to Waring and Ball requesting that either or both hold in escrow an attached document—Pinckney's resignation as mayor, to be presented to the city council after eighteen months (provided Pinckney was elected) if the editors thought he had not fulfilled his promise to reduce taxes and if they believed he had not honored his other campaign pledges. Both Ball and Waring refused, the former declaring the proposition contrary to his conception of the duties of an editor. Ball suspected the entire suggestion had been a political maneuver; he heard that his and Waring's refusal would be used as part of an advertisement.[50] The next day the Pinckney faction bought a full page of *The News and Courier* on which was printed the letters containing the pledge together with the statement that Ball and Waring had declined to act as judges.[51] Ball had no strong objection, but he did not like being "used" even in this small way. "Nothing could be more childish and silly," he said privately, "than the Maybank-Pinckney contest for mayor of Charleston."[52]

Ball voted for Burnet Maybank for the reason that his father was Ball's family physician,[53] but *The News and Courier* did not choose between the candidates. There were no important issues involved, and as an editor, Ball could maintain detachment; nevertheless, he complained that both sides accused him of being partisan. Maybank was the victor

48. Ball, Diary, VIII, 72, May 18, 1931.
49. *The News and Courier*, Oct. 5, 1931.
50. Ball, Diary, VIII, Oct. 3, 1931.
51. *The News and Courier*, Oct. 4, 1931.
52. Ball, Diary, VIII, 127, Aug. 14, 1931.
53. *Ibid.*, VIII, 109, July 16, 1931.

by a large majority,[54] but on the night of his victory he sent Ball a "curt note" requesting that his picture be left out of *The News and Courier* and that nothing be said about him in the news columns. Ball regarded his attitude as "preposterous"; but for the intercession of Waring and others, he might not have used a picture of the new mayor nor mentioned his name in an editorial. Maybank and some of his partisans appeared provoked because *The News and Courier* had not made war on their opponents. Ball held, however, that an endorsement by *The News and Courier* would have brought against Maybank the charge that he was the candidate of the South Carolina National Bank and weakened his case. Julian Mitchell, the bank president, was also one of the owners of the paper.[55]

The vigorous campaigning in 1931 had created another tense interlude in Charleston. Officers of the ships in port were asked to keep sailors aboard for the several days surrounding the election, because it was feared that a thousand sailors on the streets would add to the excitement in the town. Ball regarded the request, whether wise or not, as "a sorry reflection on the town, a confession that it is too stirred up by a wretched little political contest."[56] He mused: "Isn't Charleston funny? Especially in politics? And Charleston doesn't know it."[57]

Ball soon became one of the city's most conspicuous citizens. He was one of those invited by Mayor Grace to be in the first party to cross the new Cooper River bridge, that incredible structure with its ski-slope approaches. Although Ball had not been one of the mayor's admirers, on that occasion he wrote, "Not only for Charleston but for all South Carolina your agency in this mighty work has been of invaluable service. As a South Carolinian I am most grateful to you."[58]

Although Ball proclaimed his annoyance at the city's politics, he found the rest of Charleston life irresistible. The annual St. Cecilia Ball had changed little since he had first attended the affairs in 1895 and 1896. Dancing began promptly at nine, with supper at half-past twelve, followed by dancing until two. Men wore white gloves and ladies were properly chaperoned. One startling difference was evident, however;

54. In the contest for alderman-at-large for the fourth ward, John P. Grace was defeated by J. Albert Von Dohlen.
55. Ball, Diary, VIII, 158–159, Oct. 7, 1931.
56. *Ibid.*, VIII, 160–161, Oct. 7, 1931.
57. *Ibid.*, VIII, 97, June 22, 1931.
58. W. W. Ball to J. P. Grace, Aug. 2, 1929, John P. Grace Papers, Duke University Library.

now, during prohibition, no wines were served. Men brought whiskey to the ball and drank it in an anteroom. Still, the ball was "a dignified and beautiful entertainment where good manners prevailed, . . . the last stand of respectability . . . and serving a better purpose now perhaps than at any time in its long history, [as] a check on the too free manners of the day."[59] Ball admitted, however, that the young people preferred the cotillions at the Francis Marion Hotel. Fay Cornelia Ball, home after a brief and not very successful stage career, made her debut at the hotel during the Christmas holidays in 1928, and soon afterward attended her first St. Cecilia Ball, accompanied by her father. The Society rules forbid the presence of actresses at the ball; but, the story is that Fay, in jovial defiance, once attended with her Equity card concealed in her evening bag.[60]

"Polite society" was only one of Charleston's attractions for the transformed upcountryman. During the twenties and thirties as Southern writers rose to dominate American literature, Charleston was a literary center of some importance; DuBose Heyward, Herbert Ravenel Sass, Julia Peterkin, and Josephine Pinckney, to name a few, were among her important resident writers. Hervey Allen and Heyward were the mentors of the literary clique which included Ball's son-in-law and daughter, Clements and Katharine Ripley.[61] In 1920 Heyward and Miss Pinckney organized the poetry society which inspired the formation of similar groups throughout the South. The Poetry Society of South Carolina had a membership of four hundred and a waiting list. Ball was a friend of the literati, and for a time served as president of the Society. Samuel G. Stoney, Charleston antiquary, remembered Ball presiding in the South Carolina Society Hall—leaning back, thumbs in his vest, with an inch or two of shirt showing beneath.[62]

When people prominent in the arts, politics, and government visited Charleston, Ball met and talked with them: Henry Seidel Canby, Walter Lippmann, Stephen Vincent Benet, Robert Frost, theatrical director Rouben Mamoulian, Ben Hecht and Charles McArthur, Cyrus H. K. Curtis, Colonel E. M. House. When Ball and his daughter Eleanor

59. Ball, Diary, VII, 294, Jan. 18, 1930.

60. Fay Cornelia Ball was not the first performer to attend the St. Cecilia Ball; General Wade Hampton was reputed to have brought a well-known actress, but his prestige was so great that the lady was allowed to remain.

61. Katharine Ball Ripley's published books were *Sand in My Shoes* and *Sand Dollars*, both autobiographical, and a novel, *Crowded House*.

62. Samuel G. Stoney, in interview with author, May 8, 1959.

called on Colonel House, the two men talked about Winston Churchill. House remarked that he did not "get along" especially well with Churchill at the peace conference. Lloyd George, having failed to obtain certain concessions from House, assigned the matter to Churchill and seemed pleased, House reported, that Churchill could do no better.[63]

Ball had met Churchill a few days before. Bernard Baruch, whom Ball had seen again at several Charleston parties, asked him to be among the forty guests invited to meet Churchill at Hobcaw Barony, Baruch's winter estate near Kingstree. During the visit, Ball argued with Churchill the relative merits of Scotch whiskey and South Carolina corn.[64] He recorded his impressions of the famous statesman:

> Before luncheon I chatted twenty minutes with Churchill and he seemed sleepy. Then I sat opposite him at luncheon and he spoke with animation and force against American prohibition. Mr. Churchill met precisely in appearance and manner the mental picture that I had formed of him from reading. He is a most interesting man—he has much of the personality of the late Colonel Theodore Roosevelt, but I think that his emphasis, his dynamics, seem less of a business, more natural, than Roosevelt's. I fancy that he has more of a sense of humor. Churchill said that the American Prohibitionists should be punished, should be repulsed for what they have done to the country, for their assault on states rights and popular liberty, I like that idea.[65]

Ball loved cocktail parties and he attended many. With a drink or two and an audience, he was a beguiling guest. People seemed not to tire either of his myriad anecdotes of the state and its people or of his salty derision of the current state of life in America. One thing was certain— whether the subject was folklore or philosophy, he never wearied of talking. His pleasure in party-going was somewhat diminished, however, because Mrs. Ball would not accompany him. Since her return to Charleston, she had become a virtual recluse. She was simply no longer interested in "society." Besides her immediate family, she saw only her sisters and occasionally, a few old friends. She retained, however, her interest in the stage, and when she went out, it was usually to the theater. Ball bore his disappointment with the patience of a devoted

63. Ball, Diary, VIII, 218, Feb. 24, 1932.
64. Margaret L. Coit, *Mr. Baruch* (Cambridge, Mass., 1957), p. 330.
65. Ball, Diary, VIII, 217–218, Feb. 21, 1932.

husband and transmitted her excuses. Once, in declining the invitation of an old friend, he remarked, "I think if you will install a moving picture in your house and line the walls with cross word puzzles she would come. I can't get her to go with me anywhere."[66] But Ball went to parties—sometimes alone, sometimes with one of his daughters—and he enjoyed them.

One night at the Clements Ripley house he met Virgil Steed, a representative of Bobbs-Merrill, who asked him to write a book about South Carolina. Actually, Steed first suggested such a book as a project for the Ripleys, and they suggested that Ball should be the one to write it. But according to Steed, in a subsequent publicity release, the idea had come from a small town newspaperman he met while riding in a dirty day coach between Columbia and Charleston. During their conversation, Steed remarked:

> The question occurred to me, how such a people, with such grand leaders as Wade Hampton, John C. Calhoun, Rhett and scores of others, could have fallen from their high estate. Now all are poor. The leaders seem third-rate demagogs. The very inspiration of the place has vanished. Why?

His companion explained that it was a long story, a great story, one he always wanted to write but never would. When Steed inquired who could write it, the man replied, "W. W. Ball, editor of the Charleston News and Courier." While he was in Charleston, he called on the Ripleys and repeated the conversation. When he said he would like to meet Mr. Ball, Katharine Ripley replied, "We'll have him over. He is my father. He could write such a book, but he never will. However, do try to get him to do it."[67]

The book Steed wanted from Ball was not to be a history, but a narrative with a thread of history running through it and serving as a framework on which would be hung anecdotes and biographical sketches. Steed was not the first to encourage Ball to write a book. A decade before, Ulrich B. Phillips had suggested that "any man who can express himself with such cogency ought by all means to put his experiences, observations and judgments into a book for public enlightenment."[68] Ball had never written anything longer than an article, and for

66. W. W. Ball to Margaret B. Meriwether, April 21, 1932, Papers of Robert S. Meriwether, The South Caroliniana Library.
67. Virgil Steed's letter to the "book trade" printed in *The State*, Oct. 26, 1932.
68. U. B. Phillips to W. W. Ball, Dec. 9, 1923, Ball Papers.

a few days he hesitated. Finally he notified Bobbs-Merrill that if he could induce his daughter Eleanor to return from New York to help him, he would undertake the book. Eleanor insisted that the real reason for calling her to Charleston was that her father always wanted at least one daughter at home; but since her present job was on a short-lived women's magazine which was soon to expire, she had no reason to refuse his appeal.[69]

In February, 1931, Eleanor Ball came home and work on the book began. Her main task was to do what research was needed. Some had to be done from Ball's own collection of South Caroliniana, at the Charleston Library, or in *The News and Courier* "morgue," but most of the material for the book came from the diaries Ball had then been keeping for fifteen years. Eleanor recalled her father's routine:

Papa wrote a big chunk of the book every night, and next day I got ready material for what he wanted to write next. . . . As was his invariable habit, he wrote from after supper until late into the night. (He worked in this way almost every night in the years that followed his regular newspaper night work whether he was writing a book or not: sometimes he wrote letters, or next day's editorials, . . . or sometimes he just wrote. During various times of his life he attempted short stories (which weren't published) or special articles or whatever came into his head. Except for his diary, he always used the typewriter. He had begun typing long before it was a craft, so he never learned to use a machine properly. He typed fast, with two fingers, very inaccurately, and banged the keys with terrific force. . . . So, every night he wrote part of the book—I should say at least a thousand words at a stretch. Some nights more. Of course, what he wrote didn't always stand up in the light of day. Sometimes he would destroy what he had done— sometimes cut. But on the whole he did very little rewriting. What he had to say . . . had been written, or talked so often before— written in diaries, or in his editorials, talked with friends and in speeches. . . . As a chapter was finished it was read by, or read aloud to, my brother-in-law, Clements Ripley who was a successful author and gave Papa many valuable suggestions. My sister Katharine Ripley, who was also a professional writer, helped too; but she and my father were always temperamentally at variance and

69. Eleanor Ball Hewitt-Myring to author, July 30, 1959.

she wasn't nearly so helpful as Clem. At about midnight Papa came downstairs, where my mother was usually still up reading or sewing, and had his 'nightcap.' Except on special occasions, he had only this one drink during the day, but it was a huge one (of illicit corn whiskey at this period, but according to Prohibition standards a good brand) served with a great deal of water in an oversized glass. I had a drink with him (in an ordinary tumbler!), and then we played three *parties* of Piquet: eighteen hands.[70]

Toward the end of the writing of the book, he became impatient and, possibly, physically tired. On at least one occasion, he hurled parts of the manuscript across the room, exclaiming, "I haven't got to write this."[71] But he persisted, spurred on by Bobbs-Merrill's Mr. Steed, who, as he received the completed chapters, offered such suggestions as: "Believe your book is grand with lots of punch. Make it plenty long. Give it plenty of ginger and keep it from being confusing wherever possible."[72] Finally, after a year the book was finished; only the title must yet be chosen. After "Remembering South Carolina," "Pitchforks and Pal-mettoes," and "South Carolina: Mother of Fighters" had all been dis-carded (Ball especially objected to the latter because he was weary of the emphasis on South Carolina as peculiarly gallant and brave), author and publisher agreed upon *The State That Forgot: South Carolina's Surrender to Democracy*. In the summer of 1932 Bobbs-Merrill sug-gested postponing publication for a year in the hope that depression conditions might improve. But Ball asked them not to wait; he would like his mother to see it before she died and many of his friends were expecting it that year. He did not hope to make any money from it, anyway. His publishers relented, and in October the book went on sale at $2.50 per copy.[73]

The State That Forgot is a historical sketch of South Carolina from colonial days to the turn of the twentieth century, generously adorned with "local color" and autobiographical anecdotes. But at the heart is Ball's political philosophy; everything else is embellishment. South Car-

70. *Ibid.*
71. Samuel G. Stoney, in interview with author, May 8, 1959.
72. Virgil Steed to W. W. Ball, Jan. 4, 1932, Ball Papers.
73. Besides members of his family, Ball received critical assistance of one sort or another from Herbert Ravenel Sass, Charleston novelist (H. R. Sass to W. W. Ball, Aug. 25, 1932, Ball Papers), and from R. S. Meriwether, Professor of History at the University of South Carolina (W. W. Ball to R. S. Meriwether, March 28, 1932, Meriwether Papers).

olina had surrendered to democracy, he said, and as surrender implies defeat, so she had induced her own decline when rule by the aristocracy gave way to rule by the masses. Ball traced the democratic curse back to Reconstruction:

> My political thesis is that the Federal Government, by means of armed forces, placed South Carolina on the operating table in 1867, that in 1868 the Carpetbaggers made an incision in its body, and, by the constitution they adopted, injected into it the deadly and foreign poison of democracy, which, after causing the loathsome ulcers of Reconstruction, subtly spread through the bloodstream of the white people and killed for ever in it the inherited corpuscles of political and social health.[74]

Ball admitted that the bars had already been somewhat lowered by the Constitution of 1865. By this constitution, devised under the moderate Reconstruction policies of President Johnson and representing the will of native white elements, the parish system of representation in the state legislature was abandoned. Under that system, the older areas of the low country had been organized into districts corresponding to the parishes of the Episcopal Church. The upcountry was subdivided into counties, substantially larger than the low-country parishes. As a result, the General Assembly had been weighted in favor of the more conservative coastal districts. Abolition of the parish system had increased the strength of the smaller landowners of the Piedmont. Also, taxpaying ceased to be one of the bases for representation in the House, and the election of the governor, lieutenant governor, and presidential electors was shifted from the General Assembly to the people.

In other respects, nevertheless, the Constitution of 1865, adhered to the conservative heritage of the state. The judges and most of the state officers were still to be elected by the General Assembly. "The new constitution," said Ball, "was a long step but not a plunge in democracy."[75] The state had not utterly spurned the colonial constitution fashioned along semi-feudal lines by John Locke. "A more 'numerous democracy' had been made but a 'too numerous democracy' had been avoided."[76] South Carolina, however, was forced to scrap that constitution and devise another which would better satisfy the Radicals who had taken control of the federal Reconstruction program. Accordingly, a

74. Ball, *The State That Forgot*, p. 15.
75. *Ibid.*, p. 141.   76. *Ibid.*

convention composed almost entirely of carpetbaggers, scalawags, and Negroes, fashioned the Constitution of 1868. Ball appraised the new constitution with these words:

> The finished product of the convention was a document copied from constitutions of Northern States, especially from the constitution of Ohio. It established universal and practically unrestricted manhood suffrage, limited the term of judges elected by the Legislature so making them subservient to it, made all other officers except county tax collectors, auditors and justices of the peace, elected by the people, . . . authorized a free school system and a two mill tax to support it, prohibited lotteries and duels, . . . and provided for the opening of public educational institutions, high and low, to all persons without regard to race or color. Thus at last the rash of democracy was spread by law backed by bayonets over the body of South Carolina. . . .[77]

The state was to live under that constitution for twenty-seven years. But in 1876 occurred the Red Shirt campaigns whereby the whites regained control of their state government. That would have been a logical time for South Carolina to check her headlong plunge into democracy. But, Ball protested, no retreat took place:

> When the white men took government from the Carpetbaggers, Scalawags, and negroes [sic], they caught democracy with it and . . . [they] have been obscenely delirious from it. Hampton and his Red Shirts in 1876 'redeemed the state from negro [sic] misrule' but not from the 'government by the people' strange to South Carolina until the Carpetbaggers, black and white, brought it from the regions beyond the Potomac and Ohio. . . .[78] The Democrats 'cleaned house' without sweeping out the worst of the debris that Reconstruction left, the constitution of 1868 with its democracy [small *d*]; they accommodated themselves to it, unknowingly they fell in love with it, swallowed it hoof, hide, and hair. Occasional protests were uttered but were scarcely audible—they are still clinging to most of it and like a millstone it is clinging to them.[79]

If it was the Constitution of 1868 that had put the state on the road to political ruin, developments under Benjamin R. Tillman had taken South Carolina to the depths—or so, at any rate, said Ball. The state

77. *Ibid.*, p. 149.   78. *Ibid.*   79. *Ibid.*, p. 170.

convention of 1890 had provided for county primaries to choose delegates to the 1892 Convention. In 1896 the first statewide direct primary for the naming of candidates for United States senators, governors, and other state officers was held. Worse, the state's third post-Civil War constitution had been adopted in 1895. The men who, between 1876 and 1890, had run the government and lifted the "Prostrate State" to her feet, he argued, were members of the Bourbon Democracy who were "men of simple tastes and without exception poor," but who were described as aristocrats and "aristocrats they were in their virtues."[80] Ball summarized his damnation of the events of 1895 with these words:

> The document that came out of the convention locked the gates against the negroes [sic] and entrenched the white Democracy. In essentials it preserved all of the democracy that the Carpetbaggers and negroes [sic] had injected into the state to its undoing in 1868. Neither Reformers nor Conservatives mentioned the wisdom and necessity of returning to the system of government that ended in 1865 under which in the words of William A. Schaper, 'South Carolina, after 1816, became the real political leader and example of the South—Virginia more and more took second place.' Tillmanism brought down the temple of the fathers with a crash, it might have stood some decades longer, it might even have been restored.[81]

Steeped in the romantic vision of ante-bellum South Carolina, Ball called upon the state to readopt aristocratic government, and once again be a leader. That is the book's final plea, but it is drowned in pessimism:

> Why should not South Carolina show the way? A third of a century it was the leader of the South when the South was leading the country. It should lead again. There is small hope of that. Every political sign visible is that in the Republic South Carolina is a dead thing, harmless perhaps except to itself. . . . There is no recovery.[82]

The State That Forgot is written in a style noticeably superior to that Ball employed in his editorials; tales of Laurens County, "Colonel" Ball,

---

80. *Ibid.*, pp. 182–183. Ball did not subscribe to the term "Bourbon Democrat"; he said, "Demagogy invents an epithet and parrots it until ignorance adopts it."
81. *Ibid.*, p. 229.   82. *Ibid.*, p. 289.

and slavery on the Watts plantation, in particular, are charmingly told. The book was, for the most part, well received by reviewers. *The New York Times* said:

> Out of the fullness of the heart the mouth speaketh; a mind active and curious, a robust memory, a humor richly flavored of the soil—and the ready pen of the seasoned journalist has done the rest, rejoicing in freedom from journalistic restriction. . . . He has written about his own State—South Carolina—as no outsider would be permitted to write about it even if he could.[83]

In the Boston *Transcript*: "Few states have been subjected to so keen, so disturbing and yet so affectionate an analysis by one of her own citizens, as has South Carolina in his delightful, whimsical and at times merciless account of her doings. . . ."[84] The *New York World Telegram*'s critic remarked:

> In a confused and jabbering world, in which some want a dictator, others want a division of all private property, others want a low tariff and still others will be completely mollified by the restoration of beer, Ball's book will come as a godsend. With happy cries the political intellectuals will pounce upon it, discovering here a man of the South who cheerfully admits the worst of their accusations.[85]

Most reviewers, though they might discount his interpretation of history, treated *The State That Forgot* as an important book. The Asheville, N. C., *Citizen*, whose editor was Ball's former colleague Robert Lathan, said:

> An absorbingly interesting revelation, the more so because there is scarcely a chapter that is not loaded with the dynamite of controversy. . . . Dr. Ball is a man of wide reading. But nowhere in this record and analysis does he take the slightest account of the fact that the same processes which he describes as having operated so devastingly in the Palmetto State were operating during the same period almost from world's end to world's end. . . . This is one of the things which make the book what it is—a key, as it were, to the almost inevitable effects of walling a people in by forces against which they are helpless. . . . Wholly apart form this phase of Dr.

83. *The New York Times Book Review*, Nov. 27, 1932.
84. Boston *Transcript*, Dec. 2, 1932.
85. *New York World Telegram*, Oct. 11, 1932.

Ball's study, and leaving undebated here his conclusion, . . . this book is notable and valuable for a number of reasons.[86]

One thing was certain—*The State That Forgot* created a stir in South Carolina. State historian D. D. Wallace, who regarded Ball's despised Constitution of 1868 as a good constitution typical of the period, reminded Ball that the democratic movement was worldwide and had come to areas that had never experienced Reconstruction. There had been a strong democratic undercurrent in the state before the Civil War, held in check only by exigencies of outside dangers. Still, he admitted, "everyone" was enjoying the book and eager to discuss it.[87] Francis Butler Simkins, historian of Benjamin Tillman and the Tillman movement, informed Ball:

> The State That Forgot had made a deep impression on me. . . . You are the only South Carolinian except Governor Perry with a public reputation whom I can recall who has since the Civil War taken the trouble to write his memoirs. While I was in Columbia Christmas I heard its merits pro and con debated warmly.[88]

The State Book Store in Columbia took the following advertisement in *The Gamecock*, the student newspaper of the University:

This Season's Holiday Gift
For South Carolinians

THE STATE THAT FORGOT
by William Watts Ball

Henry Bellamann says, "Every good South Carolinian should not only read this book, but should own a copy. It will be long before such an informed intelligence and such an enchanting humanity moulds another comparable work."[89]

Professor Yates Snowden exclaimed in *The State*, "Children cry for it; old maids love it; everybody wants it." But he did not share his

---

86. *Asheville Citizen*, Oct. 26, 1932.

87. D. D. Wallace to W. W. Ball, Dec. 8, 1932, Ball Papers.

88. F. B. Simkins to W. W. Ball, March 19, 1933, Ball Papers. Benjamin F. Perry, a reluctant secessionist, was appointed provisional governor of South Carolina by President Johnson. He served from June until November, 1865. See Lillian A. Kibler, *Benjamin F. Perry, South Carolina Unionist* (Durham, N. C., 1946).

89. *The Gamecock*, Dec. 12, 1932. Novelist Bellamann later became famous as the author of *Kings Row*, published in 1940.

friend's pessimism; South Carolina would again come to the front, though she might never again play a leading role. Ball, he believed, like some theologians, "mistakes the dawn for a conflagration."[90] Other friends regretted that Ball's final chapter was so gloomy,[91] while Fitz McMaster, perhaps his warmest intimate, scolded, "If . . . your book does not make you the most hated man in South Carolina except with the Kosmos Club, . . . I miss my guess. Of course that will disturb you much!"[92]

Perhaps the soundest and most penetrating review of *The State That Forgot* was written by Henry Steele Commager, then Professor of History at New York University. In the New York *Herald-Tribune*, he said:

> [Ball is] at once one of the most distinguished and most intelligent citizens of a state less deficient in such citizens than 'The American Mercury' would have us believe. Mr. Ball is thoroughly unreconstructed . . . , takes his stand in the South of the agrarian tradition . . . , [and] he writes In Memoriam. For he confesses in the last chapter, 'There is no Recovery.' We are not here concerned with the validity of Mr. Ball's argument. As a matter of fact, it is neither clear nor consistent nor convincing, it is not systematically presented nor adequately supported, and it cheerfully ignores uncomfortable facts. It is the manner of the argument rather than the matter that arrests our attention: that manner is delightfully discursive and anecdotal. Mr. Ball has drawn on his own capacious experience and that of his family connections for illuminating stories and picturesque incidents illustrating the society and character of up-country South Carolina. His chapters on the rise of Tillman and the Agrarian Jehad, on the Dispensary System, have the rich flavor of personal experience. He has described by example rather than adjective, analyzed through anecdote rather than through statistics, and he displays his prejudices with a charming geniality.[93]

On the first anniversary of publication, *The State That Forgot* had sold only 1460 copies (all but 102 of those in the first six months), and

90. *The State*, Oct. 13, 1932.
91. D. C. Heyward to W. W. Ball, Oct. 4, 1932; Thomas D. Parker to W. W. Ball, Jan. 8, 1932, Ball Papers.
92. F. H. McMaster to W. W. Ball, Sept. 27, 1932, Ball Papers.
93. *New York Herald-Tribune Books*, Jan. 1, 1933.

Ball had received three hundred and sixty-five dollars in royalties at twenty-five cents a copy. Most South Carolinians were not readers; fewer still had a taste for provocative material. The book's small sale did not appear to disturb Ball; he expected that it would have a limited market especially during depression years. The publication of the book alone had been a great event in his family and he was flattered by much of what had appeared in the reviews. The article in *The New York Times*, he boasted, was all that he could ask, and more. He hoped the book might receive some attention in New York so that liberal and radical publications would give it "the devil."[94] As more praise came to him, he admitted, "I grow exceedingly conceited."[95]

Before *The State That Forgot* had been out a year, he had conceived an idea for a second book. A way out of the depression could be found, he predicted, through redistribution of urban population throughout the countryside. Using the automobile and rural electric power, the unemployed might settle a new frontier, a "vertical" frontier. South Carolina had countless neglected acres to contribute to such a development. It should be possible for a man to live on the land and grow his own vegetables, yet commute to a nearby factory. Ball completed three tentative chapters for "The Vertical Frontier" but abandoned his plans when he failed to receive encouragement from his publishers.[96]

Ball never again attempted writing on a large scale. And *The State That Forgot* is now all but forgotten—except by a few university professors who may recommend it to students as a rousing illustration of the reactionary view or as a classic testament to Southern idiosyncrasy. Actually it has a larger meaning for those who would understand American intellectual life and Southern history.

During the decade of the twenties, the South surpassed New England in textile manufacturing. A growing percentage of owners of Southern mills were absentee Yankees. In 1929 the region's first serious labor revolts occurred, and Communist agitators were discovered among the rioters in Gastonia, North Carolina. There could no longer be any doubt that industrialization threatened to bring permanent change. Some Southerners questioned the wisdom of continuing to heed the advocates of the "New South." If the South proceeded in remaking herself in the image of the North, would she not fall heir to those Northern problems

94. W. W. Ball to Eliza W. Ball, Nov. 28, 1932, Ball Papers.
95. Ball, Diary, IX, 17, Oct. 13, 1932.
96. D. L. Chambers to W. W. Ball, Jan. 5, 1934, Ball Papers.

from which she had fancied herself immune? Chief among the literary expressions of reaction was *I'll Take My Stand*, published in 1930. A defense of agrarianism and individualism, it was the work of twelve Southern writers, most of them associated with Vanderbilt University in Nashville, Tennessee. During the early 1920's, four of their number (John Crowe Ransom, Allen Tate, Robert Penn Warren, Donald Davidson) published *The Fugitive*, a significant magazine of poetry and criticism. Later in the decade, with the nation seemingly committed to materialism and the South in ferment, they began their quest for Southern identity. They found the good life in an agrarian society where ideals meant more than money—in the South before 1880—and they recommended it to a nation which had lost its balance.

The State That Forgot was part of the same worry, the same literary development which produced *I'll Take My Stand*. Ball was one of those Southerners whom W. J. Cash perceptively described as fearing the loss of the aristocratic ideal. They opposed "progress" because it meant the shift of leaders from the fields to the market place where they would be corrupted. Like the Fugitives, Ball found the cherished personal virtues —the code of the upcountryman—secure only in the land. But because his arena was political, he saw the happier life also dependent upon conservative government.

To be sure, Ball and the men of Nashville took a romantic view of the virtues of agrarianism, especially considering the current state of agriculture. And the older South they remembered was never so fine as they pretended. Perhaps they also knew that the forces of "progress" were too strong to resist, but they allowed themselves the luxury of rejection, and in so doing they raised some questions which defied glib answers. Stirred by painful change, Ball offered a strong defense of the aristocratic ideal still revered by many of his fellows. But he soon departed the mainstream of Southern conservatism when he remained rigidly nostalgic amidst the frustration and despair of the Depression.

CHAPTER NINE

BALL VERSUS THE NEW DEAL

At the onset of the Depression, Ball had not been particularly alarmed. After all, South Carolina, as an agricultural state, had learned to live with pestilence. During the 1920's the state had not shared in the apparent national prosperity. Boll weevils and bank failures had hardened her for the events which followed the stock market crash in 1929. Although the value of their real estate and cotton stocks declined somewhat, there is no indication that Ball and his family suffered hardships, even though, in 1932, his salary was cut ten dollars a week.[1] Ball's remedy for the nation's economic distress was strict public and private economy. In *The News and Courier* he called upon the federal government to cut expenses ruthlessly, but his emphasis, predictably, was essentially local. South Carolinians should purchase products manufactured within the state in order to promote local self-sufficiency, he urged in a manner reminiscent of the proposals of Edmund Ruffin during another time of trouble a century earlier.[2] The state government should reduce its operating costs, beginning with the public schools. The legislature could not afford to support a high school system, he argued. Besides, it was nonsense to provide every boy and girl with a secondary education. Always more European than American in his educational philosophy, he now contended that free public education should be confined to the first six or seven grades; the majority of public high schools should be abolished and some technological schools established. The state colleges should be consolidated to save money and stop their jealous competition for students and appropriations. All of these objectives could be better realized, of course, by a less democratic political system.

As W. J. Cash observed, denigrators of "progress" were critical of industry and education because they were the twin wedges splitting

1. Ball, Diary, VIII, 263, June 7, 1932.
2. Ruffin (1794–1865), the foremost agrarian reformer of the Old South and one of the first advocates of secession, advocated soil conservation as necessary for the economic self-sufficiency of South Carolina and the South during the pre-Civil War crisis.

apart the old order. Ball had already found industrialization unacceptable unless accompanied by home ownership and "vegetable garden" agriculture. Now as the staunchest traditionalist in the public life of his state, he turned his attention to the public schools. Although their leveling effect has often been overstated, Ball attacked the schools because he regarded them as social and racial democratizing agents. He launched scores of editorial jibes, many of them oblique. On a single editorial page, for instance, appeared:

The South Carolina School System

Between 1920 and 1930 the number of native white illiterates in S. C. was reduced 2,496.

The number of negro [sic] illiterates was reduced 25,357.

In 1930 the number of white illiterates was 36,143. The number of negro [sic] illiterates was 156,065.

Peculiarities of Greenville

In his charge to the grand jury in Greenville last Monday Circuit Judge G. D. Oxner said that Greenville is "the most populous county in the State and the most criminal."

Greenville's population (census of 1930) is 117,009. The whites number 89,154 and the negroes [sic] 27,855.

Greenville receives from the State school fund more than any other county receives.

In Greenville nine of ten public officers have been tried for crime in the last 10 years and some of them have been convicted.

Greenville is Circuit Judge Oxner's home. He should know his county.

On the Court House Door

For the improvement of government in South Carolina The News and Courier offers the following recipe:

Let the payrolls, with name and amounts paid, in every county and municipality be mimeographed and posted on the court house door once a month.

In every school district let the names with amounts paid to them of every teacher, janitor, bus driver, be mimeographed and posted on the schoolhouse door once a month.

Let the names, with amounts paid to them of all corporation

lawyers be mimeographed and posted on the court house door once a month. Let the terms of all contingent fee contracts between lawyers and clients, with the names of lawyers and clients be posted on the court house door.[3]

Ball's latest campaign caused the president of Clemson College to write him, "Your editorials furnish me with a genuine kick. Even your suggestion to create a Prime Minister in South Carolina is amusing. I take your paper for the sake of the editorials."[4] As Ball grew older (he was now sixty-three), he became even less respectful of the holy institutions of democracy. He seemed to delight in the furor resulting from his reflection on the usefulness of the public schools. To a Northern friend he confided:

> Virtually all the politicians, the school teachers' soviet, and many of the ecclesiastics abhor The News and Courier, but I have a lovely time writing for it and its circulation (never large from your point of view for we live in a thinly peopled land) has steadily grown, is larger now than ever in its history of 130 years "spite the depression."[5]

Ball always said that from the piazza of his summer cottage at Caesar's Head, located in the mountains that fringe the northwestern corner of the state, he could see the steeples of Charleston, see the whole state stripped bare. As he mused in his mountain cottage during the summer of 1932, he was sure that the demoralization of character manifested in numberless ways was profounder, more serious, than the financial depression—and it was more a cause than an effect of the times. He supposed that the cotton mill people were poorer, but the well-to-do still gave parties, and the farmers were being sustained by their gardens and did not suffer much. Through his editorials in *The News and Courier*, Ball insisted repeatedly that there was no acute privation, that the people were pleasure bent, and that they were "too soft" to make temporary sacrifices without complaint. When he spoke strongly against the governor's application for a Reconstruction Finance Corporation loan to help pay the cost of a highway program to relieve unemployment, he was showered with criticism. A Walterboro attorney, who reported that in Colleton County almost complete crop failures promised desper-

3. *The News and Courier*, May 3, 1933.
4. E. W. Sikes to W. W. Ball, Feb. 10, 1932, Ball Papers.
5. W. W. Ball to F. C. Norton, April 10, 1933, Ball Papers.

ate hunger come winter, charged: "If your editorials are taken literally, I fear that you are totally ignorant of the unemployment conditions in the State."[6] Ball, nevertheless, continued to stress that the solution to the depression would be found with the dispersal of the urban proleteriat: the modest expansion of the national government under the Hoover administration to provide relief and employment was not only unnecessary and degrading to the public character but a violation of a state's rights. Fitz McMaster, who "forgave" Ball because he was so fond of him, charged:

> Your theories belong to the age when cotton mill employees were chained to their machines. . . , when 'liberty' was unrestrained. The principle of 'my brother's keeper' was merely a yeast germ beginning to move. But it is marching on. . . .[7] The world has grown much better, and while there are still some that hold with you, their numbers—except in Charleston—are growing smaller. . . . The day will come when you will be regarded as the last of an old school who held to many false principles.[8]

Years later Ralph McGill, editor of the *Atlanta Constitution*, remembered those days in the South:

> Aligned with faculty members from Emory University and Georgia Tech., I traveled much of [Georgia] to spend a day investigating and half a night in argument and in question-and-answer hours. There were sharecroppers and tenants to visit. Their wretched cabins and the pitiful meagerness of their possessions and existence were eloquent evidence of the iniquities of an agricultural social and economic system which had ground to a halt. I recall thinking, with a surge of pity, on seeing them on the roads, sometimes whole families of them ragged, now and then barefooted, I had never before seen despair. There was the rough, sealy skin of pellagra victims, the thin bodies and hot eyes of the chronic malaria sufferers. We got to know U. S. Public Health doctors and technicians who encouraged us to peer through microscopes and learn to identify hookworms. We saw and we talked. . . . Gone, finally, were the myths of white-pillared mansions, and a magnolia-scented civilization. There were days, as we drove along the

6. R. M. Jeffries to W. W. Ball, Sept. 26, 1932, Ball Papers.
7. F. H. McMaster to W. W. Ball, Feb. 13, 1932, Ball Papers.
8. F. H. McMaster to W. W. Ball, July 19, 1928, Ball Papers.

rural roads, when it seemed as if distorting veils had been removed and we could, for the first [time], see the cotton South plain.[9]

There is no doubt that many suffered, but Ball would not allow himself to see them. Rather, in his public statements he deliberately minimized the hunger so evident in the state. Rigid always, Ball held that fundamental values must survive the pressures of transitory problems no matter how serious they might be. To Mayor Grace on the eve of one Independence Day he wrote, "Freedom is dangerous, beset with hazards—men who would have it must take a chance—especially the chance of poverty—at least in the present stage of human progress and for a long time to come."[10]

As the Democratic national convention met in 1932, Ball hoped that the party would adopt a platform and nominate a candidate who would end prohibition and restore government to the states and freedom to the people. He deplored the basis for Southern antagonism to Al Smith, but in that instance, at least, he faced realities; *The News and Courier* did not support Smith for the nomination. *The New York Times*, observing that "the opportunity to fight out the battle of religious liberty this year does not appear to be inviting or to promise success," declared itself to be in full agreement and offered reasons quoted from *The News and Courier*:

> It is not for the Democratic party to sacrifice itself to soothe the sting of Governor SMITH's friends. If we knew how to rebuke the snobs, knaves, hypocrites who circulated lies about SMITH, it would give us the keenest joy to do exactly that. But we see no hope of it. . . . That AL SMITH lives in a country of character and understanding so shrunken that it cannot justly appraise his value is unfortunate. It is a fact.[11]

Ball believed all the leading candidates for the Democratic nomination to be "aristocrats" and therefore disqualified from running for office in South Carolina where the "common man" was one who when in a crowd likes to be told that he is of the common people but who, if you told him so privately, would promptly knock you down. *The News and Courier's* candidate was the anti-prohibition governor of Maryland, Albert C. Ritchie. Franklin Delano Roosevelt, although perfectly accepta-

9. Ralph McGill, *The South and the Southerner* (Boston, 1964), pp. 159–160.
10. W. W. Ball to J. P. Grace, July 3, 1934, Grace Papers.
11. *The New York Times*, Feb. 28, 1932.

ble, was Ball's third choice.[12] In response to an inquiry from James A. Farley as to the sentiment in South Carolina, Ball replied that while feeling could not yet be determined, South Carolina usually jumped on the biggest bandwagon. While *The News and Courier* was whole-heartedly for Ritchie, Ball assured Farley, it had "only the kindliest disposition" toward Roosevelt.[13]

When Franklin Roosevelt became the Democratic nominee, Ball was satisfied. Roosevelt was "wet enough" for him, a clean-minded gentleman, not of "the greatest mental calibre," but with "brains a plenty to be president."[14] He lauded the Democrats editorially for declaring in favor of repeal and predicted that Roosevelt "should pass through a campaign teeming with hope and encouragement."[15] But after the Democratic victory, he admitted privately that he was concerned about what Roosevelt would do: "Perhaps [I] am somewhat reactionary myself, but I think his biggest job should be abolishing things. This country is too big and diverse for Fascism or Socialism. The only thing that will save it is a swing back to minimum government."[16] His apprehension notwithstanding, on New Year's Eve as he closed his diary for the year, he confessed, "More than usual, I say, I have enjoyed 1932, despite the depression and a carbuncle on my neck. . . ."[17]

Charleston was glum in the early weeks of 1933; stores were closing, many people had no money; Ball was not paying his current bills, and for the first time was allowing life insurance policies to lapse. Although Roosevelt's inaugural address contained the threat of assumption of temporary dictatorial powers by the chief executive, Ball applauded the speech. Ordinarily, he would have been indignant and *The News and Courier* would have roared; but Roosevelt had pointed to the congestion of population in industrial centers as an immediate cause of trouble in the United States. Ball was "with the president."[18] Two days later Roosevelt closed the banks; almost immediately Bernard Baruch passed the word to Ball and at least one other prominent South Carolinian that if the banks did not reopen soon, he would put up the capital for a new bank so that the people of the state might carry on their business.[19] Ball

12. *The News and Courier*, May 7, 1932.
13. W. W. Ball to James A. Farley, Jan. 28, 1932, Ball Papers.
14. Ball, Diary, VIII, 93, June 18, 1931.
15. *The News and Courier*, July 3, 1932.
16. W. W. Ball to W. E. Woodward, Dec. 20, 1932, Ball Papers.
17. Ball, Diary, IX, 33, Dec. 31, 1932.   18. *Ibid.*, IX, 46, March 4, 1933.
19. B. M. Baruch to W. W. Ball and Christie Benet, March 8, 1933, Ball Papers. See also Coit, *Mr. Baruch*, p. 401.

replied, expressing his admiration for Baruch's scheme, but doubting that there would be need for it because, in his opinion, most South Carolina banks were sound and would reopen.

When, after a week, the South Carolina National Bank was still closed except for deposits in and withdrawals from new accounts, Ball began an editorial campaign to have the bank fully reopened. The bank's president was Ball's brother-in-law, Julian Mitchell, and Ball was sure that both the bank, one of the state's major institutions, and the judgment of its managers was sound. *The State*, taking up the issue, reprinted Ball's plea that the South Carolina National Bank be fully reopened at once.[20] April came and the bank was still closed; the director of the state tax commission advised Ball that his check in payment of his 1932 income tax could not be accepted because it had been drawn on the South Carolina National Bank which had been closed and whose operations were still restricted. Ball lost all patience, and with an acid retort demanded his check back:

> I want my dear old check—not only is it an antique but the faith in it of my bootlegger is unshaken. If you . . . or any of your inhuman pack, will come to me, stealthily, by night, I shall undertake to demonstrate to you that the respectable bootleggers of this town are not indifferent to a check merely because the battery of a bank has run down and it has to be cranked up. . . . You will find me at 14 WATER Street where I reside in deference to my dry friends.[21]

By early May, it was apparent that the bank would soon reopen; depositors would lose something; it was all a "great shame."[22] But by that time Ball was bewildered as he surveyed the events of the famous Hundred Days. "The revolution proceeds," he noted;

> The abdication of congress, so far, is as nearly complete as it well could be. I knew, everyone knew, that a crisis was present March 4, 1933, but I could not have believed then that one-fifth of the power would be granted to Franklin Roosevelt that has been given him. . . . The federal constitution is in suspension to a great extent, and the president a dictator.[23]

20. J. A. Von Dohlen to W. W. Ball, March 18, 1933, Ball Papers.
21. W. W. Ball to W. R. Bradley, April 7, 1933, Ball Papers.
22. W. W. Ball to Eliza W. Ball, May 4, 1933, Ball Papers.
23. W. W. Ball to J. A. Hoyt, May 13, 1933, Ball Papers.

Ball found a dozen measures of the new administration objectionable (the federal dole, the subsidizing of farmers, the enormous expenditures for public works), but according to one close friend, it was Roosevelt's taking the country off the gold standard that decided Ball's future course.[24] "Did you know," he asked Fitz McMaster, "that a ring of federal officeholders is forming to control the political affairs of this state? Before 1936 federal employees will double or treble. . . ."[25] To Ball it was "goodbye to states rights."[26] Within two months after inauguration day, Ball became the first Southern editor to withdraw his support from Roosevelt. In the summer of 1933 *The News and Courier* declared war on the New Deal.

Ball began his editorial campaign cautiously. His first thrusts were directed against the government's inflationary policies: "Our sorrow is that the universe, which is to say, the gold dollar of 25.8 grains, seems to have exploded on inauguration day."[27] Farm subsidies, though they reward one group at the expense of others, he described in careful, though skeptical terms as an "experiment in social justice."[28] Although fundamentally opposed to government in business, he had no immediate objection to the Tennessee Valley Authority because it would take people out of crowded cities and put them on forty-acre farms in the Tennessee Valley—and near those farms, *little* factories might develop. At the same time he was unenthusiastic about the attempts of the state legislature to obtain federal funds for proposed power development on the Santee and Cooper rivers. The project was designed to "make every day Sunday" in South Carolina, but Ball predicted, that "sweet dream" would not be realized.[29] Ball was convinced that the South would receive scant attention from Washington to her requests. The one-party system had deprived her of political influence; she would continue to be treated as a conquered province and given the scraps from the federal table, and she would remain economically backward. Indeed, he was soon to recommend that South Carolina, in order to dramatize her plight, should withdraw her senators and representatives from Congress![30] But in response to a plea from Mayor Burnet Maybank of Charleston that he support the Santee-Cooper project lest the industrialization of Tennessee

24. T. R. Waring, Jr., in interview with author, May 13, 1959.
25. W. W. Ball to F. H. McMaster, May 13, 1933, Ball Papers.
26. Ball, Diary, IX, 59, May 14, 1933.
27. *The News and Courier*, May 2, 1933.
28. *Ibid.*, May 17, 1933.   29. *Ibid.*, May 2, 1933.
30. Ball, *The Editor and the Republic*, p. 166.

and Alabama destroy the Carolinas, Ball assured the Mayor that he did not intend to oppose public power developments in the state except to say that he was opposed to this sort of government operation in general.[31]

By the summer of 1933 Ball had begun to sharpen his attacks. "The new political economy," he wrote, "is on the verge of taking from the people their last surviving private rights. The solvent minority is called upon to support the insolvent majority."[32] In parts of the state, he informed Secretary of Commerce Daniel Roper and the Bureau of Public Relations of the N.R.A., there was much dissatisfaction with emergency relief. Planters claimed that it was demoralizing labor. In the same report, Ball told the federal authorities that in Darlington and Florence counties, some farmers refused to sign agreements to destroy part of their growing cotton. Later, "night riders" began to pull up acres of their cotton. After the sheriff's office in Florence County had been reinforced by thirty-eight special constables, no further trouble had been reported. Still, Ball admitted, the N.R.A. minimum wage might mean the economic salvation of the South if the North accepted its share of the Negro burden. Southern people, he stressed, would not pay Negroes the same as whites. Finally, Ball warned, "A disturbance of labor conditions is to my mind the one thing that might impair or destroy the solidarity of the white Democratic party in this state. . . . The Administration had better watch its step in the South."[33]

Ball thought that a reduced tariff would help the South (though he did not think reciprocal trade agreements the correct approach) and he admitted that the N.R.A. had helped the textile business in South Carolina particularly by reducing working hours; still, with the New Deal he had "no sympathy." His approach to the Depression was unchanged and, apparently, unchangeable. With the passing of each month, his hostility to the federal policies seemed to intensify. In the autumn he wrote to his friend D. F. Houston, who had had years of experience in national administration:

What government is undertaking to do is preposterous. The trouble with the United States is the decadence of the people, of the national character. The financial and industrial misfortunes of the people have been brought by the people themselves upon themselves. Government is trying to save them from the penalties of

31. W. W. Ball to Burnet R. Maybank, May 6, 1933, Ball Papers.
32. *The News and Courier*, June 18, 1933.
33. W. W. Ball to Charles F. Horner, Sept. 25, 1933, Ball Papers.

their own follies. . . . All classes of people have been guilty alike
of the follies. . . . Franklin Roosevelt is doing what he can, doing
right well, but every thinking person perceives that he is compelled
to deal in double meanings and half truths in his relations with the
people and their representatives.[34]

According to Ball's estimate, out of 1,738,765 South Carolinians, one
and a half million were more prosperous than at any time in his memory
except for 1917–1921. Opportunities were numerous; even the state's
industrial population was so close to the land that it was scarcely hungry
whether the mills ran half-time or less. But government interference had
destroyed initiative; relief had turned large towns into "concentration
camps for beggars."[35]

The suggestion of Ball and other Southerners in the conservative
establishment that salvation lay on the farm exposed their extraordinary
naïveté. Lack of capital after the Civil War had forced sharecropping
and tenancy upon the region to an extent unknown in other American
farmlands. The crop-lien merchant, often in association with the banker,
exacted maximum credit charges for seeds and supplies. In the face of
spiraling financial burdens, the boll-weevil scourge of the twenties
proved a devastating blow to the farmer. The yield of cotton per acre in
the late years of the decade was half the amount produced in 1919.
With the coming of the depression, the farmer needed something more
than the code of the upcountryman upon which to build again. Would
federal measures like the Agricultural Adjustment Act be helpful?
Would there ever be any help?

A year after Roosevelt's inauguration, Ball could see no good coming
from New Deal policies. He was bewildered by a program which was
not socialistic, communistic, or fascistic, but which struck at capitalism
and laissez-faire, and he often proclaimed himself "too old" to comprehend what was taking place. In any case, nothing had been done to
stimulate the economy; the New Deal was a failure. About Franklin D.
Roosevelt, Ball was not so certain. He avoided direct editorial attacks on
the President while he recorded his doubts in his diary. Was Roosevelt
able? He was not sure. There were signs to the contrary. He had charm,
courage, audacity; but Ball added, "He does not captivate me."[36] And
the revolution proceeded.

34. W. W. Ball to D. F. Houston, Oct. 27, 1933, Ball Papers.
35. *Ibid.*
36. Ball, Diary, IX, 153, March 2, 1934.

At least one aspect of the Congressional program, however, received Ball's hearty approval: repeal of the Eighteenth Amendment. He was quick to give editorial support with a revival of his anti-prohibition campaign. At the same time, in a letter to the *Forum*, Ball reviewed the milestones in the South Carolina liquor question; 1904, when an act was passed permitting local option between prohibition and the state dispensary, and two-thirds of the counties voted dry; 1907, when the state dispensary was abolished, and one-third of the counties took advantage of the Carey-Cothran Act which permitted the establishment of county dispensaries; and 1916, when state prohibition was adopted. Ball repeated his familiar charge that, between 1907 and 1916, drinking decreased, and general conditions had been much better then than now.[37]

In June, 1933, Stringfellow Barr, editor of the *Virginia Quarterly Review*, who had "always wanted" an article by Ball in his magazine,[38] asked for a statement on the problem prohibition repeal represented for the South, and although Ball wondered whether there would soon be any states, or any South, or whether they would disappear with the old order, he submitted his views in an essay which he called "The Dry South Dampens." The liquor controversy, he began, was but one of the reflections of the state of affairs in the South. The Civil War had released the forces of democracy in the white masses and created an aristocracy of skin. Since that time, the South had been insignificant; except for the brightness of her military record, she had become a "collection of relatively impoverished geographical divisions, receptive of alms, imitative of and envious of Northern gogetters and their ways."[39] In that atmosphere the liquor traffic had been voted out mostly by working men under ecclesiastical influence. Despite continued domination by the clergy, Southern states would now vote for repeal, not because there was any united Southern opinion on the matter, but because of debt and financial demoralization. There was liquor in circulation on which no tax was paid; legislators would follow any path that might lead out of depression. Besides, the political ecclesiastics had overplayed their role.[40]

Ball used the relationship of the church to the prohibition movement

37. *Forum*, XC (July, 1933), supp., x, xi.
38. Stringfellow Barr to W. W. Ball, Sept. 14, 1933, Ball Papers.
39. W. W. Ball, "The Dry South Dampens," *Virginia Quarterly Review*, IX (Oct., 1933), 527.   40. *Ibid*., p. 536.

as an excuse to hurl another broadside at clergymen in politics (Bishop Cannon had already been hit for his part in the election of 1928). In the "good old days," under the constitution written by John Locke for the proprietors of South Carolina and in four subsequent constitutions between 1776 and 1865, the clergy had not been allowed in politics. The Constitution of 1868, the product of a convention in which ministers, especially Methodists, were influential, had opened the doors. In the popular mind, especially that part of it which was feminine or rural, the conviction that a preacher was a divinely appointed political advisor soon became firmly lodged.[41] In the South (the Deep South, at least) one powerful and pervading political notion was a dread of the admission of Negroes as corruptive factors in elections. Another was fear of Roman Catholics, of whom rural Southerners knew little except from tales handed down. Members of the less educated clergy (and some who should know better) preached it.[42]

Ball hoped that South Carolina would support the repeal of prohibition for reasons other than practical and constitutional. A few months before, a Negro had applied for admission to the University of North Carolina on grounds that it was a state school. While the Negro was refused admission, the state, to avoid controversy, was to pay his expenses to a school outside the South. Ball feared that if the Southern states blocked repeal of the Eighteenth Amendment, Northern states might retaliate by pressing for enforcement of the Fourteenth and Fifteenth amendments. Southern people were, in his words, "playing with fire."[43]

Ball expected South Carolina to approve repeal, but when in November she legalized the sale of beer and wine while leaving stronger liquor forbidden, he responded with a petulant editorial:

As the News and Courier was the only prominent newspaper in South Carolina that carried on a long, energetic, and incessant campaign for repeal in South Carolina, it is the only prominent newspaper that may be said to have suffered a severe defeat in rejection of policy last Tuesday. How South Carolina voted last Tuesday was a matter of no significance or importance outside the State.[44]

41. *Ibid.*, pp. 529–531.   42. *Ibid.*, p. 536.
43. W. W. Ball to John A. McPherson, June 21, 1933, Ball Papers.
44. *The News and Courier*, Nov. 9, 1933.

To a Northern friend who gibed, "How come you let South Carolina vote dry?" he replied:

> Had South Carolina not gone wrong on the Eighteenth amendment, it would have been a severe blow to what I have been saying, about the general cussedness of its political condition. The state easily could have carried for repeal if the leaders in charge of the wet campaign had known how to lead and had been men commanding confidence. Charleston voted wet 22 to 1.[45]

The next year in a referendum the voters finally rejected prohibition, and in 1935 a state law authorized the sale of liquor in package stores only.

The liquor referendum coincided with the Democratic primary election of 1934, and although Ball was preoccupied with the course of the New Deal, he did not shun local politics. In the spring he was shocked to hear that certain mill owners would support Blease for governor against his principal opponent, Olin C. Johnston of Spartanburg. They would back Blease because he had favored local unions only, because they thought he could be "controlled." Johnston was identified with the interests of organized labor and regarded by some alarmists as "almost a communist."[46] Apparently Ball had no knowledge of the efforts of similar men a generation earlier to prevent the re-election of Governor Manning, else he could not now have been so astonished. In any event, his thorough disbelief is difficult to explain, for he always conceded that Tillman had enjoyed some support from the planter class. At first Ball could not believe the rumors were true; the mill executives were men he regarded as belonging to his own "class," sons of men who would not have voted for a demagogue like Blease under any circumstances. If it were all true, he hoped he would have the courage to brand them publicly as no better in mind and character than their "hands";[47] if the stories were well founded, the degredation was now complete. To Ball, here was final proof that taste and judgment—the aristocratic ideal—could not survive in the greedy environment of the New South.

Ball's determination that, once again, Blease would be denied public office was strengthened by a conversation he had that summer with Senator Byrnes, who "spoke strongly" of Blease as a senator, condemn-

45. W. W. Ball to D. L. Chambers, Nov. 10, 1933, Ball Papers.
46. Ball, Diary, IX, 196, July 29, 1934.
47. *Ibid.*

ing his servility to Senator George H. Moses, Republican of New Hampshire.[48] Ball had been so closely identified with anti-Blease feeling, however, that it seemed to him a campaign originating elsewhere would be stronger than one begun by *The News and Courier*. After he saw in the Greenville *News* an editorial describing the sort of governor the state needed, he wrote to the editors of the Greenville papers with a proposition. He offered them the prestige of leadership if they would declare for Wyndham Manning or another acceptable candidate.[49] Byrnes expressed approval of Ball's plan and disappointment when it failed to produce results.[50] Just before the first primary, *The News and Courier*, acting independently, declared that while there were other "respectable" candidates, Manning had been the only one to show the strength that would insure victory over demagoguery and disorder.[51] Manning was the son of the former governor whose life Ball had recently sketched for the *Dictionary of American Biography*. Ball believed that Wyndham, like Richard I. Manning, would treat all interests fairly, and that he was the best of the eight men in the race. Ball's endorsement of Manning was followed the next day by a reprint in *The News and Courier* of Blease's pardon record, and the next day Ball cautioned:

> There are many convicts now in the penitentiary having influential connections outside. The people who do not wish the convict influence to have weight in South Carolina had better vote against candidates who are acceptable to it. Mr. Blease has not in his campaign said that he would not repeat his pardon record of 1911–1915.[52]

But when the first primary vote eliminated Manning, Ball announced that *The News and Courier* had no candidate, that neither Johnston nor Blease was acceptable to it.[53]

Ball's determination to remain neutral wilted, however, as he became convinced that cotton-mill interests were actively supporting Blease. In the two weeks between the primaries, *The News and Courier* emerged as a supporter of Olin Johnston. Johnston's appeal for votes in class-conscious South Carolina seemed to be based primarily on his having

48. *Ibid.*, IX, 203, Aug. 18, 1934.
49. W. W. Ball to "the editors of the Greenville papers," Aug. 20, 1934, Ball Papers.
50. James F. Byrnes to W. W. Ball, Aug. 26, 1934, Ball Papers.
51. *The News and Courier*, Aug. 26, 1934.
52. *Ibid.*, Aug. 28, 1934.   53. *Ibid.*, Aug. 30, 1934.

worked in his youth as a cotton-mill operative. Ball regarded Johnston merely as the less dangerous of the two demagogues, but his chagrin at the defection of the textile conservatives spurred him to another tireless tirade against Cole Blease. The spectacle presented by the cotton-mill aristocracy in open support of Blease was a political phenomenon of the first order in South Carolina; rumors spread outside the state, and interest was aroused at least as far north as Baltimore, where the editor of the *Evening Sun* asked Ball to confirm or deny.[54]

In *The News and Courier*, Ball hammered at the injustice of smear tactics which had suggested that Johnston was a "red." Johnston, Ball stressed, was no more an enemy of property than the editor himself. Ball gave publicity to Johnston's pledge that there would be no abuse of the pardoning power during his administration. Then Ball asked, "Who of these two candidates would be the favorite of the criminals?"[55] But Ball saved his greatest scorn for that aspect of the Blease campaign which he considered fundamentally dishonest. The poor and weak had finally rejected Blease, he claimed, after three decades of empty promises. Though Ball admitted to being a "Tory," he expressed strong sympathy for the working class. Though he opposed the closed shop, he accepted as necessary the national organization of labor; and to restrict the trades union movement to local unions, as Blease had suggested, was to "tear its heart out."[56] Now, the depressed were deserting Blease, but he had found a new champion: "The strong and rich hug him to their boosums [*sic*]."[57]

Down to the eve of the decisive primary, *The News and Courier* struck continuously at the unholy alliance between Blease and a considerable element of the moneyed interests, particularly in the textile complex in the Greenville-Spartanburg area of the state. But when Johnston was the victor, Ball felt no elation. He pretended a longing for the return of Ben Tillman. Though he had opposed Tillman as a demagogue who cultivated class strife, Tillman had been a strong leader, a brilliant speaker, and a clever politician. Ball would now gladly welcome the wielder of the pitchfork into the current vacuum.[58] The Johnston-Blease gubernatorial contest of 1934 was in one respect the most unpleasant for Ball in his long public career, because he had to

54. Hamilton Owens to W. W. Ball, Aug. 31, 1934, Ball Papers.
55. *The News and Courier*, Sept. 4, 1934.
56. *Ibid.*, Sept. 10, 1934.   57. *Ibid.*, Sept. 5, 1934.
58. Ball, Diary, IX, 207, Sept. 9, 1934.

oppose hitherto anti-Bleasites like Christie Benet and Foster McKissick, men who had been his lifelong friends. But there were gratifications, too. On the last night of the campaign Blease took time to denounce Ball specifically;[59] as always, the editor was amused and warmed by his attack. A letter came from Olin Johnston thanking Ball for his support and for his dynamic editorials, which Johnston credited with bringing many "thinking people" to his support.[60] Some observers credited him with Johnston's nomination, and while he acknowledged that Senator Byrnes had also played an important part, he seemed particularly pleased to be able to report to his son-in-law that on the night of the election Byrnes had telephoned him long distance and attributed the results in the main to efforts of *The News and Courier*.[61]

Ball's involvement with local politics was transient, however; the anti-New Deal crusade soon recaptured the columns of *The News and Courier*. The *Charleston Evening Post* was the only other major paper in the state attacking the Roosevelt administration's policies, and under T. R. Waring's subtler direction, *Post* editorials lacked the bombast that characterized the comments of *The News and Courier*. Consequently, it was Ball who began to attract attention outside the state. He was proud that while he had been editor of *The State*, New York papers had telegraphed asking *The State*'s opinion on important matters, and that now they wired *The News and Courier*.[62] The Hartford *Courant*, the Boston *Herald*, and New York *Herald-Tribune* were reprinting parts of his editorials. He relished comments that his editorials were "red hot," and he smiled at the rise in the circulation figures of *The News and Courier*. His principal point of attack was the inconsistency of New Deal philosophy: "I can see the logic of Communism or Socialism, the logic of a dictatorship. . . . I can see none in a system that recognizes private profits and at the same time bludgeons the successful."[63] Ball lamented also the passing of the old federal republic as it was being replaced by a centralist system *ruled* from Washington by a greatly expanded bureaucracy. On New Year's Day in 1935 *The News and Courier* declared the "Great News Story of 1934" had been "the immense progress in the destruction of the states."

59. R. B. Herbert to W. W. Ball, Sept. 13, 1934, Ball Papers.
60. Olin D. Johnston to W. W. Ball, Oct. 3, 1934, Ball Papers.
61. W. W. Ball to Clements Ripley, Sept. 14, 1934, Ball Papers.
62. W. W. Ball to Alfred Huger, Jan. 13, 1934, Ball Papers.
63. W. W. Ball to Professor F. W. Bradley of the University of South Carolina, Sept. 6, 1935, Ball Papers.

Speaking before the South Carolina Conference on Public Affairs in Columbia, Ball called the New Deal a "frantic effort in this country to put a roof over it and regulate its inhabitants as a household."[64] The United States, he stressed, was too big, too diverse for centralism except through military rule; force had failed in the South during Reconstruction as it would always fail there. Yet the government was swelling, entering into production and taxing the people to maintain itself as a corporation. "Washington is a devil fish," he warned, "with tentacles stretching to every one of you and taking your money."[65] The United States soon would bear no more resemblance to the republic of 1929 than it would to Soviet Russia. Ball admitted that he might be an "ingrained and ingrowing reactionary with a mind shut to the new light."[66] The big change might be necessary, it might even be good (he did not think so); but, Ball urged his listeners, call it by its name: Revolution! Fitz McMaster observed that, while Ball had given a discerning address, it had been founded on utterly false doctrine: "Why should any one hesitate to call the present process REVOLUTION. The only fear that I have is that it will not go far enough to succeed."[67] In February, 1935, Ball opened an editorial campaign to have delegates to the next Democratic national nominating convention chosen by popular election rather than by party convention in the hope South Carolina's allegiance to Franklin Roosevelt could be broken.

But without doubt, as Roosevelt entered the second half of his first term, Ball was a lonely voice in loyally Democratic South Carolina. As Ball's editorials began to attract nationwide attention, they brought him both criticism and praise. The New Orleans *States* voiced objections typical of the loyal press when it condemned him for taking a narrow view of the President's spending program.[68] Support came from a variety of sources: from crackpots who regarded the administration as dominated by radicals—socialists and communists—and were therefore cheered by Ball's attacks; from states rights traditionalists like Donald Davidson, who had more hope now than he had five years before when *I'll Take My Stand*, to which he had contributed, was "generally taken as nothing more than a quixotic gesture";[69] from conservatives like Senator Harry Flood Byrd of Virginia, who was so impressed with

64. Ball, *The Editor and the Republic*, p. 178.
65. *Ibid.*, p. 182.   66. *Ibid.*
67. F. H. McMaster to W. W. Ball, Aug. 14, 1935, Ball Papers.
68. Webber D. Mott to New Orleans *States*, Feb. 18, 1935, Ball Papers.
69. Donald Davidson to W. W. Ball, May 10, 1935, Ball Papers.

Ball's editorials that he quoted from one in a speech in New York and from another on the floor of the Senate;[70] and from rich Northerners like Edward F. Hutton.

Hutton, a broker whose objections to New Deal fiscal policies inspired him to become a financial columnist for the New York *Herald-Tribune*, was the husband of Marjorie Post and Chairman of the Board of the General Foods Corporation. After Hutton saw *The News and Courier* during a stay at his plantation near Green Pond, South Carolina, he became one of Ball's friends and enthusiastic supporters. He sent one of Ball's editorials, "Declaring the New Republic," to Paul Block, president and publisher of a chain of seven newspapers that included the Pittsburgh *Post-Gazette*, Toledo *Blade*, and Milwaukee *Sentinel*. Block thought the editorial "very marvelous and courageous" and showed his appreciation by running it in all his papers.[71] Ball could not help being flattered by growing national attention, and he did not underestimate the influence of the wealthy admirers who enjoyed "old Ball's rantings."[72] At the same time, he assured his sister, with whom he was always frank, "I see a lot of the rich, and I suppose some of them think they own me. They don't."[73]

Ball's rejection of any and all who supported the New Deal caused him somewhat reluctantly, to oppose Senator James F. Byrnes. Many years later, Byrnes, after concluding his public career by serving as governor of South Carolina, could not recall "having written Dr. Ball any letters of importance."[74] But the truth is though they seldom saw each other—the two men enjoyed a rather close relationship during the time Byrnes was a rising politician in the state. Byrnes made no secret of his respect for Ball as a person and as a political editor.[75] Midway in his first term in the Senate, he wrote Ball:

> Without your wonderful assistance, I could not have been nominated. About the only hope that a man in public life can have is to render such service that he will not disappoint those who had sufficient confidence in him to contribute to his election. If I have not disappointed you, I am happy.[76]

70. Harry F. Byrd to W. W. Ball, April 6, 1935, Ball Papers.
71. Paul Block to E. F. Hutton, Feb. 13, 1935, Ball Papers.
72. W. W. Ball to Sara Ball Copeland, Feb. 20, 1935, Ball Papers.
73. *Ibid.*
74. James F. Byrnes to author, June 3, 1959.
75. James A. Hoyt to W. W. Ball, Sept. 22, 1934, Ball Papers.
76. J. F. Byrnes to W. W. Ball, June 21, 1933, Ball Papers.

What did Ball think of Byrnes? He "liked him greatly."[77] Furthermore, he doubted whether the people of the state recognized that Byrnes was the most influential South Carolinian since John C. Calhoun.[78] Ball did not suggest that Byrnes had the status of the South's hallowed ante-bellum spokesman, but he regarded him as an able man who played the game of politics well.

Although Ball took the major credit for putting Byrnes in the Senate, the editor was shy about asking for favors in return. But once, although he did not directly ask Byrnes to use his influence, he did bring to the Senator's attention the names of several men who had co-operated with *The News and Courier* and who were in line for promotion in the railway mail service.[79] When William Ball, Jr., was looking for a job and inquired whether he should write to Byrnes, Ball reminded him that he was over twenty-one and need not consult his father.[80] Ball informed Byrnes he had heard indirectly that William had written to him "something about work"; it was not his enterprise, he stated, and had been undertaken without his knowledge.[81] Some months later the younger Ball received employment in the office of the Collector of Internal Revenue. Ball conceded that Byrnes had been responsible but assured a friend, "If my influence had weight I cannot help it—I certainly did not exert it. . . . I am very friendly with Byrnes."[82]

Ball remained editorially friendly towards Byrnes until it appeared that the Senator was becoming one of Roosevelt's trusted lieutenants. As late as June, 1935, he noted with satisfaction Byrnes's declaration for a Constitutional amendment if Roosevelt thought it necessary to continue the N.R.A. and the rest of New Deal.[83] But by the autumn a change in Ball's attitude was evident. In an editorial supporting his hopeless campaign to have delegates to the next Democratic national convention elected by primary vote, Ball asked, "What course will the boss take? Shall the people be denied this primary in order that Roosevelt may be spared the risk of defeat and Byrnes given the prestige of a Roosevelt victory in the convention to help him in the primary?"[84] Ball's somewhat

77. Ball, Diary, IX, 215, Oct. 28, 1934.
78. W. W. Ball to James A. Hoyt, Sept. 24, 1934, Ball Papers.
79. W. W. Ball to J. F. Byrnes, Oct. 6, 1933, Ball Papers.
80. W. W. Ball to D. C. Heyward, Nov. 11, 1933, Ball Papers.
81. W. W. Ball to J. F. Byrnes, June 25, 1933, Ball Papers.
82. W. W. Ball to D. C. Heyward, Nov. 11, 1933, Ball Papers.
83. W. W. Ball to E. F. Hutton, June 13, 1935, Ball Papers.
84. *The News and Courier*, Sept. 29, 1935.

derogatory allusion to Byrnes as the political boss of South Carolina gave warning that, as far as Ball was concerned, his public romance with Senator Byrnes was over. He accurately predicted that if Roosevelt remained in power, Byrnes would resign before the end of his second Senate term to accept a post that would take him outside the state.[85] He had no objection to Byrnes as a person—he liked him—and he did not enjoy criticizing his course. But, to Ball, he was a taker of dictation, "another man's man";[86] he opposed "his Rooseveltianism which if not stopped, will ruin the country."[87]

The perpetually amiable Byrnes took calmly the objection of *The News and Courier*, but while he was campaigning for re-election to the Senate in 1936, he seemed to refer to people like Ball when he declared, "You are either for the Democratic party or you are against it. Everyone who calls himself a Democrat should bow to the will of the party or get out of the party."[88] Ball's retort disclaimed the obligation of Southern Democrats to vote the party line in national contests because, he claimed, the national Democratic party was now like the Republican party, a Negro party.[89] It had become clear at last—though Ball was a Southerner and Democrat, he was first and last an upcountryman.

As the time for presidential elections approached, it was obvious that Ball, although he did not abandon his previous grounds for protest, was concentrating his opposition to the New Deal on the racial policies of the Roosevelt administration. He was apprehensive of the attempts of the national Democratic party to court the Negro vote; he feared they would result in a federal attempt to enforce the Fifteenth Amendment to insure the ballot for Southern Negroes. He was particularly irked by the public statements of Eleanor Roosevelt, whose activities, in his view, did more harm than good. He described Mrs. Roosevelt as "one of those Northern women conscious of a 'mission' to befriend the American Negro."[90] Ball waged a lifelong campaign against lynching, but he did not sanction a national anti-lynching law (or the proposed child labor amendment to the Constitution) because "all federal interference with our affairs tends to complicate the race question."[91] Ball favored a Southern white man's party cut loose from the national Democrats and the national Republi-

---

85. Ball, Diary, X, 95, Sept. 13, 1936. Byrnes, re-elected to the Senate in 1936, resigned his office in 1941 to accept an appointment as Associate Justice of the United States Supreme Court.   86. *Ibid.*
87. W. W. Ball to Eliza Ball, June 8, 1936, Ball Papers.
88. *The News and Courier*, July 25, 1936.
89. *Ibid.*   90. Ball, Diary, X, 1, Sept. 16, 1935.
91. W. W. Ball to George L. Buist, Sept. 3, 1934, Ball Papers.

cans. It was entirely possible, he predicted in *The News and Courier*, that South Carolina would soon have such a party.[92]

Ball simply could not forgive Southern New Dealers for supporting an administration which fostered political equality of the races; political gains for the Negro would be a prelude to equality in industry and the acceleration of social mixing. He charged them in his diary, to be read by some future historian:

> If then time shall prove that Senators Robinson, Byrnes, Bankhead, Russell and the rest are wrong, if the troubles to the South that I have forecast shall come, they will have been guilty of betrayal of their people from motives low and contemptible. Not one among them has even tried to defend the principles underlying the New Deal.[93]

Ball could barely comprehend the manner in which South Carolinians had repudiated the code of their grandparents. On the subject of Charleston's mayor, he lamented, "Burnet R. Maybank, mayor—efficient mayor and business man and politically ambitious—is wholly committed to Roosevelt, Byrnes, The New Deal, and he is the great grandson of R. Barnwell Rhett. . . ."[94] Southerners, Ball suggested, might give Republican Senator William E. Borah his due; Borah had voted against the Wagner-Costigan anti-lynch bill and proved that, of all Northern men in public life, he was the best friend of the South in the matters that vitally affected the South.[95]

Meanwhile Ball had decided that Roosevelt was a "common demagogue,"[96] and his attacks on the President's programs became more outspoken. Sometimes a half dozen anti-New Deal editorials appeared in a single issue of *The News and Courier*. Roosevelt was aware of the perpetual fire burning in Charleston. He and Ball had not met in October, 1935, when the editor was among the crowd that heard Roosevelt speak on the grounds of The Citadel. But in January, 1936, Mr. and Mrs. Ball received a formal invitation to dine at the White House with President and Mrs. Roosevelt on February 11. The Balls declined; moreover, they made no effort to publicize the "honor" that had come to them. But later, when Fitz McMaster learned of the refusal, Ball had to explain his reasons. Fay Ball went nowhere, and certainly could not have

92. *The News and Courier*, Feb. 3, 1936.
93. Ball, Diary, X, 131, Dec. 19, 1936.
94. *Ibid.*, X, 123, Nov. 23, 1936.   95. *The News and Courier*, Feb. 3, 1936.
96. Ball, Diary, X, 89, Aug. 29, 1936.

been induced to have dinner with strangers in Washington. Ball had a cold; the trip would have been long and expensive. Finally, he admitted, had he gone to the dinner people in South Carolina would say, ". . . Ball ate the president's salt and then criticized him."[97]

At the same time Ball was invited to the White House, his daughter Eleanor was offered a government job—as a writer for the American Guide Book Series of the Federal Writers Project, W.P.A. Was this a way of taming him, Ball wondered? Upon his advice, Eleanor refused the position. It would have been humiliating for him to have a daughter employed by an agency of the Roosevelt government. His opposition to the New Deal had become an obsession.

Summer came, and the Democrats met to renominate Roosevelt. The invocation was given by a Negro Baptist minister, and later "Cotton Ed" Smith led the South Carolina delegation out of the convention in protest against the increasing attention paid the Negro vote. Ball's choice had been Senator Harry F. Byrd; Ball maintained that Byrd and Carter Glass were the two Southern men in public life who were thinkers, gentlemen, and Democrats.[98] He could see little chance of a return to the old republic under either Roosevelt or Alfred M. Landon. For forty-five years, he announced, he had been an independent; except in the free silver agitation, it had been agreeable to him to act with the Democrats; this year he would not vote.[99] On the night of the primary when Byrnes was overwhelmingly renominated, for the first time on an election night since 1890 (except when he had been out of the state), Ball did not go to the newspaper office. Only the size of Roosevelt's victory surprised him; the secret of his success, Ball ventured, was that he had been a humanitarian with the public money. He conceded that the policy of *The News and Courier* had been soundly repudiated; the voters had issued Roosevelt a "blank check."[100] Ball had his tall drink at night, read Dickens, and waited for the republic to go to hell.

97. W. W. Ball to F. H. McMaster, April 29, 1938, Ball Papers. Although Roosevelt and Ball were never to meet, Ball met and talked casually with two of the President's closest advisers: Dr. Rexford G. Tugwell, introduced to him by James F. Byrnes (Ball, Diary, IX, 203, Aug. 18, 1934); and Harry Hopkins, brought to his office by Burnet R. Maybank (Ball, Diary, IX, 225, Nov. 30, 1934).

98. W. W. Ball to Sara Ball Copeland, March 15, 1935, Ball Papers.

99. W. W. Ball to Dr. Henry N. Snyder, President of Wofford College, June 28, 1939, Ball Papers.

100. *The News and Courier*, Nov. 5, 1936.

CHAPTER TEN

CRUSADES CONTINUED

THE EDITOR grew old and his world changed. Fitz McMaster reported the large majority of the Kosmos Club heartily in favor of the New Deal. Word came from Laurens that mills were not using a single bale of cotton, their whole output being made from rayon.[1] For some years Ball often had not felt well, but his illness had been more annoying than serious; now he submitted to a prostate operation. In 1934 his daughter Fay had married; three years later the last of his single daughters wed a Britisher and went to live in England. Eleanor Ball was closer to her father than his other children, but the loss of her must have been softened by the Anglo-American alliance her marriage represented. Katharine Ball Ripley had gone to California, where her husband Clements wrote "Jezebel" for Bette Davis and scripts of other successful movies. In 1935 Ball's close friend and fellow-editor, Thomas R. Waring died; and the next year, his mother. Ever since Ball had left home they had remained close through frequent correspondence and Ball's occasional visits to Laurens. Now Katharine wrote her father, "I know it is very hard for you—that you will miss dreadfully her letters—the practical, far-seeing advice, the salty humor, and the scoldings—and I feel very sorry for you."[2]

Most significant of all, Ball's political world was disappearing. Fading now was the mainstay of his career—the threat of Blease. With the advance of education and urbanization the heyday of demagoguery passed, and new political types emerged. Ball was not prepared to cope with the complexity of the new leaders: Olin Johnston, who had some of the characteristics of the old-fashioned demagogue, but who had programs too; Burnet Maybank, who like others of Ball's own class became a conservative New Dealer; James F. Byrnes, who enjoyed a political career reminiscent of the versatile statesmen of the ante-bellum South. Later U. S. Supreme Court Justice and Secretary of State, Byrnes exhibited along the way the prevailing characteristic that Ball could not

1. A. F. McKissick to W. W. Ball, Jan. 28, 1935, Ball Papers.
2. Katharine Ball Ripley to W. W. Ball, n. d., Ball Papers.

abide: flexibility. But the fixed attitudes of the upcountryman were discredited during the Depression; to most, experimentation rather than individualism was the hope of the day. When Ball retained his ancient commitment, he entered the romantic fringe of American conservatism. At the same time, however, his feelings were typical of those harbored by the dispossessed, those whose natural security had been weakened by the introduction of "social security," those who grew to hate the man who lived at "Hyde the Loot" Park. And so Ball continued his old crusades with undiminished vigor, though his ideas were out of style, even in South Carolina.

Ball's rejection of everything associated with the New Deal soon caused a break with his alma mater. In 1938 Ball extended his long-sustained campaign against the "low level" of state government to include the state university. For some time he had believed that no officer or professor in a state college could have taken issue with any policy of the state or federal government without placing his position in jeopardy, although he offered no proof that actual coercion had taken place. Even while he had been Dean of Journalism, he had not felt completely free, although he mentioned no specific instances when he had been subject to "pressure." But when South Carolina awarded an honorary degree to Harry Hopkins, Director of the W.P.A., after the university had been promised a large grant of federal funds, Ball could not contain himself. Soon afterward, in answer to Fitz McMaster's suggestion that he add his diary to the University's manuscript collection, he snapped, "It's the last hole in which I would bury it. . . . Is it not a crawling, cringing, fawning thing at the feet of Harry Hopkins? Your suggestion astonishes me."[3] Ball assured his friend that if he had something to give to a neighboring school it would go to some place like Duke, "which has an endowment from 'economic royalists,' and is reasonably free."[4] Ball's editorials expressed his disgust with state-supported institutions and although they won him some applause from presidents of denominational schools, they substantiated the charges of others that his chronic attacks upon the state were doing irreparable damage to her reputation. In any case, when Ball announced his permanent defection, Carolina lost a man who for years had been one of her staunchest alumni.

But some things in Ball's life remained constant. He loved to tell the story that he had read in *The New Yorker* about the Northern woman,

3. W. W. Ball to F. H. McMaster, June 18, 1938, Ball Papers.
4. *Ibid.*

spending the winter in Charleston, who said to her neighbor, a native of the city, "I'm finished with the Sunday *New York Times*; would you like to look it over?" "No thank you," was the reply; "I don't know anyone in New York." Ball thought the story truly Charlestonian. Charleston did not change, or at least, not very much; and Ball continued to travel in society. In one two-week period he attended twelve parties (though he was nearly seventy) and met Ida Tarbell, who had been one of the Muckrakers, and actor George Arliss. He was the luncheon guest of Mr. and Mrs. Henry Luce at their house on the Cooper River.[5] There were the weeks every summer at Caesar's Head, where he could sit on the piazza of "Ball's Perch" and through his opera glasses watch the lights come on in Greenville, and where almost every night after he had finished working or writing in his diary, Ball played piquet with Mrs. Ball or with a daughter if she happened to be visiting.

In 1929 Eleanor Ball had learned to play piquet[6] on a visit to England. When she returned, she mentioned the game to her father, who remembered having played it with Charles Otto Witte many years before. Soon afterward Ball took up piquet again, and in his later life, he developed a "veritable passion" for the game.[7] Scores were continued, night after night, and duly recorded by Ball in his diary. From all accounts he was an incredibly bad card player, but although he seldom won he did not tire of the game. Now and then Ball would insert in the diary next to the nightly score a comment suggesting that, although he and Fay Ball played with equal skill, she had uncommon luck.

Another regular diversion for Ball was the trip to Hobcaw Barony for Bernard Baruch's traditional New Year's Day luncheon. Although Baruch had opposed deficit financing and tinkering with the currency, he was fond of the President and did not share Ball's total disillusion with the Roosevelt administration. Ball, nevertheless, considered Baruch to be his "best backer among the fiercely rich."[8] Each year Ball visited with the delegation of rich Northerners who came to spend the winter on their South Carolina plantations, and they helped spread his reputation when they went home in the spring. Under these circumstances *The News and*

---

5. Ball, Diary, X, 278–280.
6. Piquet is a card game regarded by many as among the best for two players. Popular during the Regency period in England, it still enjoys some popularity among the upper classes there. It is played much more in France, where it is a game of the people.
7. Eleanor Ball Hewitt-Myring to author, July 30, 1959.
8. W. W. Ball to Sara Ball Copeland, Oct. 5, 1939, Ball Papers.

Courier developed an enviable out-of-state mailing list. The owner of the famous Westover Plantation in Virginia suggested to U. S. Representative Hamilton Fish that he subscribe to the Charleston paper which spoke for a Jeffersonian party not looking for subsidies for farmers, and added, "Ball is the most brilliant editorial writer I have ever read. He represents the agrarian and Southern point of view in the best sense. . . ."[9]

Ball admitted with good-natured amusement to being the darling of the rich; he felt sorry for the persecuted rich as well as the persecuted Jews and Chinese.[10] He was equally aware that his almost daily preachments were making him increasingly unpopular in South Carolina. When, in 1937, he was awarded the honorary degree of Doctor of Letters by tiny Oglethorpe University of Atlanta, he commented that he should not have been introduced as standing gallantly for the traditions of the Old South, but as "the archaic editor of a fossilized newspaper in an antique town."[11] Protest mail, sometimes unsigned, came to Ball questioning his qualifications as a critic of contemporary trends. One such letter, observing that Ball enjoyed the luxury of a four thousand dollar summer cottage, charged:

> You are always telling the public to dig and plow and plant, to raise hogs and chickens and work hard and earn bread by honest sweat, and that no one who will toil like that need ever want. How would you like to do it? You must think everyone knows *how* to farm successfully.[12]

Ball responded to criticism of this sort by restating his position in stronger terms. One such editorial was astonishing, even for him:

If We Had Mussolini

Were Benito Mussolini dictator of South Carolina the South Carolinians would be compelled to raise all the wheat, oats, corn, cattle, sheep, hogs, wood, tobacco, butter, milk, cheese, chicken, turkey and other poultry, vegetables, fruits, currants, grapes, raisins, olives, wine, whiskey, brandy and beer that they consume. Just as he has reclaimed the Pontine marshes and compelled the

9. Richard Crane to the Hon. Hamilton Fish, Feb. 11, 1937, Ball Papers.
10. W. W. Ball to Sara Ball Copeland, Jan. 20, 1939, Ball Papers.
11. W. W. Ball to Sara Ball Copeland, June 3, 1937, Ball Papers.
12. "Reader" to W. W. Ball, July 27, 1937, Ball Papers.

Italians to raise wheat, he would reclaim the abandoned rice fields of South Carolina and the exports of "Carolina rice" would be as valuable as they were eighty years ago. He would probably have the South Carolinians producing indigo and possibly raising silk worms and silk. There is nothing in Italy that soil and climate do not make producible in South Carolina. If we had a Mussolini we would crow for day and produce them, importing only a few trifles like coffee and tea from foreign ports.[13]

From avowed New Dealer Fitz McMaster, critical but ever understanding, Ball received a most pertinent reminder.

Now I tell you, you do nothing but write about Roosevelt—that is the impression you give, and while I know you care nothing for adverse or favorable criticism, I am warranted in saying that one or two of your dear friends in Charleston, who think along the same lines as you do, and with whom I disagree, think you harp too much about the New Deal. You will have to diversify.[14]

Slowly, however, events were taking shape that were to make Ball less an outcast in his own state. In the spring of 1937 he was puzzled by the conduct of Senator Byrnes. He could not believe that stories of a rift between Byrnes and Roosevelt were true; yet, the Senator, in "almost open rebellion,"[15] had voted with Harry Byrd and others against an extension of the Tennessee Valley Authority. Ball was informed there was talk in Columbia that Byrnes had turned against Roosevelt, saying that the President's word could not be trusted.[16] A story dispatched to him privately by one of the news bureaus in New York (McClure's Newspaper Syndicate) listed Byrnes among those senators now opposed to the President.[17] "Reliable informants" told him that Byrnes and others had come to believe what Ball had been insisting: that an alliance of Northern New Dealers, Tammany Hall, and Negro leaders meant to control the Democratic party to the exclusion of the Southerners. Still Ball was incredulous; Byrnes had not deserted Roosevelt on the court-packing issue. But soon *The Nation*, commenting on the defeated movement supported by Byrnes which would have required local govern-

13. *The News and Courier*, July 19, 1938.
14. F. H. McMaster to W. W. Ball, Feb. 3, 1938, Ball Papers.
15. Ball, Diary, X, 182, May 16, 1937.
16. *Ibid.*, X, 178, May 1, 1937.   17. *Ibid.*, X, 184, May 19, 1937.

ments to pay at least one quarter of all new W.P.A. projects, included the Senator as part of the "stampede of Southern Senators off the Roosevelt reservation."[18]

Ball was not finally convinced, however, until he journeyed from Caesar's Head to the offices of the *Greenville News*, a paper which about six months before had begun to support the contention of *The News and Courier*, that New Deal policies were irreconcilable to Southern interests. Roger Peace, the paper's editor and a close friend of Byrnes, who had recently talked with the Senator, told Ball that

> . . . the breach between Byrnes and Roosevelt is real and substantial, that Byrnes has discovered that Roosevelt will tolerate no difference of opinion and demands complete subservience to his will. . . . Byrnes has come around to the opinion that you and I hold. . . . His present position is very uncomfortable; he is more worried than he has ever been.[19]

Ball was now ready to welcome Byrnes back into the reactionary fold; two days later he printed an editorial which indicated he was "Thinking Better of Byrnes."[20]

Byrnes never admitted an outright "break" with Franklin Roosevelt, but he did acknowledge differences with the President during this period. Although he did not like several provisions of Roosevelt's bill to reorganize the Supreme Court, or the President's procedures concerning it, Byrnes announced he would support the bill because he believed the Court was "legislating by a majority of five."[21] But after he decided that the bill could not be passed, and so advised the President, Roosevelt would not at that time agree to support a compromise bill. When Majority Leader Joseph T. Robinson of Arkansas died in July, 1937, while controversy over the court bill still raged, Alben Barkley of Kentucky and Pat Harrison of Mississippi, both friends of Byrnes, announced that they were available for Robinson's Democratic Senate post. Byrnes favored Harrison, and when the President called him in to talk over the matter, he advised the President not to interfere. Roosevelt replied that he had not taken and would not take part in the deliberations surrounding the selection of a new majority leader. But the next day a

18. *The Nation*, CLXIV (June 26, 1937), 720.
19. Ball, Diary, X, 194, July 7, 1937.
20. *The News and Courier*, July 9, 1937.
21. Byrnes, *All In One Lifetime*, p. 97.

letter the President had written to Barkley was made public. The Roosevelt letter did not mention specifically the Senate contest, but it referred to Barkley as "acting majority leader of the Senate" and stressed the need for pressing the original court bill. To the Senate and the press, the contents of the letter indicated that Roosevelt supported Barkley.[22]

Byrnes found further cause for disagreement with the President during the Congressional elections in 1938; he did not approve of Roosevelt's attempt to unseat conservative Southern Democrats who had not supported New Deal legislation in the Senate. Some of the President's closest advisers thought it unwise for him to dare to intervene in Southern politics. At the request of Harry Hopkins, Byrnes sent him a telegram intended for Roosevelt's attention, warning that interference in South Carolina affairs would boomerang. But Roosevelt would not be deterred; he undertook a "purge trip" through the South. After a visit to Georgia, where his appeal to the voters not to return Walter George to the Senate caused a flurry of resentment, Roosevelt visited South Carolina. Since Olin Johnston had been invited to ride on the presidential train, it was obvious that Roosevelt favored Johnston for the seat held by "Cotton Ed" Smith, presently running for re-election. According to Byrnes, Roosevelt promised that there would be no repetition of the Georgia incident, that he would talk about fishing. But in a brief platform speech at Greenville he quoted, out of context, a remark of Smith's which implied the Senator's belief that people like those who had gathered at the railroad station were willing to work for fifty cents a day. Roosevelt's remark prompted an aide to signal for the train to start, " but the damage had been done." Roosevelt's enemies were able to use the *Congressional Record* to show that Senator Smith had been misrepresented.[23]

Ball, of course, came immediately to the editorial defense of Senator Smith. To him, Roosevelt's attempt to remove the Southern rebels was the most important issue of the 1938 campaigns. Smith must be returned to Washington in order that the "radicals" who supported the administration would not be encouraged. "Cotton Ed" Smith has been described as "unmatched as an exponent of white supremacy, and without peer as a defender of southern womanhood."[24] Ball has been accused of supporting a man whose oratory violated the anti-demagogue principles the editor held so precious. He usually did endorse Smith, but he

22. *Ibid.*, pp. 98–99.   23. *Ibid.*, pp. 102–103.
24. Key, *Southern Politics*, p. 139.

was not deceived about his aptitudes or his accomplishments during the decades the Senator's voice rang from the stumps of South Carolina. Rather, he regarded Smith as "harmless" and useful, the lesser of evils. In the past he had been invaluable—he had been used to defeat Blease. Now he could be used for the undoing of Roosevelt.[25]

In May the campaign in *The News and Courier* started. Roosevelt had picked Johnston and Ball observed, "If the president can elect Mr. Johnston U. S. Senator from South Carolina he can elect anybody."[26] Throughout the long summer *The News and Courier* spoke for Senator Smith, warning against "a sneaking attack on the integrity of the white party and its primary."[27] Southern white people, Ball stated, were not preventing Negroes from voting; they could form their own party; so could Episcopalians, women, Greeks—if they wanted to. But the Southern white party was legal! An attack upon Smith was an attack upon the white man's party. Northern Negro leaders were the masters of the national Democratic party.[28] A vote against Smith was a victory for Walter White and the N.A.A.C.P.[29] And on the day before the primary, after State Senator Edgar Brown, chief of the "Barnwell Ring," had withdrawn his candidacy, Ball ran a front editorial:

In Terms of South Carolina

Last night Franklin D. Roosevelt, in Hyde Park, New York state, said in reference to the withdrawal of Mr. Brown from the contest in South Carolina that in his opinion "it clarifies the issue." With that the News and Courier agrees.

Mr. Roosevelt, a New York voter, further says that "one of these candidates (of the two left in the South Carolina contest) thinks in terms of the past . . . and the other thinks in terms of 1938 and 1948 and 1958." With that, too, The News and Courier agrees with the gentleman of New York.

The candidate for senator in South Carolina thinking in terms of 1938 is Ellison D. Smith.

Last Saturday, August 27, the New York Times contained this:

"La Guardia children to visit Roosevelt. . . . Mayor La Guardia arranged another visit to Hyde Park, which would include Eric" (his little boy). "In the party will also be Jean, 9, the La

25. W. W. Ball to Sara Ball Copeland, Sept. 2, 1938, Ball Papers.
26. *The News and Courier*, May 18, 1938.
27. *Ibid.*, July 23, 1938.   28. *Ibid.*
29. *Ibid.*, July 19, 1938.

Guardias' daughter, Richard La Guardia, a nephew of the Mayor, a neighborhood playmate, and the negro child." "The negro child is the son of the La Guardias' cook." "Mrs. La Guardia will accompany the children with the Mayor."

To this visiting and entertainment it is not for The News and Courier to object, for gentlemen of New York have the right to arrange these social matters for themselves.

This sort of thing is not "the thinking of South Carolina in 1938, in 1948, or in 1958." It is not thinking in the terms of Ellison D. Smith for South Carolina, and he does not "arrange" for his family to visit Mr. Roosevelt with his colored cook's child in the party.

The other candidate says that he is a "ONE HUNDRED PER-CENTER FOR ROOSEVELT."

Who shall do the thinking for South Carolina?

Shall the gentleman who votes in Hyde Park, New York?

Or shall you, the voters of South Carolina, in tomorrow's primary?[30]

Next day, the voters gave their answer; Olin Johnston was defeated and Smith's primary victory guaranteed his return to Washington. Ball jubilantly announced that Roosevelt had been deposed as party leader in South Carolina.[31] Smith, often sporting a cotton blossom boutonniere during campaigns, had long been one of the most extravagant performers in national politics. To celebrate his latest victory, he donned a red shirt and spoke to a large group of red-shirted men from Orangeburg who had gathered at the Wade Hampton statue in Capitol Square. "Cotton Ed" proclaimed to the crowd the similarities between 1938 and 1876. He wrote Ball: "It is difficult for me to put into words my deep appreciation of your sincere enthusiasm in my behalf during my race for re-election to the Senate. Just let me say, I thank you."[32]

More important, the Smith-Johnston contest had produced something of a revolution in the South Carolina press that Ball, after his years of virtually solitary dissent, found warmly satisfying. In one issue of *The News and Courier* he reprinted editorials from twenty-two different state papers (mostly weeklies) which contained varying degrees of criticism of New Deal policies.[33] V. O. Key called South Carolina politics "the

30. *Ibid.*, Aug. 29, 1938.   31. *Ibid.*, Sept. 14, 1938.
32. E. D. Smith to W. W. Ball, Sept. 3, 1938, Ball Papers.
33. *The News and Courier*, June 12, 1938.

politics of color"; indeed in the summer of 1938, the infant, slow-bloom-
ing racial controversy had contributed to a weakening of the spell the
Roosevelt New Deal had cast over the South. The President's blunder-
ing interference in the state's private affairs and the increasingly obvious
pro-Negro policies of the New Deal had produced a partial disaffection
in South Carolina that no amount of tampering with Jeffersonian traditions, however hallowed, could have engendered.

The year 1938 also saw one of the most spirited and controversial
gubernatorial campaigns in the history of the state, the last contest in
which Cole Blease played an important part. Ball believed that the
contests for senator and governor were related, all part of a grand plan
drafted by the Byrnes "machine," which he thought now controlled
South Carolina. Byrnes, according to Ball's conjecture, was backing
Burnet Maybank of Charleston for governor. In return for Byrnes's
support, Maybank would agree not to try for the Senate in 1942, when
Byrnes himself planned to run for re-election. But in 1944 Maybank
might have his chance; in that year Smith would be eighty years old and
would not be expected to run again. Smith, in turn, would agree to retire
after another six years, in exchange for the support of the Byrnes
machine against the current challenge of Olin Johnston. Thus the way
would be cleared for Maybank in 1944.[34] Ball was convinced of both the
logic and the reality of the Byrnes-Smith-Maybank alliance, because a
"frame-up" was necessary if Maybank were to be elected, considering
the still-existing antagonisms between upcountry and low country. No
Charlestonian had been elected governor since the Civil War.

Charleston newspapers naturally gave their support to Maybank. Ball
thought Maybank could win even though Blease was against him and
the Bible Belt seemed alarmed lest the evil ways of Charleston contami-
nate them. He was optimistic, although the editor of *The State* warned
him:

> You know as well as I do what constitutes the unforgivable sin of
> the Low Country. It refuses to lie about its sinning. That's the
> trouble. Sinning is all right. Even Bible Belters do it. But to sin
> and not lie about it awful. It shows indifference to hypocritical
> pretense. It shows disregard for the Almighty's wrath. Sinning
> must be behind his back. Lest he be deceived, who is safe?[35]

34. W. W. Ball to C. B. Smith of the Greenville *Post*, June 22, 1938, Ball
Papers; Ball, Diary, XI, 63–64, Sept. 11, 1938.
35. James Derieux to W. W. Ball, Aug. 2, 1938.

After the first primary had eliminated minor candidates, Maybank faced Wyndham Manning in the run-off. When Manning in a speech denounced Charleston's record of law-breaking and proclaimed his pleasure at having the support of Cole Blease, Ball was incensed. Charleston's resentment at Manning's attack did not particularly disturb him; the city had voted Bleasite more than once in the past. He was distressed, however, that Wyndham Manning was the first "gentleman" of South Carolina to give a high testimonial to Blease. Ball's opinion of Manning had dropped earlier when he had accepted a post in the Roosevelt bureaucracy—as manager of a plantation owned by the federal government in Lee County.[36] But now Manning had complimented the man who had been his father's bitter enemy. In Ball's judgment, only the Gonzales brothers had suffered more at the hands of Blease than had Richard I. Manning. Though Maybank was no pet of Ball's, the editor contributed to his campaign, in the days before the second primary, a flood of editorials characterizing Manning as pro-Blease and anti-Charleston.

The 1938 Maybank-Manning contest was used by V. O. Key to illustrate frequent tendencies in South Carolina politics. Not always but often voters have divided along upcountry–low-country lines although "voter consciousness of such differences is not sharp." The presence of large numbers of Negroes, Key observed, muffled issues between white politicians. But though there might be a lack of issues, there were plenty of candidates—sometimes six or eight, for example, in the first gubernatorial primary. As a result, South Carolina politics was multifactional. The candidate hoped to carry his home county and add the neighboring counties. From localism it was only a step to sectionalism and, often, a dual division along upcountry–low-country lines. The counties below the fall line have a sort of unity—they are wet, they have a large percentage of Negroes, and they are more dependent on agriculture than the upland counties. Maybank, the victor in 1938, carried the counties of the coastal plain (the seacoast areas by large majorities), but was able to capture only one of the northwestern counties.[37]

The vote in the gubernatorial contest was close, and Manning charged that irregularities in Charleston had given the election to Maybank. Acting upon Manning's charge of fraud, Governor Johnston ordered the city's ballots seized. Local election officials were ejected

36. Ball, Diary, X, 70, July 22, 1936.
37. Key, *Southern Politics*, pp. 131–137.

from Hibernian Hall by state guardsmen while Manning's aides copied the Charleston polling records. Excited but orderly crowds milled outside the hall for several days while the outcome remained in doubt. Ball conceded that it had been unwise for Mayor Maybank's managers to deny Manning's request that he be allowed to send observers to the Charleston polling places on election day. Charges of fraud in Charleston had been brought before, and Ball admitted that there probably had been cheating in the 1938 election. But, he judged, it would not have involved more than two thousand votes; and if that amount were doubled, Maybank would still have a majority in the state.

Ball certainly did not approve of Governor Johnston's order seizing the Charleston ballots. He had scored the Governor before—in 1935, when in a dispute with the powerful "Barnwell Ring" he had tried unsuccessfully to take control of the state highway department despite condemnation by the State House, Senate, and Supreme Court. That episode received considerable attention, enough to cause Henry Steele Commager to review the entire South Carolina political situation and brand Johnston a "dictator."[38] Now, Ball condemned Johnston's action as another incident in "the 'holy war' so valiantly waged to rekindle the fires of an ancient and poisoned hate against Charleston."[39] Besides, to Ball it was a question of whether military or civil government should rule. A week after the second primary, as Ball applauded, the state executive committee of the Democratic party disallowed Manning's pro-

38. In South Carolina where the executive is a relatively weak official, the balance of power is in the legislature. One of the phenomena of the recent political history of the state has been the power of the Barnwell Ring, so-called because of the concentration of residents of Barnwell County in key positions in the legislature. The leader of the "ring," Edgar Allen Brown, having risen to the position of president pro tempore of the Senate, was supported by his Barnwell neighbor Sol Blatt, for ten years Speaker of the House. During Johnston's first term as governor, he engaged in a contest with the "ring" over control of the highway department, an important source of patronage, whose chief was the brother-in-law of Senator Brown. Johnston, failing to persuade the legislature to oust certain commissioners appointed by a previous governor, personally announced their removal, declared the commission in rebellion, proclaimed martial law over the department, and occupied it with troops. The governor held the department for two months but was unable to uncover irregularities in its records. The Senate and House voted by large majorities to return the commission to constitutional civil authority, and their judgment was upheld by the Supreme Court. Governor Johnston had been defeated by the "Barnwell Ring," which remained antagonistic during the rest of his term. Johnston, having learned his lesson, returned to the governorship in 1942, co-operated with the legislature, and received the blessing of the "Barnwell Ring" in his successful bid for the United States Senate in 1944. (See Henry S. Commager, "A South Carolina Dictator," *Current History*, XLIII [March, 1936], 568–572.)

39. *The News and Courier*, Sept. 15, 1938.

test and Maybank was declared the victor. The mayor was welcomed back to Charleston with Roman candles amid what one observer described as the biggest celebration since Armistice Day.[40]

For his part, Wyndham Manning believed he was "counted out" in Charleston and he blamed his defeat on the editorial policy of Ball and *The News and Courier*. He made his feelings clear to Ball in a hotel conference in Charleston more than a year after the deciding primary. According to Manning, the Charleston paper had irreparably damaged his campaign by charging that he had resorted to lies and slander, and by printing many unfavorable letters while failing to print letters supporting him. He had expected his radio speech to bring an uproar from the Maybank forces, but he later wrote in a letter to Ball, "What I had not anticipated, and cannot to this day explain, was why you took part in the flurry."[41] The charge of "holy war" might have been expected from those getting pinched. But Ball was not unthinking; why could he not distinguish between an attack on a community and a campaign against the public record of a candidate who was a resident of that community?

Ball, on the other hand, informed Manning of the most serious disadvantage under which he had labored: no newspaper of general circulation had vigorously supported him, as the Charleston papers had backed Maybank. Furthermore he denied *The News and Courier* had implied that Manning was a liar and a slanderer. "Send me proof!" he urged.[42] Manning could not find proof of offensive language in his clipping file but his "recollections were clear."[43] Ball and his secretary spent three hours going through the files for the period surrounding the primaries. In no case did they find the word "lie" or "lies," and the word "slander" had appeared in no *editorial*; Manning was so informed.[44] Cordial relations were eventually restored, Manning insisting that Ball's intention to be fair was what really mattered to him, anyway.

Manning's concern with Ball's relationship to the 1938 gubernatorial campaign was proof that, though his rantings against the welfare state had made him a generally unpopular figure, Ball was not yet without some influence where strictly local politics were concerned. All of this was possible, of course, because of the schizophrenic nature of Southern politics.

40. *Ibid.*, Sept. 21, 1938.
41. Wyndham Manning to W. W. Ball, Feb. 3, 1940, Ball Papers.
42. W. W. Ball to Wyndham Manning, Feb. 5, 1940, Ball Papers.
43. Wyndham Manning to W. W. Ball, Feb. 6, 1940, Ball Papers.
44. W. W. Ball to Wyndham Manning, Feb. 3, 1940, Ball Papers.

To Ball, the distinguishing characteristic of the 1938 election was that no one dared to tell "the truth" about it. He did not say in *The News and Courier* that the success of Smith and Maybank was a victory for Byrnes and his federal office holder's machine.[45] But his attack on the "office holding industry" continued, concentrated in 1939 on the government's failure to prepare the country for war. Ball was depressed by the war and by fear for his daughter Eleanor's safety in England. He agreed with his friend Baruch that the best chance of keeping the United States out of war lay in making the country so strong that no nation would dare attack her. And so he called upon Roosevelt to stop building dams, give up the W.P.A., and to put all available revenue into national defense. Furthermore, since it appeared likely that the United States might one day enter the war on the side of England, Ball could not resist suggesting it might be wise for the two countries to reunite. Ancient wounds had healed; should not the English-speaking peoples join to fight the hostile ideologies? The idea, he conceded, would be regarded as fantastic. But why?[46]

Preoccupied though he was with the preparedness issue, Ball by no means abandoned his criticism of Roosevelt's domestic policies. After an Alabama speech in which the President asked why the South did not work toward ending her economic subservience to the North by raising money to develop trade and commerce, Ball replied, "This Is Why, Mr. President." The South would rather have her properties "in hock to the North" than under a club swung by the government.[47] After the editorial was rather widely reprinted in the East, Ball remarked to his sister, "I think I could be elected to the legislature in Southeastern Pennsylvania; that seems at the moment the seat of my political strength."[48]

Probably nothing save the loss of the gold standard worried the ultraconservatives so much as the specter of socialism they saw behind the public power issue. Ball's principal domestic concern in the late thirties was the power and navigation development being built by the state and federal governments on the Santee and Cooper rivers.[49] In

45. Ball, Diary, XI, 69, Sept. 16, 1938.
46. *The News and Courier*, Oct. 13, 1939.
47. *Ibid.*, April 6, 1939.
48. W. W. Ball to Sara Ball Copeland, May 1, 1939, Ball Papers.
49. The enabling act creating the authority and authorizing the construction project was passed by the South Carolina General Assembly and signed by Governor I. C. Blackwood in May, 1934. In July, 1935, President Roosevelt approved, in a letter to J. F. Byrnes, public financing of the project. In December, 1935, three private power companies filed injunction suits. In September, 1937, a

1934, when provisional plans for the project were announced, Ball had promised not to oppose it editorially, though it represented an expansion of governmental activities that he could not approve. Early in 1938, after the Supreme Court had declared the Tennessee Valley Authority constitutional and it appeared that the legal way had been cleared for the allocation of federal funds for the South Carolina project, Ball made

decision favorable to the project was rendered in the federal district court and upheld in February, 1938, by the circuit court of appeals in Richmond. In May the Supreme Court declared the matter closed, and in August the first contracts were let. According to a directive issued by R. M. Cooper, General Manager of the South Carolina Public Service Authority, in June, 1939, the $40,000,000 project was to be financed by direct grants from the national government ($15,435,000 from P.W.A. and $6,000,000 from W.P.A.) and the issuing by the state authority of revenue bonds totaling $18,895,000. Intended chiefly to improve inland navigation facilities and provide hydroelectric power for industrial development, allied plans called for reforestation and swamp clearance. On December 2, 1942, the state flag was raised over the control power house and the project declared substantially completed, the first state-owned hydroelectric and navigation project financed by the national government as a self-liquidating project. Besides the power plant the completed project included two reservoirs—Lake Marion on the Santee River and Lake Moultrie at the headwaters of the Cooper River—with a diversion canal 6.5 miles long connecting the two lakes; and 105 miles of minimum depth inland waterway beginning at Fort Motte, on the Congaree River below Columbia, traveling down the Congaree into the Santee, connecting through the Santee-Cooper canal with the Cooper River, and terminating in Charleston at the sea. Surveys were being made at the time of the Revolution for a Santee-Cooper canal, and the vision of a seaport at Columbia (in the dead center of the state) was an old dream; but questions as to the plan's business and economic soundness had postponed attempts until the project was undertaken as a New Deal pump-priming venture. Final execution was begun only after bitter opposition from private power interests and the owners of lands to be inundated had been overcome. Sixty-five million dollars were spent, once-splendid plantation sites were submerged; and the argument continues concerning the wisdom of the project. Critics have charged that when the project was conceived, practical inland navigation on the Eastern seaboard had been dead for a hundred years. Slow barge traffic could not compete with high speed highway and rail transportation. Hydroelectric plants, except as subordinate auxiliaries to steam-electric generators, had become almost as passé as inland navigation in the East where land costs were high and coal was available; furthermore, steam auxiliaries became necessary at Santee-Cooper because the changeable river could produce only one-quarter as much power during some months as it could in others. The middle and upcountry continued to attract industry while the low country languished, Santee-Cooper notwithstanding. Henry Savage, who knows the Santee country, has concluded: "It is all but strictly true that the expensive highest navigation locks in the United States have had no beneficial use during all the intervening years except to lift fish from the Cooper River to the lake level. . . . Although the project's supporters still hold to their blind faith in the wisdom of the undertaking, the facts . . . have long since convinced the unprejudiced that the whole project was a monstrous error, the product of anachronistic enthusiasms." See Henry Savage, Jr., *River of the Carolinas: The Santee* (New York, 1956), pp. 356–361; South Carolina Public Service Authority, *Picture Progress Story: Santee-Cooper* (Monck's Corner, S. C., n. d.), pp. 2, 230–232.

editorial appraisal of the undertaking about to begin. No advocate of pump-priming, he believed the government had no right to enter the dam-building business, but since it was already in it in a big way, South Carolina might as well get her share. One aspect of the project pleased him: the distribution of money would help Charleston and the low country. Whether or not the project should be undertaken was "a matter of which The News and Courier is without knowledge or opinion."[50]

Ball's pledge not to write anything that might endanger negotiations to set up the Santee-Copper Authority did not prevent him from criticizing the actual project, once it was safely underway. The gigantic undertaking, he scolded, had not been put into the hands of successful businessmen; it was being directed by politicians, several of whom had been notorious business failures.[51] He doubted that the people of the state would buy revenue bonds issued by the authority. If the investing public believed in the project, it would not have waited for the government to sponsor it. The tendency of some of the W.P.A. workers in Aiken County to get drunk—to go on "sprees at the taxpayers' expense"—caused Ball to inquire whether a social problem had been created anywhere in South Carolina when a private corporation had built a mill or a dam.[52] And, of course, Ball studiously reported the strong objections being raised to the feasibility of the entire project. What industries would come to the low country after Santee-Cooper power became a reality? What guarantee was there? That line of attack brought Ball into an open feud with Clark Foreman, Director of the Power Division, P.W.A.

In a letter to Ball, Foreman agreed with the editor that the chief immediate benefit from the Santee-Cooper project was the increased income of the people of South Carolina. But the experience of T.V.A. showed that industries were drawn by cheap power. It was not now necessary to say which industries would ultimately locate in South Carolina.[53] But, Ball insisted in *The News and Courier*, there was doubt as to how much industry the power authority had really brought to the Tennessee Valley. According to some estimates, Tennessee trailed other states which had no public power. Ball described the only benefit to the low country so far: "A tourist in Church street scatters nickles and dimes. The dancers snatch them. There is a temporary boom in the lollypop and

50. *The News and Courier*, Jan. 5, 1938.
51. *Ibid.*, April 6, 1939.   52. *Ibid.*, April 25, 1939.
53. Letter of Clark Foreman, *The News and Courier*, Oct. 19, 1939.

sucker trade. Government is the tourist scattering $40,300,000. The News and Courier is all for it."[54] Foreman, shocked by Ball's characterization of the people who received employment because of Santee-Cooper as a "bunch of street urchins making monkey-shines on the curb for a few tourist-tossed pennies," responded:

If you are confused by the Santee-Cooper project . . . I'm afraid there isn't much I can do to help straighten things out in your own mind. There are leaders in the South who are not bewildered and confused, but who speak with conviction of its destiny. . . . I don't believe they will be able to supply you with detailed charts of minutely figured blueprints. But if you would counsel with some of them, they might hold your hand and calm your uncertain fears.[55]

When Ball chose to regard several of Foreman's statements as an official declaration that public power was the policy of the United States, Foreman reminded him Santee-Cooper was a South Carolina project entitled to federal funds, adding, "If this is state socialism, then it is socialism by the state of South Carolina."[56] Ball retorted, in the last instalment of the argument:

In his letter in The News and Courier October 19, Director Foreman said:
'The Santee-Cooper project is grounded in the public ownership and control of power.'
The policy of the government of the United States is either for or against the public ownership and control of power.
Goodbye, Mr. Foreman.[57]

Throughout 1939 Ball's editorial criticism of Santee-Cooper followed the familiar pattern: steadfast, repetitive, outspoken. The authority, he accused, was controlled by politicians; it was wasteful and extravagant. Late in the year even some of his close friends began to suggest that it was time to end the campaign. The relentless gibes, they feared, would cause the authority to move its offices from Charleston to a city with a friendlier atmosphere. Ball was not worried; the authority would not dare lose its friends in the low country; besides, if Senator Byrnes allowed the offices to be removed, he would lose the support of Charles-

54. *The News and Courier*, Oct. 19, 1939.
55. *Ibid.*, Oct. 26, 1939.   56. *Ibid.*, Oct. 28, 1939.
57. *Ibid.*

ton and the low country in his next contest for re-election to the Senate.[58] But late in February, 1940, it was announced that the Santee-Cooper offices would indeed be moved to Columbia. The authority stated that the Charleston office had been preliminary, was no longer needed, and that it had not been closed in order to punish Ball. But there were many who were not convinced; the move meant the loss to Charleston of several hundred precious jobs; and the editor of *The News and Courier* was blamed. Mayor Lockwood warned, "It seems that . . . the constant nagging of the newspaper on the authority and everything the New Deal is for has brought this thing to a head. . . . The next thing you are going to do is lose your Navy Yard."[59]

At noon on the day the impending move was announced, Ball was visited by a delegation from the Charleston Retail Merchants Association who demanded that, in the absence of evidence indicating fraud, Ball refrain from further attacks upon the Santee-Cooper Authority. Now the editor faced his sternest test; the freedom of the press and the independence of the editor, subjects of decades of his philosophizing, were threatened. Ball was adamant; he would not submit to pressure. He would resign, if his publishers so desired, but he would not change his stand. His integrity, the integrity of every editor, was at stake. From the description of an eyewitness, the delegation had entered Ball's office determined; when they left, they were "whipped."[60]

Immediate approval came from publisher Manigault. He assured Ball:

> At this time I want to make it plain to you that I am thoroughly in accord with your editorial policies. I am asking no change in them whatever. I do hope you will agree with me that this is no time for us to back fire. The threat of the federal government to punish any community is more than I can stand.[61]

Other support came in dozens of congratulatory letters, came from people who disagreed with his views but commended his ethics. Among those who wrote were John W. Davis, who had been the Democratic presidential nominee in 1924, and Wyndham Manning, who said, "I expected you'd stand up under the avalanche."[62] Newspapers also gave

58. Ball, Diary, XI, 203, Nov. 3, 1939.
59. *Time*, XXXV, No. 12 (March 18, 1940), 53.
60. T. R. Waring, Jr., in interview with author, May 13, 1959.
61. R. M. Manigault to W. W. Ball, March 2, 1940, Ball Papers.
62. Wyndham Manning to W. W. Ball, March 2, 1940, Ball Papers.

the story prime space, a Savannah paper announcing in a prominent headline, "Editor W. W. Ball Refuses to Yield."[63] The *Greenville News*, the Columbia *State*, and the Greenwood *Index-Journal*, gave Ball strong endorsement in his own state.

The Santee-Cooper affair had all the aspects of an important news story, and press comment on Ball's stand gave him more national publicity than he had ever known. *Newsweek* announced: "Editor's Anti-New Deal War Rocks Staid Old Charleston." *The News and Courier*, said *Newsweek*, was one of the fiercest New Deal lambasters in the country. Ball was pictured sitting at his disorderly desk twirling his watch chain, a foe of Roosevelt and a man willing to "die for states rights."[64] In *Time* Ball was portrayed as a baggy-suited editor, devoted to Southern womanhood and states rights, whose bosom was invigorated by the temperament of old Charleston. The magazine also quoted Ball as saying, "There has been some discussion as to whether or not Mr. Roosevelt reads the editorials in *The News and Courier*. Why, if he had been following them since June 1933, when the New Deal first was doubted, the country wouldn't be in the fix it is now."[65]

The excitement in Charleston died quickly. Ball felt that he had received more favorable comment for his unequivocal defense of a free press than for anything else he had ever done. There was no doubt that the somewhat overdramatized accounts in the national news magazines had swelled his ever-sensitive ego. And a few days after Ball turned the accusers from his office, the capstone of the entire affair was set in place. J. L. M. Irby, fired as chief of the power project's land acquisition department, claimed that he had been put on the "altar of sacrifice" and called for a special inquiry to determine "responsibility for the incompetence, mismanagement, and waste of public funds" so as to prevent "a scandal and a stench."[66] Acting upon Irby's charges, Governor Maybank asked the General Assembly to investigate the Santee-Cooper Authority. Ball expected that the state legislature would "whitewash" the authority, but Irby's disclosures had made the politicians uncomfortable. And for the moment *The News and Courier* was "on top of the world."[67]

Although he felt immense pleasure in the strong role taken by the

63. Savannah *Morning News*, March 2, 1940.
64. *Newsweek*, XV, No. 12 (March 18, 1940), 44–46.
65. *Time*, XXXV, No. 12 (March 18, 1940), 52–53.
66. *Newsweek*, March 18, 1940, p. 46.
67. W. W. Ball to Sara Ball Copeland, April 5, 1940, Ball Papers.

press in the Santee-Cooper affair, in a recent essay entitled "Of Chiefs and Staffers," Ball had lamented the decline of "personal" journalism and the tendency of editorial opinion to become mechanical under the influence of syndication. The old personal ties between an owner and his editor were disappearing. In forty-seven years, he recalled, he had never had a contract; yet his chiefs always stood by him. Still, he conceded, the editor had only a delegated voice, and the last word must belong to the publisher. Ball was evidently thinking ahead to the next presidential campaign, because at the same time he was reflecting publicly on editor-publisher relationships, he pledged privately, "As I write tonight, my resolution is that I shall oppose Rooseveltism and Roosevelt in 1940 even if it be necessary to resign the editorship of The News and Courier."[68]

Ball had known Wendell Willkie for several years before he emerged as a candidate for the Republican presidential nomination in 1940. Willkie was president of the Commonwealth and Southern Corporation, and business brought him, two or three times a year, to Charleston, where the local power company was a subsidiary of his corporation. In the fall of 1939 Willkie, who liked to sit and talk with Ball,[69] asked the editor to arrange a dinner party so that he might meet the Charleston literary colony. Ball expressed surprise that this "economic royalist" had a fancy for literature and was interested in entertaining the local literati. He, nevertheless, made the arrangements for the man he "knew well and liked";[70] and in February, 1940, Willkie, accompanied by a representative of Bobbs-Merrill and by Mrs. Irita Van Doren, book critic of the New York *Herald-Tribune*, came to Charleston, where he was host to a group of writers which included Clements and Katharine Ball Ripley, who had returned from Hollywood to settle permanently in a house on Lamboll Street.

By May petitions supporting Willkie for the Republican presidential nomination were circulating in Charleston. Although Ball did not sign them (he would commit himself only in the columns of *The News and Courier*), he confided to friends that Willkie's political opinions on main questions were acceptable to him and he would rejoice in Willkie's election. In 1932, if the editor of *The News and Courier* had not supported Roosevelt, a scandal would have resulted; but now prominent

68. Ball, Diary, XI, 49, Aug. 15, 1938.
69. Wendell Willkie to W. W. Ball, Aug. 21, 1939, Ball Papers.
70. W. W. Ball to Sara Ball Copeland, Sept. 21, 1939, Ball Papers.

Charleston men could wear Republican buttons without being insulted. For the present, however, neither Ball nor the newspaper was committed to Willkie.

After Willkie was nominated in June, Ball began to move slowly toward an outright endorsement of the former Democrat who generally supported Roosevelt's foreign policy but attacked the New Deal domestic record. Out of the 350,000 whites who voted in primaries, Ball thought he saw 100,000 who would vote against Roosevelt. Their ranks might be doubled by a strong leader if he were aided by a well-financed local campaign. He doubted, however, that Willkie's managers would consider the state worth attention. Still, there seemed to be considerable enthusiasm for Willkie in Charleston, and in early July Ball addressed that sentiment. If Willkie people meant business, he announced, they must organize an electoral ticket of Independent Democrats.

Until a short time before Democratic party regulations would have prevented such a development. The famous Rule 32 had stipulated that all registered Democrats must pledge, when they voted in the primaries, to support the nominees of the party in the general elections, state and federal. Voters submitted to rigid controls of this sort only because they seemed necessary to preserve white rule. But in 1938, out of resentment over the racial policies of the New Deal, the state convention repealed that part of Rule 32 which required South Carolina Democrats to support the party's nominee in presidential elections. South Carolinians would not follow the state's Republican leaders, Ball observed; there was need for an independent Jeffersonian Democratic party in national affairs.[71] He applauded Willkie's nomination, pointing out that no candidate of either party in seventy-five years had visited the state so often, and proclaimed him to be the "American candidate."[72] At the same time he carefully emphasized that Willkie was not *really* a Republican and had never been active in Republican politics. No fewer than four separate editorials in a single issue of *The News and Courier* presented Willkie as an enlightened Democrat in revolt against the administration.[73] However Ball chose to represent the situation, the fact was that for the first time in his life he was backing the presidential nominee of the Republican party.

In mid-July a group of Willkie supporters called on Ball to discuss a state campaign. Some of them thought that it would be unrealistic to

71. *The News and Courier*, July 14, 1940.
72. *Ibid.*, June 29, 1940.   73. *Ibid.*

make any effort beyond a demonstration—and that for the effect it would have in other states. South Carolinians, if they wished to vote for Willkie, should be left to vote for the Republican electors.[74] Ball disagreed and continued his editorial campaign for independent Democratic electors. Finally, to that end, on August 1 more than two hundred delegates convened at the South Carolina Society Hall in Charleston to organize the state Jeffersonian Democratic party. Almost simultaneously, *Time* magazine printed a picture of the "New Deal-hating" Ball and reported his support of Willkie as indicative of anti-Roosevelt rumblings in the normally Democratic Southern press.[75]

Ball's campaign for Willkie in *The News and Courier* was strangely passive. It did not stress Willkie's qualifications so much as it relied on familiar accusations against the New Deal; his approach was more anti-Roosevelt than pro-Willkie. He concentrated on the third term issue and the administration's Negro sympathies. He even requested the *Chicago Tribune* to send him stories of the prominence of Negroes in the Democratic convention while it was in session in Chicago.[76] And he tried to make capital of Senator Byrnes's popularity by publicizing the frequently repeated rumor that Roosevelt had refused to consider Byrnes as a running mate because the Senator had converted from Catholicism to Episcopalianism, and was, therefore, religiously controversial.[77] Perhaps Ball was disappointed that Willkie had not taken a firm stand for states rights; perhaps the editor thought more votes could be swayed by continuing his prodding of those aspects of Rooseveltism that seemed likely to irritate local sensitivities. In any case, as the election approached, *The News and Courier* had much more blame for Roosevelt than it had praise for Willkie.

Ball extravagantly overestimated the size of Willkie's following in

74. Ball, Diary, XI, 287, July 13, 1940.

75. *Time*, XXXVI, No. 13 (Aug. 5, 1940), 13.

76. Ball, Diary, XI, 291, July 16, 1940.

77. It is generally believed that although Roosevelt favored Byrnes as a running mate, both in 1940 and 1944, he submitted to pressure from labor leaders and party chiefs who believed that as a Southerner he was unacceptable to Negro and certain liberal voters and unacceptable on religious grounds to many others because of his former Catholicism. Most observers also believed that Byrnes was therefore disgruntled at what he considered the failure of the party to reward him for his long service as party peacemaker and go-between. But Byrnes denied that Roosevelt had "dumped" him because of his religion: "The President said he knew that some people were doubtful about the wisdom of nominating me because of my religious history, but that he did not agree. . . . To me the discussion was embarrassing and with emphasis I said that I was determined not to let my name be presented" (Byrnes, *All In One Lifetime*, p. 119).

South Carolina, and Roosevelt carried the state by an overwhelming majority. Although there were three slates of Willkie electors (the Jeffersonian Democrats and the rival Republican factions), Willkie showed strength mostly in Charleston County, where he carried three precincts. It was small consolation for Ball that his own ward, at least, had gone for Willkie. Furthermore, in spite of his insistence that they should continue to function in state politics, the Jeffersonian clubs faded with the defeat of their presidential candidate.

In midsummer Ball had expected a Willkie victory, but by election eve he had changed his mind. For the first time in his editorial career he had not even listened to election returns. That night he wrote to his sister in Laurens:

> The hour is 8:35 P.M. Election returns are coming in. I am in the house alone; Fay has gone to a play. I do not turn on the radio; it may be that the result of the election is now known, or will be soon; I shall learn it soon enough. I do not expect other than the election of candidate Roosevelt; the election of Willkie would give to me a surprise. I have no faith in "democracy" [little "d"], and the government of the United States has placed the balance of power in the hands of mendicants. I suppose the inmates of any county alms house would vote to retain in office a superintendent who fed them well and gave them beer. As for South Carolina, the South, it is decadent, spiritless; it is not even a beggar of the first class. The United States dodged, it ran to cover, it would not face the music in 1933. There will be "no recovery" until it has passed through the stages of suffering and agony, of one kind or another.[78]

---

78. W. W. Ball to Sara Ball Copeland, Nov. 5, 1940, Ball Papers.

CHAPTER ELEVEN

THE EDITOR'S LAST CAMPAIGNS

THE EARLY FORTIES were years of continuing frustration and disappointment for W. W. Ball. In his mid-seventies, he complained that now when he walked in Broad Street, he did not see half a dozen of his early companions in Charleston. He was distressed by the dispersal of his family and he worried over the problems of his children. The separation from her husband and ultimate divorce of Fay, his youngest daughter, caused him deep torment. South Carolina was then the only state which did not recognize divorce, and Ball had been one of those most active in support of the status quo.[1] He was also an active Episcopal layman and once was sent by his parish as a delegate to the church's national conference. Devoted to the old-fashioned polite standards and possessed by a strong sense of family unity, he was torn by his own complete distaste for divorce and concern for his child's happiness. Always gentle with her, he was, nevertheless, for a time, close to heartbreak. Perhaps, also, he was reminded of his own criticism of the divorces of the Roosevelt family and rendered even more uncomfortable.

Ball was getting tired, and often now he threatened to resign his responsibilities as editor and continue only as an editorial writer. Somewhat piqued that he had no share in employment policies of the paper and critical of the news department's tendency to neglect state and local news, he accused his publishers of thinking him fit for nothing more than running the editorial department. At the same time, the quality of his editorial writing had declined. His sentences had never been famous for clarity or crispness. Sometimes now they were hopelessly verbose; for example:

> In South Carolina a newspaper compares present political conditions reported in penal institutions, as secretly related to and talked of under breath in the industrial commission, as recorded in executive abuse of the power to pardon, as corruption and bribery in primary elections to which the governor and many others have

1. In 1947 the legislature passed an amendment to the state constitution establishing four grounds for divorce. Final ratification came in 1949.

borne witness, to the government of the carpetbaggers, scalawags and negroes in 'Reconstruction.'[2]

Of course, Ball was not well; recurring prostate trouble had made a second operation necessary. But even when he did not feel well, he boasted that he wrote four-fifths of the copy. Always proud that he was a "quantity producer," he could still write "three times the quantity of any man on my staff."[3]

Ball's discomforts fortunately did not destroy his sense of humor. Perhaps his favorite story concerned the visit, some time before, of two of his daughters to Paris. At a party, Fay and Eleanor were asked by a guest about the legendary Charleston entertainments. Fay replied that the St. Cecilia Ball was still being held and its old customs observed. At that point, another guest joined the group and asked the topic of conversation. When "The balls of Charleston" was the reply, she remarked, "I've always heard that they are a lovely and charming family." Ball concluded that the kinship between the St. Cecilia balls and the Water Street Balls was established in Parisian society. Ball was also flattered to report to his sister that he had received a letter from a Charlestonian who lived far away but loved to hear from home; he begged the editor to continue his subscription to *The News and Courier*, promising to pay when he returned to Charleston after the expiration of his term in the Oklahoma state prison.

Ball did not often go now to public functions. He liked to describe himself as the forgotten man, uninvited to official banquets, partly because those who sent such invitations had learned he would not come. But he continued to go to parties, to attend the meetings of the Plantation Society, and he took his turn as president of the Charleston chapter of the English Speaking Union. There were still the conversations with the old friends who were left. Sometimes Bernard Baruch would come to call; once, at Baruch's suggestion, they walked to the Battery, where they talked on a bench in the sun. And, in good health and bad, Ball maintained his unfaltering crusade against the New Deal. When the war which he had dreaded finally came to the United States, his personal thoughts rested ultimately on the familiar recriminations:

The president will speak at ten o'clock; I do not like to listen to speeches or other deliverances by radio, and I shall not hear him. He should have spoken two years ago, the night of the day that

2. *The News and Courier*, Feb. 5, 1943.
3. W. W. Ball to Sara Ball Copeland, July 13, 1942, Ball Papers.

Germany invaded Poland, September 1, 1939, and driven the Americans to spend every dollar on military preparation—and he would have begun in 1938 had he heeded the advice and urging of Bernard Baruch. However, an election was in front, and the W.P.A. and C.C.C. boys had to be fed and kept fat for it. Never was deeper disgrace for a country, in its management, than the disgrace of waste and corruption the last eight and a half years. I would not say that there has been stealing, not great stealing, but the buying of the whole people with gifts and offices has been the colossal form of corruption. . . . The American symbols are the night clubs of New York, the playboys and playgirls of Hollywood and the White House family with its divorces and capitalization of the presidential office to stuff money into pockets. I think that none of these are representative of the Americans; I hope and believe that there is still strength and backbone, that therein and thereby we shall defeat the Japanese and all others who attack.[4]

The News and Courier adhered steadfastly to its traditional policies: states rights; tariff for revenue only; strict construction of the Constitution; a federal government whose duties were confined to defending the republic against foreign attack and to preserving peace and free commerce among the states. Fazed neither by depression nor by war, the "Old Lady of Broad Street" persisted in her jealousy and suspicion of all governments that set up welfare, dogood, and handout agencies. Consequently, the attack on the New Deal waste and spending continued. In passing, Ball congratulated James F. Byrnes on his appointment to the Supreme Court, but he could not hide his pique. Byrnes, the editor boasted, had been useful in the past to *The News and Courier* in contests where the respectability of South Carolina was at stake. "With the exception of a period in 1937 and 1938, Mr. Byrnes as senator has been a faithful follower of the president," Ball added.[5] Now, he was being rewarded by his master.

Of all those associated with the Roosevelt administration, however, no one aroused such fury in Ball as did Harry Hopkins. A friend and neighbor reported to Ball that she had attended a dinner party in Washington where she had met Hopkins, who asked, "You live in Charleston; will you tell me why does the editor of *The News and*

4. W. W. Ball to Sara Ball Copeland, Dec. 9, 1941, Ball Papers.
5. *The News and Courier*, June 13, 1941.

Courier so dislike me?" She replied simply that Ball was a "crusading" editor. Ball claimed not to dislike Hopkins, but to regard him as the embodiment of the fantastic in government: a man who "on his own initiative never produced a dollar," a welfare worker who now was the greatest spender of the taxpayers' money.[6] Although Ball had a great prejudice against Hopkins, he wanted to be just; and he recorded with satisfaction Baruch's opinion that, though Hopkins was a man of ordinary talents, he did not possess first-rate ability.[7] When Roosevelt made Hopkins Lend-Lease administrator, Ball was "driven to despair."[8]

A full year before the end of Roosevelt's third term, Ball was again active in attempts to organize a Southern Democratic party. It was the spring of 1944, however, before the movement was underway in earnest. Through public contributions (Ball gave one hundred dollars), the anti-Roosevelt faction hoped to finance an advertising campaign in newspapers and on radio. The independent white Democrats would not present candidates in the primaries, but offer only a ticket of presidential electors pledged not to vote for Roosevelt. They might back a favorite son for president, or they might better co-operate with the similarly minded in other states in support of someone like Senator Harry Byrd of Virginia. Though Ball worked for the success of the movement with his editorials, he refused to attend organizational meetings or serve on committees. To do so would have compromised his editorial independence. Nevertheless, by May anti-Roosevelt Democrats had held their first meeting in Columbia, with nineteen counties represented, and made plans for a state convention. The Southern Democratic party had been reborn.

At almost the exact time that the anti-Roosevelt movement got rolling in South Carolina, the President himself was a visitor in the state. He had come to rest and fish at the plantation of Bernard Baruch, about sixty miles from Charleston. Ball has been characterized by Baruch as being a "bitter" foe of the New Deal, a man who never spared his vocabulary to make clear exactly where he stood. Baruch recalled later an incident that occurred when Roosevelt came within range of the editor's fire:

The News and Courier was one of the newspapers the President got every morning with his breakfast tray. Shortly after the Presi-

6. Ball, Diary, XII, 113, June 2, 1941.
7. *Ibid.*, XII, 87, April 19, 1941.   8. *Ibid.*, XII, 88, April 21, 1941.

dent's arrival editorials lambasting him began to appear daily. When I saw how much this irritated Roosevelt, I went to Ball and told him I thought he ought to stop the editorials while the President was there. I explained to Ball that my feeling had nothing to do with his right to express his opinions, but that it was not a gracious way of treating a guest in South Carolina.[9]

Ball had unqualified respect for his friend Baruch, but he could not slacken, particularly since he insisted that he had not said anything personally unkind about Mr. Roosevelt. To Ball, it was an "irreconcilable conflict," and the tone of his editorials did not change markedly during the President's sojourn.[10]

Roosevelt's presence also touched Ball in a way that gave vast amusement to his friends in Charleston. At a party the Commandant of the Charleston Naval District asked Ball if he knew where his son, a lieutenant in the Coast Guard, was stationed. When Ball replied, "At Georgetown, I suppose," Admiral Jules James remarked, "No, he's not; if you knew what he was doing, you would want to kill him; I have sent him on a mission." At first puzzled, Ball finally realized that his son was guarding the President.[11] Other friends informed Ball that when Roosevelt was told that W. W. Ball, Jr., was the skipper of the patrol boat that would take him fishing, he had no objections. And when Admiral James asked Roosevelt if he would like the editor of *The News and Courier* invited to a dinner party which was contemplated but never held, the President was reported to have replied, "Yes, invite him, I'd be glad to meet him; I read all that he writes."[12]

Ball accepted gracefully the jests about his son's being assigned to the President's service. He even printed a story about the whole affair in *The News and Courier*.[13] But the paper was as seriously dedicated as ever to the prevention of Roosevelt's re-election. The first results of Ball's campaign, however, were distinctly discouraging. In the senatorial primary in late July, though *The News and Courier* warned that a vote for Olin Johnston was a vote for Roosevelt, Johnston was the victor by more than twenty thousand votes over all opposition, including the veteran E. D. Smith. After thirty-six consecutive years in the Senate—a record surpassed only by Francis Green of Rhode Island—Smith was too

9. Bernard Baruch, *My Own Story* (2 vols.; New York, 1957), I, 272.
10. Ball, Diary, XIII, 69, April 20, 1944.
11. W. W. Ball to Sara Ball Copeland, May 3, 1944, Ball Papers.
12. Ball, Diary, XIII, 72, May 17, 1944.
13. *The News and Courier*, May 8, 1944.

old at seventy-eight to meet the challenge of the "carnival"; nor could he match Johnston's efforts to provide legislation to preserve the white party.

Smith's departure was still another sign of the passing of an era. Descendant from a line of cotton planters, his single constructive purpose in the Senate had been to secure legislation beneficial to cotton farmers. Though he endorsed most of the administration's farm measures, he opposed virtually everything else in the New Deal program. Author of some of the rawest racial oratory ever heard in the South, he hit hardest when cotton prices were lowest. Described variously as "bulky, ponderous, grumpy, grizzled, baggy-faced and crusty,"[14] he has been called the last of the "spittoon Senators."[15] Within months after Cotton Ed's defeat, he was dead. The primaries would be quieter now.

Although Ball's candidate, Augustus S. Merrimon, trailed the field in the 1944 primary,[16] *The News and Courier* continued to urge the election of independent Democratic electors. Persistently, Ball branded the national Democratic party as a Negro party and reminded his readers that the electoral college had been devised as a defense for small states. If eleven to sixteen Southern states withheld their electoral votes, they could assure respect for their political policies. A vote for Roosevelt was a vote for the Fair Employment Practices Commission. The South's only hope was for her white citizens to stick together and vote for electors pledged to Harry Byrd.[17] All parties but the Southern Democratic party were mixed—white and Negro.[18] But in spite of the untiring efforts of *The News and Courier*, aided principally by the Greenwood *Index-Journal*, the anti-Roosevelt movement did not develop. Ball declined to be an elector, although supporters of his editorial policies expected him to head the ticket.[19] Very few people made financial contributions; the Southern Democratic party could not wage an effective campaign. Once again South Carolina gave solid support to Roosevelt and the Democratic party.

14. Adjectives used in *Time* magazine and collected by Leonard N. Plummer (John T. Salter, ed., *Public Men In and Out of Office* [Chapel Hill, N. C., 1946], p. 345).

15. Heywood Brown in *The New Republic*, XCVI (Sept. 14, 1938), 157.

16. On February 28, 1944, columnist George Sokolsky wrote Ball, asking about Merrimon's prospects. Ball replied that Merrimon had been consistently opposed to Roosevelt, but would not predict whether or not he had the power to lead an anti-New Deal movement.

17. *The News and Courier*, Oct. 16, 1944.

18. *Ibid.*, Oct. 1, 1944.

19. J. K. Breedin to T. R. Waring, Sept. 5, 1944, Ball Papers.

Ball's considerable efforts in behalf of the abortive political revolt still left him time to pursue older objectives. He urged that since degrees from the state-supported colleges were not accepted as first class, aid to these schools should be abolished. All state schools except The Citadel, he charged, were part of the state political machine, and as proof he offered: "The wedding of colleges and politics in South Carolina is complete. The election of State Senator and Trustee H. R. Sims to the presidency of Winthrop was the unblushing confession of it."[20] Ball, however, was somewhat embarassed in his charge that state college professors did not have freedom of speech. The day before Ball had printed an editorial to the effect, *The News and Courier* had published a letter from a Citadel professor critical of American foreign policy and calling upon Congress to reduce tariffs and open up world trade.[21] Ball had not seen the letter, and he admitted that his editorial had been untimely, but he insisted it was the first time in years that a letter from a state college professor on a controversial subject had been printed in a newspaper.

Ball's continued unflattering observations on the quality of state politicians brought him a stinging letter from Reverend E. W. Cantwell, secretary to Governor Johnston. Ball had apparently at one time insinuated that the Board of Pardons, of which Cantwell had been chairman, ought to be investigated. Later Ball suggested he and Cantwell join in a front-page editorial asking for an inquiry into pardons and paroles under Johnston. When Cantwell offered to co-operate with the understanding that if no fraud was proved Ball would allow the pardon board to dunk him in Charleston's Colonial Lake, the editor refused the proposition. Now, Cantwell charged,

> You have acted as an old woman and should be branded as a common scold. Your actions toward me shows [*sic*] that you do not have any conception of the democratic way of life. You feel like the Tory of old. . . . I have defended you all over the State. There has been a rumor that you were half-crazy. I have denied this to everyone that I have met.[22]

T. R. Waring, Jr., Ball's nephew and a member of his staff, had earlier reported on his return from a trip to Columbia that Olin Johnston had

20. *The News and Courier*, June 23, 1944.
21. Letter of Augustus T. Wilson in *The News and Courier*, Aug. 19, 1947.
22. E. W. Cantwell to W. W. Ball, June 17, 1943, Ball Papers.

said that people considered the editor of *The News and Courier* to be a "crazy man."[23]

But by the mid-forties, personal antagonisms and minor issues were fading in the face of the South's mounting racial anxiety. Back in October, 1940, in an article in the *South Atlantic Quarterly*, Ball observed that there had been no lynching in the United States in the year ending May 3, 1940. The reason for the "Improvement in Race Relations in South Carolina," he judged, was the movement of the races away from contact with each other, the ultimate completeness of segregation.[24] But at that moment, the "second Reconstruction" was already underway. For the generation following the establishment of legalized segregation and acceptance by the counts of all but the most blatant caste discrimination, the racial issue remained virtually dormant. Now, however, emerging forces combined to force open the entire issue. The Negro migration northward had begun in earnest with World War I. By 1940 a small Negro professional and white-collar class resided in a number of Northern cities and it used its growing political power to win greater equality of treatment there. Because New Deal programs were designed to advance employment and security, including that of Negroes, most Northern Negroes abandoned their historic allegiance to the Republican party. In cities like New York, Chicago, Philadelphia, and Cleveland the Democratic political machine depended heavily upon the Negro vote.

Their new economic and political strength allowed Negroes to mount a serious attack upon segregation, particularly as it had been legalized in the educational, travel, and political institutions of the South. Acting chiefly through the N.A.A.C.P., Negroes brought a series of test cases before sympathetic federal justices. On the eve of World War II segregation in interstate transportation facilities began to crumble as the Supreme Court ruled that denial of a Pullman berth to a Negro when such facilities were available to whites was a violation of the Interstate Commerce Act.[25] Simultaneously, in a case dealing with ballot-box tampering by state officials in a primary election, the Court held that the federal government could regulate a state primary where such an election was the instrument for choosing candidates for federal office. Inherent in that decision of course, was the threat that the Court would

23. Ball, Diary, XII, 261, March 19, 1943.
24. Ball, *The Editor and the Republic*, p. 195.
25. Mitchell v. United States, 313 U. S. 80 (1941).

ultimately use the Fifteenth Amendment to nullify the white primary.[26]

In the early days of the "Negro Revolution," Ball wrote scores of editorials insisting that Negroes be paid equal compensation for equal service, teachers, included—always with the clear understanding that separation be maintained. Eschewing the phrase "white supremacy" in favor of "white separation," he once remarked, "No respectable person in the South wishes the negroes [sic] to have anything less than justice, but justice does not mean intermingling, political or social."[27] Demands for federal anti-poll tax legislation brought from Ball a strong denial that the poll tax had an important influence on voting practices in South Carolina. It was not a deterrent to registration, he said, because the tax was only one dollar and did not apply to men and women sixty years of age and over. Besides, large numbers of whites, as well as Negroes, did not take the trouble to register. Of course, his principal objections to repeal of the poll tax were that it would swell an already greatly overexpanded electorate, and at the same time represent "a cowering under the whiplash of Northern Liberals."[28]

In 1942 Ball stirred up a minor tempest when he declared in an editorial that in the *Physicians' Handbook on Birth and Death Registration*, a pamphlet issued by the United States Bureau of Census in 1939, doctors were informed that babies of racially mixed parentage should be registered as white if either parent was white. Did this practice, he asked, encourage amalgamation of the races? Furthermore, he could not resist mentioning that the pamphlet bore the name of Harry Hopkins, who had been Secretary of Commerce.[29] The editorial, and others which followed, captured the interest of Senator Theodore Bilbo, the notorious racist from Mississippi,[30] but it also evoked a letter of protest from the director of the Census Bureau. Instructions, Ball was told, applied to races of parents, *not* of children; the latest (1942) edition of the manual stipulated that when *parents* are white and non-white, the race of the non-white should be coded as Negro. The race of the children was a matter to be determined by the bureau. The director regretted the misunderstanding, and promised that language would be sharpened to

26. United States v. Classic, 313 U. S. 299 (1941).
27. W. W. Ball to Braxton H. Tabb, Jr., June 1, 1944, Ball Papers.
28. W. W. Ball to Nelson M. Shipp, Jan. 30, 1945, Ball Papers.
29. *The News and Courier*, Oct. 31, 1942.
30. Sen. Theodore G. Bilbo to W. W. Ball, Nov. 29, 1942, Dec. 30, 1942, Ball Papers.

avoid any possible misinterpretation in future editions, but added, "Despite the fact that this booklet has been in use for several years by many thousands of physicians, no criticism similar to yours has ever been raised from any part of the United States."[31] Ball followed with an editorial blaming the confusion on the ambiguity of the language in the pamphlet, but expressing relief at the explanation. He also reprinted an editorial from the *Greenville News* which remarked, "Recently a newspaperman in another section of the state threw a few conniption fits." After describing the affair, the upcountry paper guessed that the Census Bureau's explanation "ought to quiet the minds of any who may have got 'het up' over this 'sensational exposure!' "[32]

Ball began to receive many anonymous letters, mostly from Negroes denouncing *The News and Courier* for cruel injustices to the colored race.[33] His editorial evaluating "The New Negro Politicians" drew sharp criticism from the state chairman of the colored Progressive Democratic party.[34] And when Roy Wilkins, editor of *The Crisis*, the periodical issued by the N.A.A.C.P., requested a conference with Ball on the Negro question, the editor was polite but cool. His general rule, he replied, was to say nothing on public questions that he did not say in the columns of *The News and Courier*. If Wilkins came to Charleston, Ball would be glad to see him, but Wilkins must not be disappointed if Ball had little or nothing to say.[35] To Ball's mind, *The News and Courier* was trying not to inflame the racial issue, "endeavoring to avoid printing anything that would stir angry feeling between the white and the colored people."[36] Yet it seemed to a variety of critics that Ball's editorials were producing the opposite result. A college student wrote the editor:

In a recent issue of your paper I noticed the words 'pro-negro [sic] administration' or something to that effect. I am definitely not a New Deal sympathizer but neither am I one to promote or aggravate the racial problem with which we are faced today. I consider your phraseology to be such an antagonizer. I feel that it is the duty of every newspaper to do everything within its ability to bring

31. *The News and Courier*, Nov. 13, 1942.
32. *Ibid.*, Nov. 19, 1942.
33. W. W. Ball to Sara Ball Copeland, July 13, 1942, Ball Papers.
34. John H. McCray to W. W. Ball, Sept. 9, 1944, Ball Papers.
35. W. W. Ball to Roy Wilkins, April 28, 1944, Ball Papers.
36. W. W. Ball to Mrs. H. W. Frampton, July 3, 1944, Ball Papers.

about a solution to this problem rather than aggravate it. I sincerely feel that you are doing anything but this.[37]

A Charleston woman who had admired Ball's editorial courage was distressed by his incessant hammering at the Negro question.[38] Day after day, Ball had more than one editorial on the subject. And from his old friend Fitz McMaster came perhaps the most damning indictment of all. After the United States Supreme Court had handed down its decision in the famous Smith *vs.* Allwright case and Ball had roared his dissent, McMaster wrote: "A member of the Kosmos club, not at the Kosmos meeting but outside, a few days ago told me in soberness that he believed you had done more to stir up trouble with the Negroes than any other man in the State."[39]

There was no doubt that Ball's racial attitudes were more reactionary than those he expressed as a younger man. Perhaps it was a natural accompaniment of old age; perhaps, as has been suggested, he was conforming to the harsher philosophies of his publishers.[40] More likely, he foresaw the destruction of the last remaining institution of the old society. Whatever the reason, he now spoke like a militant racist.

"White supremacy will be maintained in our primaries. Let the chips fall where they may," Governor Olin Johnston shouted to one hundred and seventy members of the General Assembly called in special session in April, 1944.[41] A few days before the revolution in civil rights had reached the heart of Southern politics when the United States Supreme Court, in Smith *vs.* Allwright, declared the white primary unconstitutional.[42] Deciding a case in a Texas primary, the court compelled the admission of Negroes to Democratic primaries, but resistance was concentrated in South Carolina, Mississippi, and Alabama. The South Carolina legislature responded to the Governor's challenge by drafting a constitutional amendment, later approved by the voters, repealing all laws regulating the primaries and, in effect, granting the Democratic party the status of a private club. With the attempt to circumvent the decision of the court by the repeal of primary laws, South Carolina left the administration of her major elections to the discretion of the party.

37. Cadet N. A. Baker to *The News and Courier*, published Nov. 28, 1943.
38. Susan Pringle Frost to W. W. Ball, Aug. 17, 1943, Ball Papers.
39. F. H. McMaster to W. W. Ball, May 28, 1944, Ball Papers.
40. George Buchanan, Dean of the School of Journalism of the University of South Carolina, in interview with author, June 23, 1959.
41. *The News and Courier*, April 15, 1944.
42. 321 U. S. 649 (1944).

The lifting of state controls increased opportunities for fraud, but corruption was regarded as the lesser danger.

Ball, in *The News and Courier*, remarked, "The white primaries in South Carolina having been stripped of legal definition and recognition, the danger of negroes [sic] breaking into them does not exist."[43] For a long time, Ball chided, *The News and Courier* had been saying that the Democratic party was in reality a private club and not a part of the state's legal establishment. But it had taken a Supreme Court ruling in a Texas primary to bring that fact to the attention of the governor's office. Now there must be a special legislative session at considerable expense to the taxpayers "to take action the advisability of which a high school boy of average intelligence might have foreseen long ago."[44]

The threat to the white political monopoly in South Carolina posed by the Supreme Court's ruling had little impact, however, on the election of 1944. The state had found temporary safety by deeming the business of the Democratic party a private affair; by the scheme which became known as the "South Carolina plan," she hoped to avoid further federal involvement with her domestic institutions. Longstanding loyalties to the national Democratic party held; Ball's entreaty in behalf of a white Southern Democratic party went virtually unheard.

After the election a temporary lull ensued in the dispute over the voting rights of the Negro. Ball gave thanks in 1945 for the end of a war that had both stirred and depressed him. But the shifting climate of the postwar years provided the greatest challenge ever to the set of his mind. Franklin Roosevelt and Cole Blease were gone—both had died during the war—and Ball could no longer berate them. Ball acknowledged the passing of Roosevelt with a front-page editorial:

The American, the World's, Sorrow

In the presence of death, of their president, in war their commander-in-chief, the people of the U. S. bow in sorrow. First of all, with deep respect, they sorrow with his widow, his daughter and his four soldier sons. They can do nothing that will assuage the grief of the wife and children, beyond saying that, in this time, millions of them know, as they have not known in long years before, what sorrow is.

The Americans well know that in this war the president's days

43. *The News and Courier*, April 16, 1944.
44. *Ibid.*, April 19, 1944.

and nights have been filled with unceasing strife for the defense of his country and the safety of his countrymen. They forget their disagreements of opinion, remembering only that a man not young in years and not for many years in vigorous health, has worked with unfaltering diligence and has exposed himself on sea, on land and in the air to perils as well as discomforts for their sake.

Mankind, with the exception of men of nations who, to us Americans, seem to be enemies of Mankind, share in this loss that has come to the people of the United States. The death of the president of our republic is the sorrow of all the men and women of the world not lost to understanding of the righteousness, that in the world should prevail.

The News and Courier, as an American voice, speaks for the people of South Carolina, the people of Charleston, saying that with the family of the president and all persons closely and affectionately associated with him, they respectfully and deeply mourn.[45]

When Ball treated the death of the President strictly as the passing of a war leader, he took the only course which allowed the editor to be generous without being hypocritical.

War's end found Ball, once again, in an extraordinarily weak position. One prominent Charlestonian, in a letter to the son of a former editor of *The News and Courier*, claimed:

Personally, I like Mr. Ball and am on the friendliest terms with him, but I do not either sympathise or agree with his narrow and very provincial point of view. It is indeed tragic to see how this newspaper has completely lost the influence which it once had. During your father's editorship it was a great power in the State and had national recognition. Both Hemphill and Lathan maintained its position by their vigorous and incisive editorials, although political conditions and the growth of "The State" in Columbia did lessen its general influence. Under Mr. Ball's guidance it has sunk to a point where, even in local matters, its views carry but little weight with the public.[46]

But the war had given impetus to the Negro movement and thus pro-

45. *Ibid.*, April 13, 1945.
46. Nath B. Barnwell to F. Warrington Dawson, Oct. 14, 1946, F. W. Dawson Papers, Duke University Library.

vided Ball with a final great issue for crusading and with new "villains" in the form of Harry Truman and an assortment of federal judges.

During World War II the labor shortage increased the demand for Negro workers and opened the way for their penetration of craft unions. At the same time the Roosevelt administration included anti-discrimination clauses in war contracts and employed large numbers of Negroes in the federal bureaucracy. Not long after the end of the war, President Truman ordered the desegregation of the armed forces. And with the coming of the Cold War, it became imperative to rid American democracy of its abuses in order to counter Communist propaganda attacks. The "second Reconstruction" accelerated as sectional arrangments became the target of a national mission. In 1946 the Court again used the interstate commerce clause to invalidate a Virginia statute requiring racial segregation on public buses moving across state lines.[47] The next year court decisions reopened the entire issue of Negro suffrage.

In the summer of 1947 Judge J. Waties Waring, a Charlestonian of impeccable connections, ordered in U. S. District Court, Charleston, that South Carolina conscientiously open her primaries to Negroes.[48] A case had been brought from Richland County, where managers of the primary had refused to permit Negroes to vote. The plaintiff charged that the Democratic party controlled choice in South Carolina elections —every governor, senator, representative, assemblyman since 1900 had been a Democratic nominee.[49] In finding for the plaintiff, Waring reminded the people of his state that whether universal suffrage was desirable was not the point—it was the law. South Carolina was the only state which then conducted a primary election solely for whites. Representation of the Democratic party as a private club was pure sophistry; private clubs or business organizations did not vote for and elect a president of the United States. Judge Waring's position was unequivocal, his language stern:

> It is time for South Carolina to rejoin the union. . . . I am of the opinion that the present Democratic party in South Carolina is acting for and in behalf of the people of South Carolina; and that the primary held by it is the only practical place where one can

47. Morgan v. Virginia, 328 U. S. 373 (1946).
48. Elmore v. Rice, 72 F. Supp. 516 (1947). Judge Waring was the younger brother of Ball's long-time friend and associate T. R. Waring, whose wife, *née* Laura Campbell Witte, was the sister of Fay Ball.
49. There was a Republican representative from Georgetown County until 1902.

express a choice in selecting federal and other officials. Racial distinctions cannot exist in the machinery that selects the officers and lawmakers of the United States; and all citizens of this state and country are entitled to cast a free and untrammeled ballot in our elections, and if the only material and realistic elections are clothed in the name 'primary,' they are equally entitled to vote there.[50]

Local resentment against Judge Waring was overwhelming, and it found articulation in the steady flow of Ball's editorials. If Negroes voted in white primaries, what would happen in those counties where Negroes outnumber whites? Scalawags there would court the Negro, flatter him, buy him. Another Red Shirt campaign would be necessary.[51] Should Waring's decision be upheld upon appeal, there was only one alternative. South Carolina must abandon completely the name "Democrat," divorce itself from its national party affiliation, and re-establish a white man's political club under a new title. "It is inconceivable," Ball said, "that things have yet come to the point where the right of privacy of assemblage can be restricted by government fiat."[52] A white people's party should hold a convention to "frame and adopt rules and regulations for the nomination of public officers by county and state conventions in the event that the decision that negroes [sic] cannot be kept out of primaries shall be sustained by higher courts."[53] Why was Governor Strom Thurmond hesitant and J. F. Byrnes silent? Why had not the "Barnwell Ring" provided legislative direction? "The present seat, throne and fortress of dumb-stricken kings," Ball remarked, "is in Barnwell, S. C."[54] A stand must be taken now, the editor implored, because the ultimate aim of the hostile forces was the mixing of the races.

In August attorneys for the South Carolina Democratic party won a stay of Judge Waring's July 12 order. Postponement was granted by District Judge George Bell Timmerman after lawyers for the party had complained that Waring's ruling had been "so general in nature" as to be "confusing."[55] His decision applied to all Negroes while the defendant in the case had been the Democratic party of Richland County only.

50. *The News and Courier*, July 13, 1947.
51. *Ibid.*, July 16, 1947.   52. *Ibid.*, July 13, 1947.
53. *Ibid.*, July 17, 1947.   54. *Ibid.*, July 22, 1947.
55. *Ibid.*, Aug. 20, 1947.

When the circuit court of appeals upheld Waring's decision, and the Supreme Court refused to review the case, a desperate search began for still another device to prevent political integration.

Although the overwhelming majority of white Southerners were devoted to the caste system regulating race relations, by this time rival attitudes had developed. One group—smaller, quiter, and without effective leadership—advocated accommodation; the larger group defiantly rejected compromise. In 1948, in spite of the plea of *The Columbia Record* that further proposals in that direction were beneath the dignity of both the party and the state, the Democratic state convention decided upon a plan. The white party would be retained, but a Negro, outside the party, would be allowed to vote in Democratic primaries if he pledged, among other things, that he was not a member of another party, that he opposed a fair employment practices law, and that he believed in the social and educational separation of the races.[56] Thus Negroes might become active in South Carolina politics only by swearing away any interest in their own advancement. Pushed by the N.A.A.C.P., the case found its way again to Judge Waring. His patience exhausted, Waring threatened imprisonment to those who tried to render the law of the land inoperative in South Carolina. The time had come, he repeated, when racial discrimination in political affairs must stop.

But already an earnest and vital independent political movement was underway, in protest against the civil rights program of the Truman administration and the attitudes of the liberal court. The sort of Southern party Ball had envisioned for a decade was, at last, in the making. Naturally, Ball was one of the most frenetic spokesmen for the irreconcilables. In a ringing front-page editorial early in January, 1948, Ball declared both major parties to be pro-Negro. A white South that "crawls on its belly, submits and begs," cried Ball, was the laughingstock of the two great parties. Two-party government was a fetish; there was "nothing in it." John Quincy Adams had been elected president by the House of Representatives. Rutherford B. Hayes was elected by a majority of one vote in the electoral college. Abraham Lincoln and Woodrow Wilson were presidents who had not received the support of the majority of the voters. A convention of Southern white Democrats should now be held to determine how the South might exercise influence in the choosing

56. Some counties, in defiance of the state convention, enrolled both white and black in the Democratic party.

of the next president. Of 531 electoral votes, 140 were in the South; yet, the North, East, and West treated the South as a slave province.[57]

Other papers joined Ball in the demand for action; the Columbia *State*, like *The News and Courier*, called for a Southern third party. State Senator R. M. Kennedy, Jr., advised, however, that it was not necessary to form an independent party. Instead, the state should boycott both national conventions and offer its electoral votes to that party whose platform was in the South's best interests.[58] On January 19, in the state Democratic party's biennial convention, Governor Strom Thurmond[59] was nominated for the office of president of the United States. The state's national convention votes were to be withheld from Harry S. Truman. If Truman were nominated, South Carolina would not support the national party in the electoral college. The state had not spoken so sharply since 1860; it would bolt rather than accept Truman. At the same time Governor Fielding L. Wright of Mississippi issued the call to revolt at the western end of the Deep South.

On February 2, 1948, President Truman requested Congress to take action on civil rights legislation. A few days later a conference of Southern governors at Wakulla Springs, Florida, adopted a resolution condemning Truman's civil rights program and setting another meeting in forty days to discuss means to counteract it. Thurmond described his resolution, adopted over those of Governor Wright and Jim Folsom of Alabama, as putting the governors on record as "being shocked" by both political parties trying to entice "an infinitesimal pressure bloc to vote for one party or the other."[60] The Southern governors' conference also named its own political action committee, headed by Thurmond, which was to go to Washington during the forty-day "waiting period" to demand concessions to "white supremacy" from President Truman. About two weeks later a delegation of governors met with Howard McGrath, National Chairman of the Democratic party. When McGrath gave a flat "No" to their request that Truman's anti-discrimination proposals be withdrawn, the governors of South Carolina, North Carolina, Texas, and Arkansas called on Democrats to join in a revolt against Truman. The South, they announced, was not "in the bag" anymore.

Ball, in a letter to the New York *Herald-Tribune*, sought non-South-

57. *The News and Courier*, Jan. 9, 1948.
58. *Ibid.*, Jan. 17, 1948.
59. Thurmond, running as a mild progressive, had been elected governor in 1946 over James McLeod, the anti-Roosevelt, anti-New Deal candidate.
60. *The News and Courier*, Feb. 8, 1948.

ern support for the anti-Truman movement. There was more at stake than the South's racial arrangement. The proposed second conference should not be confined to Southerners or governors but should attract all those interested in preserving the rights of states against federal penetration. The United States would be better, he exclaimed, if the election of the president went to the House, where all states have one vote and the "city states" could not dominate the proceedings. To this cause he welcomed even the Progressive party:

> Repugnant as are the policies and plans of the Henry A. Wallace party to me, I would rejoice to see its candidate receive a sufficient number of electoral votes to throw the election of President to the House, though preferably that would be accomplished by states supporting another candidate.[61]

Meanwhile, Ball cheered on Strom Thurmond. He wrote the governor: "In my opinion you have made an admirable statement of the spectacle that has 'shocked' the South, which 'outrage[s] and insult[s]' our people."[62] From day to day, the editor promised, the course that should be taken by the people of the state would be outlined in *The News and Courier*. In his editorials Ball complimented Thurmond for "burning his bridges," for coming to the fore in leading Southern opposition to Truman. He advised his readers, "South Carolinians should not forget that their governor went to the front when the fighting was heaviest and before the outcome was decided."[63]

While Ball heaped kindness upon the governor, his treatment of Senator Olin Johnston was even rougher than usual. In truth, Johnston, though a Roosevelt liberal in all else, had not been one in racial matters; but Ball was blinded. Senator Maybank, the editor declared, had replaced Johnston as the defender of South Carolina mill workers. Johnston had boasted that he had been a mill boy, but he had left the mills to become an attorney. The day before Truman had delivered what Ball described as the President's "mixed race" speech, Johnston had told an audience in Columbia that Republicans were responsible for anti-Southern measures, while the Senator knew of Truman's antagonism toward the South.[64] This latest attack evoked from Johnston in Washington an official reply which Ball duly published in *The News and Courier*:

61. New York *Herald-Tribune*, Feb. 22, 1948.
62. W. W. Ball to Strom Thurmond, Feb. 16, 1948, Ball Papers.
63. *The News and Courier*, March 20, 1948.
64. *Ibid.*, Feb. 4, 1948.

Dr. W. W. Ball, without conscience continues to be abusive and insulting through the columns of his newspaper. In his lead editorial of February 4 he again voices a lie when he accuses me of supporting the national administration's consistent campaign to break down the social customs of the South.

I have always ignored these personal attacks against me, these efforts to injure my character and reputation. There have been several instances of clear libel, but I have foregone my right of recourse through the courts simply because I did not care to indulge in the indignity of a legal squabble with a cynical, calloused, bitter and doting old man whom the world has moved on and left behind.[65]

In his statement Johnston also condemned Ball for having supported the Haskellite Movement in 1890. In doing so, the Senator was reiterating a charge brought several months before by the Anderson *Independent*. In an editorial the New Deal-Fair Deal upcountry paper had said:

Let's see now, we believe history records that Editor W. W. Ball, of the Charleston *News and Courier*, attended the Haskell convention in South Carolina back before the turn of the century. The purpose of that convention was to put out an independent ticket, woo the Negro votes, in an effort to defeat BEN TILLMAN.

People in this area who have always favored race segregation, (both social and political), are wondering if he isn't just the man needed to campaign for the Democratic party in the doubtful states, where the Negro votes must be wooed?

Isn't he an experienced wooer?[66]

Ball journeyed to Laurens but could not locate the files of the *Advertiser* that would disprove positively the *Independent*'s contention. The error, he judged, had originated in D. D. Wallace's three-volume history of the state. Wallace, in a letter to Ball, admitted the inaccuracy[67] and the editor so informed the Anderson paper. He had not supported the Haskellite defection, though it had been an honorable movement; he did not consider it a defamation to be associated with it; but he wanted the record put straight.

The Ball-Johnston feud was but an indication of rising feeling in the

65. *Ibid.*, Feb. 7, 1948.
66. Anderson *Independent*, Nov. 25, 1947.
67. D. D. Wallace to W. W. Ball, Dec. 13, 1947, Ball Papers.

South as the national nominating conventions approached. In May a conference at Jackson, Mississippi, with Thurmond keynoting, made plans for still another meeting, in Birmingham, Alabama, if the national convention of the Democratic party adopted a civil rights platform. But, in Ball's estimation, though the great majority of white people in the state were opposed to Truman, political conditions in South Carolina were so utterly confused that anything could happen before the November elections.[68]

Events of mid-July, however, were to have an important crystallizing effect. Judge Waring ruled that Democratic party enrollment books must be kept open to all persons irrespective of race, color, or creed. Ball countered with the suggestion that all enrollments be temporarily stopped and lack of funds might be given as the excuse:

How to Stop the Club Enrolling

The enrollment of persons in Democratic clubs costs money. The extension of time of enrollment is expensive.

The clerks are paid. How much it costs to continue to enroll voters is no matter.

It costs money. Whose money is it?

It is money voluntarily contributed to an unincorporated political society.

The treasurer is the trustee of the society's, the party's, funds.

By whose authority does he hire clerks in Charleston or other counties to keep open offices and enroll persons in clubs?

No federal court has pointed a way by which money can be raised to pay costs of enrollment.

Money contributed by candidates is voluntarily given. No person is compelled to be a candidate and put up an entrance fee.

Some of the money in the hands of county Democratic Committees was contributed by citizens who would not have contributed it had they suspected that it would be used to pay clerks for enrolling colored citizens.

Can a federal court order the treasurer of the carpenters' or the plumbers' union to pay out money for purposes not in the plans and policies of the union and not ordered by them?

68. W. W. Ball to Kent Hunter of the Washington, D. C., Hearst Bureau, July 1, 1948, Ball Papers.

Federal decisions have not proposed any method for paying the costs of keeping open enrollment offices.

Treasurers can refuse to hire enrollment clerks and to buy enrollment books.

Clerks can refuse to work in enrollment offices unless their pay is guaranteed.

Who guarantees it?

In every one of the 46 counties, it is the power of the Democratic clubs to close their offices. Why should their clerks work for nothing?

This Democratic party (it should drop the name), we repeat, is not a corporation, it is not a legal entity.

Is any member of it subject to a court's order unless it be directed to him as an individual?

Will any federal court give orders to the treasurer of a society or party about how he shall spend its money? To a Masonic lodge or a church?

The News and Courier is not denying the possibility that some day or other federal courts will take over the management and operation of all political societies and administer their finances. Not yet has that time come.

The enrollment offices of Democratic clubs in South Carolina can close today. Federal courts are not financing them.[69]

Two days later Judge Waring ordered the abolition of the South Carolina Democratic party's voters oath, the ruling contained in a preliminary injunction against state party officials. His orders also stated that the expense of keeping registration books open was a problem for party officials to solve. Harold R. Boulware of Columbia, one of the two Negro lawyers who presented the case before Waring, said that the mention of expenses was an afterthought and would not have been included if *The News and Courier* had not "shot off its mouth."[70]

At the same time the Democrats in Philadelphia selected both Harry Truman and a civil rights plank for their platform. Immediately afterward, states rights advocates convened in Birmingham in a meeting that V. O. Key described as more a conference than a convention: "The gathering consisted of the big brass of the Democratic party of Mississippi, of Conservative leaders of Alabama, of Governor Thurmond of

69. *The News and Courier*, July 17, 1948.
70. *Ibid.*, July 20, 1948.

South Carolina and his entourage, and a miscellaneous assortment of persons of no particular political importance from other states."[71] From that assemblage emerged the States Rights party which nominated Strom Thurmond as its candidate for president.

Ball followed immediately with his editorial "Thurmond for President." The Governor, Ball proposed, was a man of no less stature than the other candidates (which in Ball's mind may have been faint praise). If the South united behind Thurmond, Truman would lose all its electoral votes and the election might be thrown to the House of Representatives, where with the votes of the South and the West, a man such as Thurmond would have a real chance. Whatever the outcome, the national parties would learn a lesson they would not soon forget—the "Solid South" would no longer be a dependable political factor. "In the electoral college," Ball advised, "lies the only chance to save the South for Southerners."[72]

While Ball praised Thurmond, he continued to emphasize the unfortunate role played by Judge Waring. When the Supreme Court upheld Waring's judgment, his son-in-law dispatched congratulations, adding, "I can't wait to see what my pal Billy Ball has to say about it."[73] Ball's jabs were frequent, varied, and sometimes petty. He reported that the Lawyers Guild, which included the influential Negro leader Thurgood Marshall, had tendered Waring a reception; readers were left to draw their own conclusions. Ball also gave prominent coverage to the resolution introduced in Congress by Southerners asking for an investigation looking toward the impeachment of Waring. The charges against Waring sprang from a persistent piece of Charleston gossip. In 1945 Waring divorced in Florida his wife of many years; Ball believed it to be the first divorce of a man in a prominent official post in the history of South Carolina, colony or state. He later married a woman not acceptable to Charleston society. His judicial decisions, many charged, were designed as retaliations against the neighbors who had snubbed him and his new wife. Official demands for Waring's impeachment, however, were based upon a somewhat more legalistic argument:

The state of South Carolina has a divorce law. [Divorces at this time still were not granted under state law.] The people of that

71. Key, *Southern Politics*, p. 335.
72. *The News and Courier*, July 19, 1948.
73. Stanley Warren to J. W. Waring, April 20, 1948, J. Waties Waring Papers, Howard University Library.

state would like to know how Judge Waring can obtain a separation from a lady to whom he has been married for approximately 30 years, remarry and serve on the federal bench in that great state.[74]

As Judge Waring withstood the scorn of his neighbors, he remarked, with an unmistakable note of sadness:

I have lived all my life in Charleston and try to see over the fog of prejudice which has engulfed this land of ours since the fall of the Confederacy, the horrors of the Reconstruction period and the years of blackness that have resulted. I have tried to do what little has come my way to see that the Negro receives justice in the court where I preside.[75]

Waring was not the only one to have his motives impugned. The Anderson *Independent*, in a bitter editorial, claimed that Ball's extreme dislike of the Roosevelt administration had been caused by the dismissal of W. W. Ball, Jr., from his job with the Department of Internal Revenue. Wilton E. Hall, editor of the paper, asked Ball to

Tell us about your son—didn't he hold a federal job for a time, upon your petition to JAMES F. BYRNES, and haven't you been lambasting BYRNES for years because he wasn't able to keep the young man connected with the succulent federal payroll?

And didn't you once draw a fat check for editing a book for the State of South Carolina? Why you tax-eating bureaucrat![76]

Ball's hide was too old and thick, however, to be punctured by such charges. While the Anderson *Independent* opposed him and the Southern political rebellion, and important papers like *The Columbia Record*, the Columbia *State*, and the Spartanburg *Herald* remained uncommitted, *The News and Courier* and the *Charleston Evening Post* went to work for the States Rights party. August came, and for the first time in an important election, Negroes in South Carolina voted in substantial numbers (approximately 30,000 of 215,000 votes were cast by Negroes). By then, Ball was in the midst of his last great editorial campaign. As was his custom, he printed political editorials daily. On one hand, he attacked Truman and the Democrats, keeping white mill

74. *The News and Courier*, July 30, 1948.
75. J. W. Waring to Rebecca West, Aug., 1948, J. Waties Waring Papers.
76. Anderson *Independent*, Sept. 9, 1948.

workers stirred up over the danger to them of a Fair Employment Practices Commission. On the other hand, he emphasized the national rather than the sectional aspects of the platform of the States Rights party; consequently, he spurned the term "Dixiecrat." When the Anderson *Independent* termed the States Righters "Oilycrats" because of the support they received from oil money, Ball countered by describing the party of Truman and Barkley as "Mixiecrat." But though Ball was editorially in the front line, perhaps because of old age and failing health, he had not participated, behind the scenes, in the actual organization of the Southern resistance movement as he had in 1944 when attempts had been weak and abortive.

In 1948 Ball had the right issue at the right time.[77] As his son-in-law told him that summer, "The weather is mighty hot, and so is politics. . . . People who have been damning you for years are enthusiastic."[78] And when South Carolina was carried for Thurmond and the States Rights party, Ball considered the outcome a triumph for the policy of *The News and Courier*. Even though victory for the States Rights party in the four Southern states with the largest percentage of Negroes[79] did not prevent the election of Truman, a victory had been won in South Carolina that would be valuable "if the leadership shall be capable of utilizing it."[80] In *The News and Courier*, Ball registered a plea, eloquent but forlorn, that the States Rights party must not be allowed to disintegrate. It must flourish, and its national characteristics must be emphasized.

Thurmond and Ball had, of course, been in contact during the previous months. But when the difficult campaign was over—one in which Ball became involved in some of the nastiest backbiting of his long career—Strom Thurmond paid his debt. He wrote Ball:

> Now that the smoke of battle has cleared away, I wish to express my sincere appreciation for the fine cooperation and splendid service you rendered during our fight for States' Rights. You did a

77. Besides voting in national elections, South Carolinians in 1948 were considering two state constitutional amendments. *The News and Courier* advised "vote no" to an amendment which would legalize divorce. It suggested "vote yes" to an amendment which would reduce the governor's power to pardon criminals, a step Ball had advocated for many years. Both amendments were approved by the voters.

78. Clements Ripley to W. W. Ball, July 22, 1948, Ball Papers.

79. South Carolina, Mississippi, Alabama, Louisiana.

80. W. W. Ball to Sara Ball Copeland, Nov. 7, 1948, Ball Papers.

magnificent job, giving freely of your time and talents, and I shall be eternally grateful to you for your patriotic service in behalf of our great cause.

Although we did not win the presidency, we have shown the political leaders of this nation that the South can be independent. With courage, persistence and determination our case will ultimately win.[81]

Like Thurmond, Ball found satisfaction in recent events, whether they be regarded in terms of victory or defeat. In *The News and Courier* he sang, "Last Tuesday, November 2, South Carolina became an unchained state. . . . Hail, hail! To South Carolina free!"[82]

81. Strom Thurmond to W. W. Ball, Nov. 8, 1948, Ball Papers.
82. *The News and Courier*, Nov. 5, 1948.

CHAPTER TWELVE

"DAMNED UPCOUNTRYMAN"

A FEW WEEKS after Ball concluded his campaign for the States Rights party, he observed the eightieth anniversary of his birth. It had been more than twenty years since he had returned to *The News and Courier*, and he had long since became a "Charleston character." Ball—a short man with prominent nose and determined eyes—was a familiar figure as he chatted in Broad Street, occupied regularly pew thirty-seven at St. Michael's, strolled the Battery in his perpetually rumpled clothes. Ball's suits looked unpressed because when he retired, he habitually tossed his jacket onto a chair seat, then sat upon it to remove his trousers. Also, during the summer, Ball arranged his suit coat to provide maximum ventilation; consequently, his jacket often looked as though it had been slung over one shoulder.[1] Perhaps the editor was not so popular a tourist attraction as the mythical Catfish Row of Porgy and Bess, or Rainbow Row, with its single houses painted in a profusion of pastels, but he was certainly the town's most distinctive inhabitant. In 1945 he sat for a sculptor who made the clay model of his head which was eventually placed in the Gibbes Art Gallery in Charleston. John Gunther in his travel book *Inside U. S. A.*, described him as "a saltily picturesque character" who liked to say that he was the last surviving Jeffersonian Democrat, and whose views, "idiosyncratic in the extreme," were expressed in editorial paragraphs that were "full of prejudice and pith."[2]

It did not trouble Ball that he was so often regarded as a curiosity, out of touch with his times. The old-fashioned black bow ties that he wore were no longer commercially manufactured, so he had them specially made. He calmly accepted his first social security check, though his model of a Democrat was still John Randolph of Roanoke, who was suspicious of government. Ball was equally undisturbed by charges that his editorials were unrealistic. He liked to boast that *The News and Courier*, like the New York *Sun* in the days of Charles A. Dana, was

1. W. W. Ball, Jr., in interview with author, May 11, 1959.
2. John Gunther, *Inside U. S. A.* (New York, 1947), pp. 726–727.

published "for the entertainment of its editor."[3] Ball went his way and told his stories. A colleague once remarked that Ball seemed to use a box of matches every time he lit his pipe—each time he struck a match, he would begin to talk, and the match would go out. His grandson recalled automobile trips from Charleston to Laurens when Ball had a tale for almost every big house along the road.

Ball found amusement also in playing "childish games" with himself: spotting out-of-state car licenses during the tourist season in Charleston; matching the number of cars he could see from his Caesar's Head piazza coming up the highway from Greenville on a Saturday night against the ones he had seen on a previous Saturday.[4] He remained devoted to piquet; once he and Fay Ball played on, unperturbed, as firemen rushed through the house to combat the effects of a minor furnace explosion.[5] And of course he still met the world's famous when they came to Charleston. One evening, which he especially treasured, he described for Josephus Daniels:

> I wish you might have been at my house a week ago when Lord and Lady Astor called. We had a delightful evening. The Lady and I became old friends between the front door and the living room. When, at 11 o'clock, she was putting on her coat she suddenly made a dive from the living room to the dining room and snatched a banana. Then Mrs. Ball gently asked his lordship if he would have a banana and he gently said that he would. So they both had a banana, being teetotalers as to liquids and tobacco they had declined other refreshment.[6]

To the end, Ball retained the personal characteristics which won those who could not sympathize with his philosophy. He never took himself so seriously that he could not make a joke at his own expense. One day Gallant Bess, the educated movie horse, visited the editorial rooms of *The News and Courier*, coming upstairs on the elevator. Ball and the horse posed for a picture, which someone suggested should be sent to *Editor and Publisher*. Ball remarked that the photograph ought to be captioned "Two Intellectuals."[7] He roared when he recalled an evening when dinner guests brought their ten-year-old grandson. All were eating

3. W. W. Ball to F. H. McMaster, Dec. 13, 1949, Ball Papers.
4. Eleanor Ball Hewitt-Myring to author, July 30, 1959.
5. Margaret Ball Hickey, in interview with author, May 8, 1959.
6. W. W. Ball to Josephus Daniels, March 15, 1946, Ball Papers.
7. Ball, Diary, XIII, 191, Dec. 26, 1946.

when the boy, who was a reader of magazines, announced to his astonished elders: "Do any of you have syphilis? If so, please leave the room. We are going to stamp it out!"

There were dozens of testaments to his kindness and generosity; he was never too busy to talk to young writers and researchers who sought his help. In appreciation, Margaret Coit dedicated to him her biography of Bernard Baruch. Gentility and politeness were among his several obsessions; his niece could not imagine her Uncle Billy ever being rude to a woman. He had equal regard for propriety, however, and there were only two people in Laurens he thought entitled to address him as "Billy," and one of them was his brother-in-law.[8] Around the newspaper office he tried to maintain a stern reserve as he cautioned, "We're running a prudish newspaper," or shouted, "Go out and infuriate somebody; stir up the animals; nobody is mad at us; the paper is slipping." But his co-workers knew that underneath the apparent strictness there was abundant warmheartedness.

For years Ball had been threatening to retire, and the matter had been discussed between him and his publishers, but after each conference the editor had decided to stay "a while longer." For two years after the major effort of 1948, he hung on. During the waning months, Ball continued to press for a return to the convention system of nominating candidates, now that the federal courts had altered the function of the Southern primary. He had no objection to a few enlightened and substantial Negroes voting and holding office, as had been the case before the introduction of the primary in the 1890's.

Ball continued also to report and comment upon the activities of Judge and Mrs. Waring. Both suffered continual social persecution, but the Judge's Yankee wife, especially, gave measure for measure to her tormentors. Elizabeth Waring, a dedicated civil rights advocate, exasperated Charleston by flaunting her admiration of the Negro race. Privately, she kept scrapbooks filled with clippings of Negroes who had been acclaimed, whether for winning literary prizes or foot races. Publicly, she proclaimed Southern whites morally decadent and spiritually inferior to Negroes. And in a talk before a small group in a Negro Y.W.C.A., she abandoned all caution.

"Blazing like a flamethrower,"[9] she spoke:

8. Beaufort Copeland, in interview with author, June 5, 1957.
9. *Time*, LV, No. 5 (Jan. 30, 1950), 18.

My very dear friends, it was brave of you to invite me to speak here, and brave of all of you to come to hear me, for the White "Powers that Be" have done everything underhanded in their power to keep me from speaking to you Negro people, even to defaming Judge Waring's and my character. But we only feel sorry for them, for their stupidity, as it will hurt them, and not us, for it is apparent to everyone what their real motive is in not wishing me to speak—FEAR of the Judge and me. We to them are like the ATOM BOMB WHICH THEY ARE AFRAID WE WILL USE TO DESTROY THEIR SELFISH AND SAVAGE WHITE SUPREMACY WAY OF LIFE. AND THEY ARE QUITE CORRECT. THAT IS EXACTLY WHAT THE JUDGE AND I ARE DOING. . . .[10]

Ball informed his sister, "It's torn Charleston wide open of course. . . ."[11] (And later) "In Charleston are no new scandals, though it is a rare day in which one hears no story about the judge and Mrs. Judge."[12]

Waring's treatment by the local press so disturbed him that he notified *The News and Courier*:

My experience with the lack of fairness and editorial integrity of the Charleston newspaper combination leads me to refuse to furnish any interviews or to authorize any quotation or run the risk of misquotation. The newspapers are, of course, privileged, and have the right to obtain and publish any authorized opinions or statements or any acts of mine. They also, of course, are entirely free to express their opinions of me and my judicial views, acts, or doings. But I do not feel it safe to give my personal opinions to be garbled to suit the propaganda purpose of so biased a newspaper. If I should have occasion to give any press release at any time, I shall prefer using some newspaper of a higher standard.[13]

The controversy lingered until 1952, when Waring retired from the federal bench at the age of seventy-two. Soon afterward he and his wife moved to New York.

Although he had been bewildered by the actions of the Warings, it was somewhat more pleasant for Ball to acknowledge his last rapprochement with James F. Byrnes. One of the few Southern politicians since

10. Jan. 16, 1950. Original copy of the speech is in J. W. Waring Papers.
11. W. W. Ball to Sara Ball Copeland, Jan. 19, 1950, Ball Papers.
12. W. W. Ball to Sara Ball Copeland, Nov. 23, 1950, Ball Papers.
13. *The News and Courier*, June 30, 1949.

the Civil War able to rise to transcend the limitations of regionalism, Byrnes had resigned as Secretary of State in 1947 and returned to Columbia. Although now he had little or no contact with Byrnes, Ball still believed that he had been, more than any other, responsible for Byrnes's early political success. And when *The News and Courier* began a reprint of Byrnes's *Collier's* article entitled "Crisis Government Can Ruin Us," warning that big government, big spending, and big borrowing were dangerous as continuous policies, Ball gave the series a hearty editorial send-off.[14] If nothing else, the compliments to Byrnes appeared to scotch the frequently repeated Charleston gossip that he had been forever marked by Ball for failing to safeguard his son's federal employment.

Meanwhile, disagreements grew over the format of the editorial page. Young T. R. Waring, Ball's principal assistant, thought that the bulk of the editorials should be reduced. They were too long, too repetitive, and discouraged reading. He suggested Ball write a personal column, continue to direct and contribute to the editorial page, but allow a more flexible and attractive package.[15] Ball consented to a three- to four-inch limit for editorials and agreed to conform to it as an experiment, but he rejected radical changes. In a fervent restatement to Waring of the traditions of the press, Ball acknowledged that a newspaper must live and make money. But editorials must be purposeful, and not primarily designed to sell papers or advertising copy. Editorials, of course, discouraged most readers; they could not compete with "funnies." But a newspaper should not habitually bend to the trend in reading. The power to repeat, to din, to hammer, was the principal advantage a newspaper possessed, and it should not be abandoned because a reader was lost or an advertising buyer dissuaded. And if what the newspaper said was less important, less influential than the sayings of an individual featured in its columns, then the paper would be better not to have editorials at all. He disliked all columnists, Ball confessed, because their columns spoke only for their authors, not for the newspapers that carried them.[16]

By 1950 it was clear that Ball's faltering health made his retirement imminent. He was not well enough in March to attend the funeral in Columbia of his oldest friend, Fitz McMaster. On January 1, 1951, Ball

14. *Ibid.*, March 5, 1950.
15. T. R. Waring, Jr., to W. W. Ball, Dec. 14, 1949, Ball Papers.
16. W. W. Ball to T. R. Waring, Jr., Dec. 15, 1949, Ball Papers.

surrendered the editorship of *The News and Courier*. Under the terms of his departure, he was to be paid the same weekly wage, for which he was to contribute editorial paragraphs and—in spite of his disapproval of columnists—to write a column which was to be called "Or Do You Remember?" While Ball had been its editor, the paper had risen from sixth to third in circulation among the state's dailies. Now Thomas R. Waring, Jr., became the paper's fifth editor. Ball, with a sigh, guessed that Waring would not be as combative as he had been or, as a former colleague had put it, not as "mean" as Billy Ball.[17]

Ball received many kind messages, but perhaps none was more gratifying than the copy of the resolution, dignified by the state seal, which was adopted by the South Carolina House of Representatives on January 11, 1951. This commendation, voted by many who were his political enemies, said, in part:

> Many of his readers disagreed with his views on political questions but all recognized him as an editor of ability and a man of courage. Upon his retirement as editor of The News and Courier, we acknowledge his achievements in the field of journalism and the contribution that he has made to free and independent thinking in this state, and wish for him many more years of useful and happy living.

Throughout most of the next two years Ball continued to go to his office at *The News and Courier*, where he wrote editorials and paragraphs for his column. But as his physical condition gradually deteriorated, many of his editorials had to be rewritten. How it must have stung to have paragraphs returned marked "rejected by editor." To his sister he lamented, "They don't like for me to write editorials except in the column over my initials."[18] By January, 1952, Ball recorded himself in positive opposition to the editorial policy of *The News and Courier*: "I hold that the opponents of the national 'Democratic' party cannot honorably send delegates to its nominating convention, participate in its negotiation and proceedings and then if its decision be adverse to their wishes, try to defeat the nominees of it in the November elections."[19] Ironically, at this time the *Evening Post* and *News and Courier* Company had begun construction of a new building located, not south of

17. W. W. Ball to Sara Ball Copeland, Dec. 30, 1950, Ball Papers.
18. W. W. Ball to Sara Ball Copeland, March 1, 1952, Ball Papers.
19. Ball, Diary, XV, 16, Jan. 28, 1952.

Broad Street in Ball's "politer part" of town, but uptown on Columbus Street. Ball, during the cornerstone-laying ceremonies, had placed a few masses of mortar on a plate which he had first laid in an opening in the cornerstone. In June, when the papers moved to their new quarters, Ball was pathetically concerned lest his old desk not be moved from Meeting Street. Even when he found it in the new place, obtrusive amidst the modern office furniture, he did not feel at home.

Ball was then suffering almost unrelieved pain from the gastric ailments that had begun troubling him in early manhood. His digestive troubles had become so severe that several visits to the hospital were necessary; blood transfusions were continued throughout the summer. On September 6, he went to the office for the last time. A few days later, his writing hand began to stiffen and cramp. On September 30 he dictated his last column. On the same day, he made the last entry, almost illegible, in the journal he had kept for thirty-six years: "I had dinner downstairs, having dressed myself and made the trip without help. I am tired; Dr. O'Hear encourages me."[20] Two weeks later, at ten minutes past midnight on October 14, 1952, William Watts Ball died.

That morning *The News and Courier* carried Ball's obituary in black-bordered columns on its front page. Accolades from important citizens soon followed. Bernard Baruch wired: "There was no greater devotee to America and what he thought it stood for. No one had greater courage in expressing his views and expressing them so well. There are too few like him left. He will be missed by us all."[21] Press reaction was remarkably unanimous in tone and approach. A Columbia paper remarked:

> Great editors, fighting editors, are judged by two criteria: one, the success of their editorial campaigns and, two, the animosities they arouse. By both criteria, although at different times, . . . he has made his impress upon South Carolina and South Carolina history.

Perhaps he knew he fought a losing battle, the *Record* concluded, but he fought on for the joy of fighting and for the enemies he made.[22] The *Atlanta Constitution* described him as "the only completely honest reactionary since 1865."[23] *The New York Times*, in reporting his death,

20. *Ibid.*, XV, 41, Sept. 30, 1952.
21. *The News and Courier*, Oct. 16, 1952.
22. *The Columbia Record*, Oct. 16, 1952.
23. *Atlanta Constitution*, Oct. 16, 1952.

observed that Billy Ball had often been called the last of the great editorial personalities.[24]

Without doubt, in press circles Ball was a legend in his own time—the outstanding exponent of lively and cantankerous journalism. When he retired temporarily to become Dean of Journalism at the University, his political prestige in the state was at its height. After he came back he became increasingly more outspoken in his reaction and, consequently, less consistently influential in state affairs. But it was then, after his return to Charleston, that he received limited national recognition for his campaigns against Prohibition and the New Deal and for his support of the States Rights party. It was during those years of flamboyant rejection that he gained a little of the attention that he craved but could not reconcile with his philosophical devotion to the principle of editorial anonymity. It was the furor surrounding his late extremism that led one prominent South Carolinian to remark that Ball's editorship of *The News and Courier* was "the most important in the history of the state since the heyday of the ante-bellum *Mercury*."[25] Even those who disagreed with everything he ever wrote regarded Ball as a state institution. The Anderson *Independent* had been Ball's harshest critic during his old age; it had classically described Charleston as the place where ". . . Dr. Ball and chronic dyspepsia run together to form The News and Courier."[26] And yet, the *Independent*'s publisher admitted, "I, too, am very fond of the G. O. P. (Grand Old Person)."[27]

But Ball was more than a fighting editor; he was an important contributor to American anti-democratic thought. In his book and in his many speeches, editorials, and pamphlets, Ball attacked the doctrine of equality. The propounders of democracy had said that since the American government was based on the theory that all men are created equal, if men were equal, they had an equal right to rule. The equality of man, Ball thought, meant equality before the law, which did not guarantee to all men an equal share in shaping the laws by which they were to be governed. The notion that men were equal was always a fallacy to him—differences in background, intelligence, and education prevented it. In government by the "enlightened" Ball saw the only answer to the problems that confronted his state and country.

24. *The New York Times*, Oct. 15, 1952.
25. Herbert Ravenel Sass in *The News and Courier*, Jan. 11, 1953.
26. "Other Men's Opinions," *The News and Courier*, Dec. 11, 1946.
27. Wilton E. Hall to Leon Harris, Sept. 23, 1948, Ball Papers.

A healthy scorn for the myth of equality was a characteristic shared by some of Ball's contemporaries who also sought to expose the failures of democracy. True democracy, said Ralph Adams Cram,[28] meant three things: abolition of privilege, equal opportunity for all, and utilization of ability. Universal suffrage and free public education had turned democracy into mediocrity.[29] Irving Babbitt[30] also claimed that during the nineteenth century in the United States the meaning of democracy had been gradually but steadily distorted. A conflict had arisen

between those who maintain that the popular will should prevail, but only after it has been purified of what is merely impulsive and ephemeral, and those who maintain that this should prevail immediately and unrestrictedly. . . . If democracy means simply the attempt to eliminate the qualitative and selective principle in favor of some general will based in turn on a theory of natural rights, . . . it will result practically, not in equality, but in a sort of inverted aristocracy. . . . One should, therefore, in the interests of democracy itself seek to substitute the doctrine of the right man for the doctrine of the rights of man.[31]

Walter Lippmann attempted to explain the reason for the difference between present-day and eighteenth-century democracy:

Had democrats admitted there was truth in any of the aristocratic arguments they would have opened a breach in the defenses. And so just as Aristotle had to insist that the slave was a slave by nature, the democrats had to insist that the free man was a legislator and administrator by nature. They could not stop to explain that a human soul might not yet have, or indeed might never have, this technical equipment, and that nevertheless it had an unalienable right not to be used as the unwilling instrument of other men. The superior people were still too strong to have refrained from capitalizing so candid a statement.[32]

28. Ralph Adams Cram (1863–1942) was an architect and social critic who sought to apply the grandeur and symmetry of Gothic architecture to contemporary political and social life. Among his architectural accomplishments is the Cathedral of St. John the Divine in New York City.

29. Ralph A. Cram, *The Nemesis of Mediocrity* (Boston, 1917), p. 23.

30. Irving Babbitt (1865–1933), editor, scholar, and critic, was for many years Professor of Classics and French Literature at Harvard University.

31. Irving A. Babbitt, *Democracy and Leadership* (Boston, 1924), pp. 245–247.

32. Walter Lippmann, *Public Opinion* (New York, 1946), pp. 193–194 (reprint).

The great democratic fallacy, Lippmann continued, had been its preoccupation with the origin of government rather than with the results. The democrat has assumed that if political power could be derived in the right way, the effects would automatically be good. "His whole attention," said Lippmann, "has been on the source of power, since he is hypnotized by the belief that the great thing is to express the will of the people, first because expression is the highest interest of man, and second, because the will is instinctively good."[33] In the end, Lippmann judged, what determined the quality of a civilization was the use made of power, not the nature of power itself.

It remained for H. L. Mencken to bring democracy to the level of the absurd. He remarked: "It came into the world as a cure-all, and it remains primarily a cure-all to this day. Any boil upon the body politic, however vast and raging, may be relieved by taking a vote; any flux of blood may be stopped by passing a law."[34] And with his caustic wit, he concluded, "I confess for my part, that it greatly delights me. I enjoy democracy immensely. It is incomparably idiotic, and hence incomparably amusing."[35]

There is no evidence to indicate that Ball corresponded with any of his fellow critics except Walter Lippmann, and his exchanges with Lippmann were few and superficial. But he certainly shared their view that government to be effective and efficient must be based on a limited electorate. He always felt that the masses of common people were not capable of ruling themselves wisely. Back to Calhoun! Back to Aristocracy!

Ball, like Jefferson, saw in the growth of big cities the concentration of laboring populations which would breed crime and political corruption. Yet Jefferson during his last years conceded the inevitability of industrial and urban development. Jefferson made adjustments to the demands of the hour, but Ball was more like John Randolph of Roanoke, whose course was inflexible. Ball advocated a return to the agrarian life to accompany the return to aristocracy. It was time for a return to pioneering, time for the exploration of a new frontier—the unused, potentially useful agricultural land that Ball called the "vertical frontier." The word "return" was the cornerstone of his philosophy. In this respect he resembled other social critics of his day. Cram, like Henry

33. *Ibid.*, p. 235.
34. H. L. Mencken, *Notes on Democracy* (New York, 1926), p. 196.
35. *Ibid.*, p. 211.

Adams, found utopia in the Middle Ages. He hoped for the development of a natural aristocracy, and suggested titles of nobility to designate proven leadership ability, offering as an example "Sir Mark Twain."[36] They all demanded a new leadership, a new governing class. Ball found his in the educated property owner. Mencken remarked that democracy, in order to separate the good that was in it theoretically from the evils that beset it practically, must invent and install a genuine aristocracy.[37] It was this aristocracy that Ball sought to re-establish in South Carolina to serve as an example to the nation. He called upon his state to enforce strictly her existing qualifications for voting, to tighten them, and to educate her people that there was no injustice in relating property holding to the ballot. He was a self-admitted and prideful reactionary.

Ball was often criticized for ignoring the facts of life. Without doubt there was truth in the charge. While he was boasting that cotton mill workers never enjoyed better living conditions, two-thirds of them lived in slum or near slum housing. He was also scored for dissipating his editorial influence in pursuit of goals that could not be attained. Too often he was guilty. Could South Carolina, or any other state, have withstood pressure for the democratization of government, a movement that had begun in America long before 1776? And, as Alexis de Tocqueville said, when a nation modified the elective qualification, sooner or later that qualification would be entirely eliminated. Was there even the slightest chance that the trend could be reversed? On the other hand, Ball's suggestion that the United States was too big, too diverse for centralized government is not without relevance to contemporary problems. Recent trends in joint federal-state planning—in co-operative federalism—rescue him from assignment to the world of utter fancy.

Ball was a product of old South Carolina where the four pillars of the social order were "ancestors, possessions, occupations and education."[38] And there he stood as the changes of the atomic age swirled about him. Death spared him the sight of the first public school integration in the South, the desegregation of public accommodations, and other manifestations of equal rights for Negroes. Moreover, already apparent during his last years was the acceleration of industrial development in South Carolina and with it the emergence of a new group of businessmen who

36. Ralph A. Cram, *The End of Democracy* (Boston, 1937), p. 211.
37. Mencken, *Notes on Democracy*, p. 206.
38. Rosser H. Taylor, *Ante-Bellum South Carolina: A Social and Cultural History* (Chapel Hill, N. C., 1942), p. 7.

were prepared to give ground in the civil rights controversy because, presumably, racial trouble discouraged industrial investment. The future of race relations in South Carolina and elsewhere seemed to depend more and more upon the outcome of the new competition between racism and materialism. The cause of white supremacy—the great Southern unifier—lost strength and its future appeared uncertain. The rise in industrial wealth also put farther beyond reach Ball's utopian state of dedicated farmers. Yet even as the factories of North Charleston multiplied, he was glad that rich Northerners occupied the nearby rice plantations until such time as they might again come into demand for agriculture.[39] Few public men today would have his approval—perhaps Senator Strom Thurmond, who changed his registration from Democrat to Republican. Ball would have approved of that.

What more fitting habitat than Charleston could there be for such a man? He once remarked, "I am what I am, a most Charlestonian person."[40] Still, even Charleston was not the same. Some of her fine old residences had necessarily been converted into rooming houses. The tourist, ubiquitous in the spring, could find family antiques for sale. The city's young leaders often now deserted the Battery for new ranch homes in the suburbs. The banker and the merchant more frequently ate "lunch" at half-past twelve; fewer Charlestonians sat for three o'clock dinner.

Much as Billy Ball loved what remained of old Charleston, he remained sentimentally attached to the upcountry where he was born and reared. "However devoted to Charleston I am," he confessed, "I don't like it that there is never any red clay on my shoes."[41] He enjoyed the frequent chiding of his Charleston cronies that he was just a "damned upcountryman." Surely he possessed in abundance the qualities of independence and individualism that the upcountry is supposed to breed. And as abstract ideals, his devotion to political honesty and personal liberty are beyond question. But as the upcountry code was his strength, so was it his weakness. Thus he became a spokesman for a shrinking band of romantics. Undeterred, he preached traditional conservatism while the old liberal-conservative dichotomy lost its viability in American democracy. Political realism demanded recognition of a new rivalry

39. Jonathan Daniels, *A Southerner Discovers the South* (New York, 1938), p. 326.
40. Ball, Diary, XIII, 230, March 14, 1948.
41. W. W. Ball to Gerald Johnson, Oct. 28, 1938, Ball Papers.

attuned to the welfare state—a competition for public support not between men who were either liberal or conservative, as Ball understood
the terms, but between men who varied in their degree of commitment to
the liberal line. But Ball saw no reason to adjust principles, formed
before he was grown, to changing circumstances; exactly the opposite—
the times must be shaped to conform to tradition.

Margaret Coit, admittedly a devotee, composed the eulogistic poem
which appeared in *The News and Courier*:

> We shall not see him again.
> We shall not climb the long and twisting stair
> To the old corner office where
> The round church looked in the dusty window pane.
> And in the shade of the brick walls beyond
> Calhoun sleeps beneath magnolias and rain.
>
> We shall not see him again.
> That cameo head, that bright, sharp eye,
> The old-fashioned, twisted, black bow-tie,
> Or hear the voice, so full of humor and of pain
> Turn time back, bring back our glorified past . . .
> The Red Shirts ride with Hampton once again.
>
> We shall not see his like again.
> He was our past, our present, one,—
> Our dreaming Charleston in the Southern sun,
> He, who out of the red hills and foot-hills came,
> Bearing aloft the banner Calhoun bore.
> For him, St. Michael's bells are tolling in the rain.[42]

The two upcountrymen, Calhoun and Ball, were indeed remarkably
alike; they were both martyrs to lost causes. Ball's career was built upon
a wistful gesture. Amidst the problems of mid-century America, the
dream of a simpler life has unquestioned appeal. Ball was a symbol of
that reverie. Throughout his lifetime he stubbornly insisted that it was
not impossible to go back. But in his heart he knew otherwise; he
admitted as much in *The State That Forgot*. The republic of quality was
dead; the new democracy was strange and vulgar; and there was no
recovery.

42. *The News and Courier*, Oct. 18, 1952. Miss Coit's biography, *John C
Calhoun: American Portrait*, was published in 1950.

BIBLIOGRAPHY

Sources

Manuscripts

Diary of William Watts Ball. 15 vols. Duke University Library.
Papers of William Watts Ball. Duke University Library.
Papers of Francis Warrington Dawson. Duke University Library.
Papers of Nathaniel B. Dial. Duke University Library.
Papers of John P. Grace. Duke University Library.
Papers of James Calvin Hemphill. Duke University Library.
Papers of David F. Houston. Harvard University Library.
Papers of August Kohn. The South Caroliniana Library.
Minutes of the Kosmos Club. 2 vols. The South Caroliniana Library.
Papers of Robert S. Meriwether. The South Caroliniana Library.
The News and Courier Collection. The South Carolina Historical Society Library.
Papers of James Henry Rice, Jr. Duke University Library.
Papers of Yates Snowden. The South Caroliniana Library.
Minutes of the University of South Carolina Board of Trustees, June, 1923.
Papers of Governor Strom Thurmond. The South Caroliniana Library.
Papers of J. Waties Waring. Howard University Library.

Books, Articles, Pamphlets

Ball, William Watts. *A Boy's Recollections of the Red Shirt Campaign of 1876 in South Carolina.* Columbia, S. C., 1911.
————. "The Dry South Dampens," *Virginia Quarterly Review*, IX (October, 1933), 526–537.
————. *The Editor and the Republic.* Edited by Anthony Harrigan. Chapel Hill, N. C., 1954.
————. *An Episode in South Carolina Politics.* N. p., 1915.
————. *Essays in Reaction.* Columbia, S. C., 1923.
————. "The Industrial Revolution in South Carolina," *Sewanee Review*, XIX (April, 1911), 129–137.
————. "Richard Irvine Manning," *Dictionary of American Biography*, XII (1933), 251–252.
————. "South Carolina's Dispensary System," *Forum*, XC (July, 1933), supp. xi.
————. *The State That Forgot.* Indianapolis, 1932.
————. *A View of the State.* Columbia, S. C., 1913.
Baruch, Bernard. *My Own Story.* New York, 1957, 1960. 2 vols.
Byrnes, James F. *All In One Lifetime.* New York, 1958.

McCravy, Edwin P. *Memories*. Greenville, S. C., 1941.
Robertson, Ben. *Red Hills and Cotton*. Columbia, S. C., 1960 (reprint).

Interviews and Personal Correspondence

W. W. Ball, Jr., interview with the author, May 11, 1959.
George Buchanan, interview with the author, June 23, 1959.
James F. Byrnes, letter to the author, June 3, 1959.
Beaufort Copeland, interview with the author, June 5, 1957.
Sara Ball Copeland, interview with the author, June 5, 1957.
Eleanor Ball Hewitt-Myring, letter to the author, July 30, 1959.
Margaret Ball Hickey, interview with the author, May 8, 1959.
Beatrice Ravenel, interview with the author, May 11, 1959.
William Y. W. Ripley, interview with the author, May 12, 1959.
Samuel G. Stoney, interview with the author, May 8, 1959.
Thomas R. Waring, Jr., interview with the author, May 13, 1959.

NEWSPAPERS

Anderson (S. C.) *Independent*, November 25, 1947, September 9, 1948.
Asheville (N. C.) *Citizen*, October 26, 1932.
Atlanta Constitution, October 16, 1952.
Boston *Transcript*, December 2, 1932.
The Charleston (S. C.) *American*, July 28, 1918.
The (Charleston, S. C.) *News and Courier*, April 8, 1895, December 25,
    1895, June 2, 1909, June, 1927–October, 1952.
The Charlotte (N. C.) *Observer*, July 24, 1922.
The Columbia (S. C.) *Record*, March 6, 1930, October 16, 1952.
The (Columbia, S. C.) *State*, August, 1913–September 1923, January 4,
    1925, April 15, 1927, October 13, 1932, October 26, 1932.
Greenville County (S. C.) *Observer*, March 13, 1930.
Greenville (S. C.) *Piedmont*, March 11, 1930.
Laurens (S. C.) *Advertiser*, 1891–1893.
The Lynchburg (Va.) *News*, September 14, 1922.
(New York) *Herald-Tribune*, January 1, 1933, February 22, 1948; *New
    York Herald-Tribune Books*, January 1, 1937.
The New York Times, June 1, 1909, August 9, 1924, August 20, 1924,
    November 25, 1928, February 28, 1932, October 15, 1952; *The New
    York Times Book Review*, November 27, 1932.
New York World Telegram, October 11, 1932.
(Richmond, Va.) *Times-Dispatch*, September 13, 1922.
The Yorkville (S. C.) *Enquirer*, December 23, 1923.

SECONDARY WORKS

Babbitt, Irving A. *Democracy and Leadership*. Boston, 1924.
Burts, Robert M. "The Public Career of Richard I. Manning." Unpublished
    Doctoral Dissertation, Vanderbilt University, 1957.
Cash, W. J. *The Mind of the South*. Vintage Edition, New York, 1960.

Clark, Thomas D. and Albert D. Kirwan. *The South since Appomattox*. New York, 1967.

Coit, Margaret L. *Mr. Baruch*. Cambridge, Mass., 1957.

Commager, Henry S. "A South Carolina Dictator," *Current History*, XLIII (March, 1936), 568–572.

Cralle, R. K., editor. *The Works of John C. Calhoun*. New York, 1857. 6 vols.

Cram, Ralph A. *The End of Democracy*. Boston, 1937.

———. *The Nemesis of Mediocrity*. Boston, 1917.

Crawford, Geddings H. *Who's Who in South Carolina*. Columbia, S. C., 1921.

Current History Association. *Who's Who in South Carolina, 1934–1935*. Columbia, S. C., 1935.

Daniels, Jonathan. *A Southerner Discovers the South*. New York, 1938.

Easterby, James Harold. *A Guide to the Study and Reading of South Carolina History*. Columbia, S. C., 1949.

"Editor, Old Style," *Time*, XXV, No. 12 (March 18, 1940), 52–53.

"Editor's Anti-New Deal War Rocks Staid Old Charleston," *Newsweek*, XV, No. 12 (March 18, 1940), 44–46.

Ezell, John S. *The South since 1865*. New York, 1963.

Foster, Jack. "Palmetto Profiles: W. W. Ball," *South Carolina Magazine*, No. 3, March, 1948, pp. 14, 27.

Guess, William Francis. *South Carolina: Annals of Pride and Protest*. New York, 1960.

Gunther, John. *Inside U. S. A.* New York, 1947.

Hemphill, James C. *Men of Mark in South Carolina*. Washington, D. C., 1907–1909. 4 vols.

Hennig, Helen Kohn. *Great South Carolinians*. Chapel Hill, N. C., 1940, 1949. 2 vols.

Historic Charleston Foundation. *Charleston's Historic Houses*. Charleston, S. C., 1957.

Historical Commission of South Carolina. *South Carolina Bibliographies*. Columbia, S. C., 1949. Nos. 1–4.

Hofstadter, Richard. *The Paranoid Style in American Politics and Other Essays*. New York, 1965.

Hollis, Daniel W. *University of South Carolina*. Columbia, S. C., 1951, 1956. 2 vols.

Jacobs, Thornwell. *Red Lanterns on St. Michael's*. New York, 1940.

Key, V. O. *Southern Politics in State and Nation*. New York, 1949.

Kirk, Russell. *The Conservative Mind*. Gateway Edition, Chicago, 1960.

———. *John Randolph of Roanoke*. Chicago, 1964.

Lander, Ernest M., Jr. *A History of South Carolina, 1865–1960*. Chapel Hill, N. C., 1960.

Leland, John A. *A Voice from South Carolina*. Charleston, S. C., 1879.

Lippmann, Walter. *Public Opinion*. New York, 1946.

Malone, Dumas. *The Public Life of Thomas Cooper*. New Haven, Conn., 1926.

McGill, Ralph. *The South and the Southerner*. Atlantic–Little Brown Edition, Boston, 1964.

Mencken, H. L. *Notes on Democracy*. New York, 1926.

N. W. Ayer and Son's Directory, Newspapers and Periodicals. Philadelphia, 1910, 1927.

Ravenel, Beatrice St. Julien. *Architects of Charleston*. Charleston, S. C., 1945. Introduction by W. W. Ball.

Ravenel, Harriott Horry. *Charleston, the Place and the People*. New York, 1907.

Rossiter, Clinton. *Conservatism in America*. New York, 1955.

Salter, John T., editor. *Public Men In and Out of Office*. Chapel Hill, N. C., 1946.

Sass, Herbert Ravenel. *Outspoken: 150 Years of The News and Courier*. Columbia, S. C., 1953.

Savage, Henry, Jr. *River of the Carolinas: The Santee*. New York, 1956.

Schaper, William A. *Sectionalism and Representation in South Carolina*. Washington, D. C., 1901.

Simkins, Francis B. *A History of the South*. New York, 1953.

———. *Pitchfork Ben Tillman*. Baton Rouge, La., 1944.

———. *The Tillman Movement in South Carolina*. Durham, N. C., 1926.

——— and Robert H. Woody. *South Carolina during Reconstruction*. Chapel Hill, N. C., 1932.

South Carolina Archives Department. *Articles in Periodicals and Serials on South Carolina Literature and Related Subjects*. Columbia, S. C., 1956.

South Carolina Public Service Authority. *Picture Progress Story: Santee-Cooper*. Moncks Corner, S. C., n. d.

Spain, August O. *The Political Theory of John C. Calhoun*. New York, 1951.

Taylor, Rosser H. *Ante-Bellum South Carolina: A Social and Cultural History*. Chapel Hill, N. C., 1942.

——— and Raven I. McDavid, editors. *Memoirs of Richard Cannon Watts*. Columbia, S. C., 1938.

Turnbull, Robert J. *A Bibliography of South Carolina, 1563–1950*. Charlottesville, Va., 1956–1960. 6 vols.

Twelve Southerners. *I'll Take My Stand*. Harper Torchbook Edition, New York, 1962.

Viereck, Peter. *Conservatism Revisited*. Collier Books Edition, New York, 1962.

Wallace, David D. *The History of South Carolina*. New York, 1934. 4 vols.

———. *South Carolina, A Short History*. Chapel Hill, N. C., 1951.

Waring, Laura Witte. *You Asked for It*. Charleston, S. C., 1941.

Woodward, C. Vann. *Origins of the New South, 1877–1913*. Baton Rouge, La., 1951.

Writers Program of the Works Project Administration. *South Carolina, A Guide to the Palmetto State*. American Guide Series, New York, 1941.

INDEX

Abbeville, S. C., 11
Abney, Ben L., 56
Adams, Charles Francis, 53
Adams, Henry, 232–233
Adams, John Q., 213
Adger College, 18–19
Agrarianism, 5, 152
Aiken County, S. C., 190
Alabama, 208, 214, 218
Alexander, Rev. J. W., 20
American Federation of Labor, 113
Anderson *Independent*, 221
  on W. W. Ball, 216
  on Judge J. Waties Waring, 220
Ansel, Martin F., 48
Arkansas, 214
Arliss, George, 177
Asheville Citizen, 99
Astor, Lord Waldorf and Lady Nancy,
  visit W. W. Ball, 224
Atlanta Constitution on death of W.
  W. Ball, 229

Babbitt, Irving, 231
Ball, Beaufort Watts, 8–12, 14–15,
  18–19, 23, 32, 42, 69, 80
Ball, Eliza, 17, 19, 30, 54, 112, 135,
  175
Ball, Fay Witte, 37–38, 50, 103, 141–
  142, 173–174, 224
Ball, William Watts
  on Charles Francis Adams, 53
  on agriculture, 81
  in American Historical Association,
  53
  Anglophilism, 85–86, 199
  as assistant editor of *The News and
  Courier*, 44–51
  attacked, 78, 106–107, 121, 155–
  156, 178–179
  and Bernard Baruch, 90, 177, 199
  and Cole Blease, 56, 77–79, 97–
  101, 110–111, 165–168
  and J. F. Byrnes, 104–105, 114–
  115, 135–136, 170–173, 200,
  226–227
  on Charleston politics, 137–139

Ball, William Watts (*cont.*)
  character and customs, 30, 199,
  223–225, 233
  children of, 40–41, 44, 52, 82, 90,
  119–120, 140, 142–144, 171,
  174–175, 177, 198–199, 202,
  220, 227
  and Winston Churchill, 141
  on the clergy, 163–164
  as columnist, 228
  as country editor, 30
  and Josephus Daniels, 107
  named Dean of Journalism, 103
  on Depression, 151, 153, 155, 157,
  161–162, 179
  on N. B. Dial, 79, 104, 112
  diary begun, 68
  on Dispensary system, 47–48
  on divorce, 198
  editor of *Charleston Evening Post*,
  33–39
  editor of *Greenville News*, 39–40
  editorship of *Advertiser* begun, 24
  editorship of *The News and Courier*
  begun, 122
  editorship of *The State* begun, 60
  education of, 12–13, 18–20, 22–23
  on education, 154–155, 204
  eulogy to, 235
  evaluation of, 5–7, 95, 152, 176,
  230–235
  experience with daily press, 30–31
  and "gold" Democrats, 36, 101
  and Ambrose Gonzales, 92–97, 103,
  105
  and Wade Hampton, 17
  and Haskell movement, 27
  and Homes-Haile murder-suicide,
  91–92
  honors, 18, 81, 90, 178
  on Harry Hopkins, 176, 200–201,
  206
  on Industrial Revolution, 58–59
  on labor organization, 131–134
  as lawyer, 23–24, 41
  and Walter Lippmann, 232
  on lynching, 29, 172, 205